Money, Politics and Power

The Nine Years' War with France was a period of great institutional innovation in public finance and of severe monetary turmoil for England. It saw the creation of the Bank of England; a sudden sharp fall in the external value of the pound; a massive undertaking to melt down and recoin most of the nation's silver currency; a failed attempt to create a National Land Bank as a competitor to the Bank of England; and the ensuing outbreak of a sharp monetary and financial crisis.

Histories of this period usually divide these events into two main topics, treated in isolation from one another: the recoinage debate and ensuing monetary crisis and a 'battle of the banks'. The first is often interpreted as the pyrrhic victory of a creditor-dominated parliament over the nation's debtors, one that led very predictably to the ensuing monetary crisis. The second has been construed as a contest between whig-merchant and tory-gentry visions of the proper place of banking in England's future. This book binds the two strands into a single narrative, resulting in a very different interpretation of both. Parliamentary debate over the recoinage was superficial and misleading; beneath the surface, it was just another front for the battle of the banks. And the latter had little to do with competing philosophies of economic development; it was rather a pragmatic struggle for profit and power, involving interlocking contests between two groups of financiers and two sets of politicians within the royal administration. The monetary crisis of summer 1696 was not the result of poor planning by the Treasury; rather it was a continuation of the battle of the banks, fought on new ground but with the same ultimate intent – to establish dominance in the lucrative business of private lending to the crown.

Richard A. Kleer is an Associate Professor in the Department of Economics, and Dean of the Faculty of Arts, at the University of Regina, Canada.

Financial History

Series editors: Farley Grubb and Anne L. Murphy

Money, Politics and Power

Banking and Public Finance in Wartime England, 1694–96

Richard A. Kleer

Routledge
Taylor & Francis Group

LONDON AND NEW YORK

First published 2017 by Routledge

2 Park Square, Milton Park, Abingdon, Oxfordshire OX14 4RN
52 Vanderbilt Avenue, New York, NY 10017

Routledge is an imprint of the Taylor & Francis Group, an informa business

First issued in paperback 2019

British Library Cataloguing-in-Publication Data
A catalogue record for this book is available from the British Library

Library of Congress Cataloging-in-Publication Data
Names: Kleer, Richard A., author.
Title: Money, politics and power: banking and public finance
in wartime England, 1694–96 / Richard A. Kleer.
Description: Abingdon, Oxon; New York, NY: Routledge, 2017. |
Includes index.
Identifiers: LCCN 2016057297 | ISBN 9781138036666 (hardback) |
ISBN 9781315178431 (ebook)
Subjects: LCSH: Finance, Public—Great Britain—History—
17th century. | Banks and banking, British—History—17th century. |
Monetary policy—Great Britain—History—17th century. |
Financial crises—Great Britain—History—17th century. |
Great Britain—Politics and government—1689–1702.
Classification: LCC HJ1012 .K54 2017 | DDC 336.4109/032—
dc23LC record available at https://lccn.loc.gov/2016057297

ISBN: 978-1-138-03666-6 (hbk)
ISBN: 978-0-367-88882-4 (pbk)

Typeset in Times New Roman
by codeMantra

To Ben Vandezande, a gifted teacher who inspired in me a love of history

Contents

Illustrations

Figures

Table

Preface

This book took me a long time to finish because I had a lot of learning to do along the way.

It was a few summers before I realized that I couldn't piece my story together from the fragments, however tantalizing, to be found in the large pamphlet literature of the period. I knew from day one that these were political documents, written for partisan or at least self-interested purposes. But for quite a while I assumed that all my authors knew what they were talking about and that if I was having trouble understanding them, it must be because I wasn't working hard enough. It was Chris Fauske, an English-lit scholar whose research interests overlapped a little with mine, who eventually disabused me of this notion. Drawing on his familiarity with the work of Jonathan Swift, he helped me see what I had been too naïve to recognize: that a lot of the pamphlet writers of the period were just putting on a good show, making it up as they went along about subjects they didn't really understand.

Once over that hump, it didn't take me long to encounter another. I had planned originally to make an extensive study of the many coinage-related debates that occurred in England during the Nine Years' War, culminating in a reinterpretation of the politics of the Great Recoinage. I proceeded at first on the assumption that proposals for raising the coin were a standard strategy of opposition parties for slowing the progress of financial measures through parliament. I had worked up more than half a manuscript along these lines before I realized that my proposed line of interpretation wasn't going to see me home.

Unsure where to head next, I set the project aside for what I thought would be a short time. I started work instead on another topic that had always interested me: Britain's South Sea Bubble of 1720. That research, which also brought me perilously close, for a time, to sinking into the scholarly quagmire that is the French Mississippi Bubble of 1719–20, turned out to take far longer than I had anticipated. But in the process I discovered that the gold and silver coin coursing through the British Exchequer was of pivotal importance for financial corporations like the Bank of England and the South Sea Company. Eventually I realized this was the key ingredient missing from my reassessment of the Great Recoinage.

So, once I had finished writing about the Bubble, I returned to my work on the recoinage with renewed optimism. It still took me quite a while to pull all the pieces together. But this time around I knew I was on the right track, allowing me to settle back and enjoy the journey.

I don't pretend with this book to have produced a definitive interpretation of the recoinage debates. I am all too aware how my sense of a given dispute sometimes changed dramatically after stumbling upon just one additional piece of documentation. I wrote the story, rather, that seemed to me to deliver the best possible fit with the evidence I was able to find.

Acknowledgements

I want to thank those participants in the series of biennial colloquia, 'Money, Power and Print: Interdisciplinary Studies on the Financial Revolution in the British Isles' (organized by Chris Fauske, Ivar McGrath and myself), who encouraged me on this project over the years. They understood, without me having to explain, why I found it interesting and wanted to tell my story from the viewpoint of contemporaries rather than through the lens of present-day economic theory. That kind of moral support was invaluable. Special thanks go to Chris Fauske, with whom I had many conversations on this subject over the years and who gave me helpful feedback on Chapter 11. Since I was an obstinate and often obtuse correspondent, he must not be held in any way responsible for the flaws in my interpretation of the contemporary political situation. Dwyryd Jones kindly agreed to meet with me in the project's earliest days and was most encouraging. Colin Brooks shared his very entertaining take on John Locke's politics and character. Stuart Handley and Henry Horwitz generously provided copies of a few key contemporary letters. Gaye Morgan of Codrington Library (All Souls College, University of Oxford) helped me far beyond the call of duty. I am grateful finally to the University of Regina for giving me latitude to carry on with a project that took so long to come to fruition and for funding me to visit the relevant archives and buy images of key manuscripts. I especially want to thank the provost, Tom Chase, for approving the year of administrative leave that I needed to finish this book.

Abbreviations

BEA	Bank of England Archive
BL	British Library, London
CJ	Journals of the House of Commons (Great Britain, Parliament)
CSPD	Calendar of State Papers, Domestic (Great Britain, Public Record Office)
CTB	Calendar of Treasury Books (Great Britain, Public Record Office)
LJ	Journals of the House of Lords (Great Britain, Parliament)
NA	National Archives, London
RCHM	Royal Commission on Historical Manuscripts (Great Britain)

1   Introduction

Overview

Recently I had the pleasure of reading Timothy Howard's book, *The Mortgage Wars: Inside Fannie Mae, Big-Money Politics and the Collapse of the American Dream*. His account overturned almost everything I had previously believed about the role of Fannie Mae in the financial crisis of 2007–8. A common storyline in the post-crisis literature was that Fannie Mae, a quasi-government agency, lay near the root of all that evil. For it had built its massive empire on the strength of a dangerous new financial product: the subprime mortgage. Few surprises then that in 2008 the US government had to put that agency into conservatorship in an effort to save the financial sector from imminent disaster. But on Howard's telling a very different story emerges. Until a wholesale change of management was forced upon Fannie Mae in 2004, the company had in fact been operating responsibly and safely. It was private mortgage lenders who were pushing the envelope, subjecting the new financial technology to pressures it was never meant to bear. But through an intense lobbying campaign those private lenders managed nevertheless to persuade regulators that Fannie Mae was the problem. By this means they weakened the corporation's grip on the industry and were able to assume a much larger role in a very profitable a line of business. In short, the financial crisis resulted from an industry turf war. Previous accounts, Howard noted, 'have almost completely missed this fact – ironically because they have had to rely on materials produced to gain political advantage in that battle, which are deliberately inaccurate and almost impossible for outsiders to decipher or entangle'.[1]

In this book I similarly attempt to reverse the received view about another, much older big-money power struggle. Since the 1930s the story of England's so-called 'Great Recoinage' of 1696–99 has been told as one of intellectual dogmatism triumphing over sound, practical reasoning. In the midst of a long and expensive war, the nation's silver coin having dwindled to half its normal size, parliament chose to have it all melted down and restored to full weight. Parliament also had to decide whether at the same time to devalue the pound. Treasury Secretary William Lowndes, approaching the matter pragmatically, laid out a convincing case for devaluation. But the government, foolishly, chose to follow the advice of philosopher John Locke, who was driven by little more than intellectual dogmatism, to hold fast to the pre-war value. Consequently, in mid-1696 the nation was plunged into a depression as severe as it was unnecessary. But in constructing this narrative, historians built principally from the large outpouring of pamphlets and broadsides published at the time. These documents, though great fun to read and chockfull of factual claims, turn out to be terribly unreliable guides. Crafted for partisan political purposes, they were the mere outcroppings of underlying, intersecting power struggles between two political camps and two groups of financiers. In the study now before you, I've worked to put those struggles front and centre. In particular, I emphasize a key decision faced by parliament that year: where to find the money for a large, new war loan. If the money were borrowed, as many were hoping, from a proposed new bank, the political consequences would have been enormous. The Bank of England would probably have become a minor player, destined to disappear once its charter expired in 1706. The Commons would have gained a great deal of influence and decision-making power. And control over the administration would have shifted back toward the tory camp. The recoinage debate, I will show, was only a concealed means of fighting this much larger battle. I demonstrate too that the received view has things almost exactly backwards: that for several months it was the administration itself that pressed to devalue the pound.

Howard, having been Fannie Mae's Chief Financial Officer for many years, knew the inside story of his industry from personal, workaday experience. I've had to assemble my alternative account by means far more indirect. Little has survived from the correspondence of the period. Fortunately we have a very extensive collection of Locke's letters, published less than forty years ago and still being mined. But besides that and a smattering of official correspondence pertaining to army finances, we have only the odd assortment of letters, mostly from minor figures, printed in various reports of the Royal Commission on Historical Manuscripts. Nor do we have the benefit of diaries or published memoirs from any of the leading politicians, or even records of parliamentary debates. The best available source of this kind is a history compiled many years later by Gilbert Burnet, an Anglican bishop with close ties to the court. But it wasn't terribly helpful for my purposes since the good bishop had little interest in public finance and was to boot strongly biased to the whig cause. Fortunately we do have two sets of diplomatic reports, both of which offer detailed, day-by-day summaries of parliamentary debates and court politics. They were written, in French (the *lingua franca* of the day), for the Dutch States General and the court of Brandenburg (both allies in the war against France) by N. l'Hermitage and Frederic Bonnet respectively. Since matters of public finance were always central to the politics of the day, these reports are often a rich, though not always entirely reliable, source of information. One MP, Narcissus Luttrell, did keep a personal record of daily news highlights; unfortunately he wasn't close to the court or very well-informed about financial matters. For the rest I have had to guess at what might have been going on behind the scenes. For this kind of reconstructive work, the most helpful sources were: contemporary pamphlets (subject to the limitations just described) and London newspapers (unfortunately, complete runs have survived for only two or three and they seldom wrote of economic issues); the printed journals of the House of Commons and House of Lords; the rather sparse manuscript minutes of the Cabinet, Treasury (alas missing for the period 1692–95), Bank of England and National Land Bank; the accounting records of the Treasury, Bank of England and of a deputy paymaster for the English army in Flanders; a complete set of Treasury payment orders; and a couple of small manuscript collections of public-finance proposals submitted to Commons committees or to the treasury lords. The biographies of Commons MPs collected in the four *History of Parliament* volumes for this period were also indispensable tools.[2]

It is never easy to catch sight of power. When at its highest pitch, it is often completely invisible. In our period it became a little more evident than usual because, the war having put economic and political systems alike under considerable strain, some groups were struggling to retain, or even to regain lost, power. Even so, the role of power in the Great Recoinage remains hard to discern. To aid with this problem, I paid close attention to contemporary economic institutions and practices. For I have found that they offer far more reliable and revealing testimony than written documents. Pamphlet authors often succeeded in concealing their objectives, using rhetoric to whip up sentiment for ends not announced. But it is almost impossible to hide the purposes of economic institutions, since their very design speaks volumes. And accounting records are also very reliable guides, since they were never expected to be seen by anyone other than insiders.

This is the main reason why the first half of the book is almost all economic history, though of an old-fashioned kind: institutional rather than theory-driven. In my estimation we can only properly understand the politics of money and public finance during our period if we first become thoroughly familiar with the underlying economic institutions and their stress points. You will therefore be introduced to England's systems of public revenues, expenditure and borrowing; to the design and operations of the Bank of England; to foreign bills of exchange (the primary mechanism by which England funded an army fighting on the continent); and to the three most important 'projects' (a contemporary term that translates roughly as 'proposals for joint private-public business undertakings') for land banks (which proposed to lend to the state using new paper currencies secured by title to agricultural rents). I've written these chapters to be accessible to non-specialists. I believe they are worth reading for their own sake; there is considerable pleasure to be had in understanding how such institutions worked. But I also tried to restrain myself, providing only as much detail as you will need later in the book to follow my arguments on subjects more political.

A short history of histories of the recoinage

I embarked upon this study in reaction to the histories I had read of the Great Recoinage. So to explain my aims in writing the book, I first need to introduce you, ever so briefly, to the broad outline of those histories.

The Recoinage Act of 21 January 1696 has received a lot of scholarly attention over the centuries. This is mainly because it has been viewed as the opening instalment of a long-running debate over whether the value of the British pound should periodically be adjusted to reflect changing economic circumstances. In 1696 parliament opted to leave the value of the pound unchanged. For two or so centuries, this was lauded as a wise decision – setting an example long followed by British policy-makers facing a similar choice.[3] The classic statement of this view is Thomas Macaulay's long and detailed narrative of the recoinage in his grandiloquent *History of England from the Accession of James II* (first published in 1849). For him the decision not to devalue was yet another instance of the marked improvement in England's political fortunes after the Glorious Revolution of 1688. A recoinage plan that would retain the integrity of the pound was jointly conceived and executed by England's two most eminent intellectuals (Locke and Isaac Newton) and two leading politicians, Charles Montagu (Chancellor of the Exchequer) and John Somers (Lord Keeper of the Great Seal, the highest legal office in the country). The latter two, bold and far-seeing, carried through parliament the statutes needed to reform the currency, against demands from timorous opposition politicians to delay action until the end of the war or at least to soften the blow by simultaneously devaluing – an expedient that would have cost England its monetary honour.

But in the twentieth century there was a shift in attitude on the part of economists, if not of policy-makers. After the first and second world wars, the administrations of the day decided to try to restore the British pound to its pre-war value, or something near it. This meant having to unwind the effects of substantial wartime price inflations and so put the country through long and painful depressions. On both occasions officials eventually relented, choosing five or six years later to devalue the pound by substantial amounts. Interpretations of the recoinage of 1696 changed very markedly after the first such episode. Beginning in the 1930s, most economic historians now maintained that, at least on the level of economic theory, Lowndes had had the better of Locke by far. Locke allowed the logic of his argument to seduce him into thinking that a metallic currency's value was some kind of natural constant. He failed to grasp Lowndes' essential insight that in fact the value of money was inherently variable and that this might necessitate periodic, offsetting changes in the official standard. Nor did Locke foresee that keeping to the old standard would cause a sharp deflation and an economic depression.[4] On this interpretation, the severe monetary troubles of summer 1696 were the very predictable consequence of Locke's intellectual rigidity. Twentieth-century commentators differ about whether Locke was also wrong in practice. By and large, those writing prior to the second world war maintained that despite his theoretical failings, he had made a telling practical point: meddling with the currency might destroy public faith in its stability and would open the door to endless further manipulations. Among more recent writers, by contrast, the consensus seems to be that Locke was altogether wrong and that it would have been better had Lowndes' advice been taken instead; England would have experienced less deflation.

These earlier analyses troubled me on several counts. First, they all viewed the recoinage controversy through the lens of later developments in British monetary policy. I wondered what I might find by approaching the episode through the eyes of contemporaries. Second, I found the accounts of twentieth-century economic historians unsatisfying because they: a) treated the question of the appropriate Mint standard as a simple technical problem (for which there were right and wrong solutions) and largely ignored the distributive issues involved – vices common among economists;[5] b) seemed uninterested in, and certainly could not account for, why parliament had taken what was in their estimation the wrong approach (while Locke may have been dogmatic, the Commons didn't need to follow his advice); and c) rested upon some key factual errors. The last point needs some explaining. Ever since Macaulay, historians had believed that the recoinage design eventually decided upon had been recommended by Locke and Newton and implemented jointly by Montagu and Somers. But some 25 years ago Kelly discovered, after a careful reading of Locke's correspondence, that this view was entirely mistaken. He established that in fact the administration had been internally divided on the issue and opted in the end for a course of action to which Locke himself was opposed and that only Newton supported.[6]

So in setting out to study the Great Recoinage I aimed to approach it as much as possible on the terms in which contemporaries would have understood it, leave ample room for issues of politics and distribution and develop an interpretation consistent with Kelly's important new findings.[7] That quest eventually resulted in a book in which the recoinage has been pushed from the centre of attention. I slowly learned that the debate over devaluation could not be understood in isolation – that its final outcome was determined by two concurrent struggles for power, one in the banking industry and the other within the administration. In the end the book became more about those contests than anything else.

Over the last half century or so the recoinage debate and its attendant pamphlet literature have been carefully examined by a small army of historians. I offer the following short overview for those interested in learning more on their own. In *British Monetary Experiments, 1650–1710*, Horsefield offered a short narrative of the recoinage and assessed the quality of theoretical reasoning in a representative cross-section of contemporary publications on the subject. The book's greatest merit for scholars of the recoinage is its extensive, meticulous bibliography of primary sources. Li's analysis in *The Great Recoinage of 1696–9* is similar to Horsefield's, though his book concentrates more on the sequence of events and less on the pamphlet literature. In their short study, *Political Parties in the Reigns of William III and Anne*, Burton, Riley and Rowlands report upon and analyze several previously unpublished House of Commons 'division lists' (records of how MPs voted, or were expected to vote, on a given issue), two of which are very closely related to the recoinage. This shed some much needed light on the inner workings of the Commons during a period that is notoriously poorly documented. In *Parliament, Policy and Politics in the Reign of William III*, Horwitz provided an updated narrative of the recoinage, refined on the basis of several important manuscript discoveries and his very extensive knowledge of parliamentary politics during this period. In *War and Economy in the Age of William III and Marlborough*, Jones offered a penetrating interpretation of the specific economic pressures contributing to clipping and the need for a recoinage. The book is still more valuable for historians of the recoinage in its expert and detailed descriptions of the actual institutions and mechanisms by which English military funds were transferred to Europe. Finally, in his Introduction to *Locke on Money*, Kelly provided a detailed narrative of the recoinage, updated in light of his very careful re-reading of the textual and manuscript evidence. To all these authors I am very grateful; without their work this study simply would not have been possible.

A short sketch of English parliamentary politics

In the second half of the book, the chapters covering the slow progress of monetary and financial statutes through the Houses of Commons and Lords, I assume a basic familiarity with contemporary English parliamentary processes. In this section I provide a little background for those who may need it. My account concerns England alone; I leave aside the kingdoms of Ireland and Scotland over which William also ruled.

The preeminent political event of the period was the so-called Glorious Revolution of 1688. In that year William of Orange, a Dutch prince, led a military invasion of England, ousted King James II in a coup at first almost bloodless and eventually took over the throne himself, jointly with his wife and James' daughter, Mary. William had been invited to England by a cross-party coalition of seven prominent statesmen, concerned like so many others that James' rule was threatening religious and civil liberties. They were especially worried that the nation would become a Catholic state allied with France, then the most absolute of monarchies and the world's leading Catholic power. After William arrived in London, James retreated at first to Ireland and then, after a decisive defeat by William's forces at the River Boyne, to France. There he maintained a court in exile for many years. Once declared king, William led England into an aggressive and very expensive war against France, one that lasted until 1697. But William's regime was never entirely secure; there was always the distinct possibility that James might try to reclaim his throne. James' supporters back in England, termed Jacobites, were constantly at work behind the scenes attempting to undermine the war effort and foment domestic unrest. So leading politicians had to walk a delicate line. If they acted too aggressively in support of William's cause, they would be in grave danger should James ever return. But if they worked too much in opposition to the court (a common strategy for gaining high-level appointments), they might be suspected of being closet Jacobites.

The political nation at this time was divided into two main camps: whig and tory. The parties formed in the 1670s during the rule of Charles II. The main dividing line between them was religious.[8] Tories were strong supporters of the Anglican church, tending to see it as the one true faith. Whigs were either Anglicans who recognized other protestant denominations as full members of the christian faith and supported official toleration of their religious practices, or themselves 'dissenters' – the contemporary term for more aggressively protestant denominations, such as presbyterianism. The two groups also divided along political lines. Tories tended to see monarchs as divinely ordained, upheld their power to the fullest and were ardently committed to the principle of hereditary succession. The more radical whigs favoured a social-contract view of monarchy and were prepared to depart from the strict line of hereditary succession if rulers had violated their implicit contract with the people. The whigs should therefore have been the natural party of government under William, since he was a Calvinist, had actively invaded England and was an heir to the throne only by marriage. Indeed, tory principles were sorely tested when it came time for parliament to declare him king (though it helped that the monarchy was bestowed jointly upon him and Mary). Some Anglican clergy, so-called 'non-jurors', refused to swear an oath referring to him as England's 'lawful and rightful' king; for this act of civil disobedience they were deprived of their livings. But William did his best to keep the peace and was very deliberate in bringing politicians of both stripes into his administration. After a short while, when opposition from whig politicians (sorely disappointed that they were not running the new regime) became too great, he even decided to give the bulk of power to the tories. Not until 1694 did the whigs (or rather a whig faction led by a handful of young, ambitious and influential men that contemporaries called the 'junto') begin to dominate at court. Even then, William moved in this direction only reluctantly; he continued to prefer a government that was as balanced between the two parties as possible.

Parliamentary procedure was very different than it is today. Voting did not run along strict party lines; there were no party whips and in principle, individual MPs were free to vote as their consciences dictated. This made it difficult, and a matter of constant negotiation, to secure the majorities needed for outcomes vital to the court, especially appropriate levels of funding for the military and taxes that could be counted upon to generate the requisite revenues. The court used three main techniques to obtain majorities. First, it assigned the role of being a House 'manager' to those MPs gifted in public speaking, able to influence the undecided vote by sheer force of rhetoric.[9] Since potential managers were usually brought on side with the offer of some lucrative public post, either for themselves or for relatives or clients, the competition for such positions was keen. Able speakers typically advertised their suitability for the role by demonstrating that they could stymie court measures. This gave rise to a general category of politician that l'Hermitage labelled 'the ill-intentioned': disgruntled MPs who, seeing themselves as deserving of office but having been denied it thus far, worked to advertise the harm they could do to the court's legislative program. Second, on key issues, court managers might strike bargains with MPs to buy their votes. This could take the form of court support for bills important to large blocs of members. At one point, for instance, the administration traded support for an act to hold parliamentary elections every three years to get ample funding for the army. Or court managers might engage in mild forms of corruption, targeting individual MPs with the offer of minor offices, pensions or other monetary bribes. Third, good managers needed to be able to take the pulse of the House and deliver bills whose specifics aligned with the sentiments of the average MP. For instance, excise taxes, which required royal officials to personally inspect manufacturing sites, were always highly unpopular; it was much easier to propose taxes that MPs or their colleagues could supervise themselves. For all these reasons, the battle of parties was not always what it seemed. Pamphlet writers would often invoke high-minded principles for ends rather ignoble. Hence one of the maxims of state of George Savile, first Marquess of Halifax and a leading minister under Charles II: 'That parties in a state generally, like freebooters, hang out false colours; the pretence is the publick good; the real business is to catch prizes; like the Tartars, wherever they succeed, instead of improving their victory, they presently fall upon the baggage'.[10]

Terminology and conventions

In this section I provide short explanations of a few key terms that will recur throughout the book but that may not be familiar to non-specialist readers.

First a few words on currency units. The principal English monetary unit of account, then as now, was the pound. At the time the pound was divided into 20 shillings and the shilling in turn into 12 pence. In all references to English money I use the original currency units, rather than converting to decimal, since they feature so prominently in the pamphlet literature. I also use the abbreviations standard at the time, so that by a reference like '5s. 2d.' I mean: 5 shillings and 2 pence. English coin bore no stated denominations. The various types were distinguished from one another only by their metal (gold or silver), size and stamped effigies. Silver coins had fixed official values. So, for instance, the largest silver coin, the crown piece, was always worth 5s. By contrast, gold coins were allowed to fluctuate in value and went at whatever price the market decided to set upon them. For much of our period the largest gold coin, the so-called 'guinea', was valued at 21s. 6d. But in 1695 its market price rose to 30s., where it remained for close to a year. The fact that coins lacked any stated denomination made it possible, in principle, for the government to decree new values for them overnight. So, for instance, during our period it was proposed to increase the official rating of the silver crown by 20 percent to 6s. 3d., and all the other, smaller silver coins in proportion.

English coins were of two basic types: what contemporaries called 'hammered' and 'milled'. The two differed in having been made by hand (beaten with a hammer) versus with a mechanical press (what contemporaries called a 'mill'). Being handmade, hammered coin was somewhat irregular in shape and weight. It also lacked the fluted and inscribed edges given to milled coins. The latter were designed to protect coin from 'clipping' (the act of stealing small slivers from the outer edge – a lucrative trade when done in sufficient volume). For fluting made it easy to see when a coin had been clipped – something impossible to detect with hammered money. Milling was a relatively new process that became the standard in England only in the 1660s. After that time, all newly-manufactured coin, both silver and gold, was milled. But for various reasons most of the new milled silver coin quickly disappeared; circulation was dominated rather by older, hammered coins from the reigns of Elizabeth through Charles II. Over time, as clippers plied their trade, this hammered money gradually shrank. By the beginning of the war the problem was not yet too bad; on average it weighed about 85 percent of normal. But the pace of clipping picked up during the war, so that by 1696 hammered money had lost about half its original weight.

I refer to English statutes using the usual scholarly convention. For example the citation '5 & 6 W. & M., c. 20' means: the twentieth statute passed during the session of parliament held during the fifth and sixth years of the reign of William and Mary. Using this reference system, the full text of the relevant acts can always be found in Great Britain, *Statutes of the Realm*, which is organized in strict chronological order. The relevant period of the latter collection has been digitized and made freely available by British History Online, which took care to note the year of reign and chapter numbers for every statute.

During our period England was on the Julian calendar while continental powers used our Gregorian calendar. The Julian calendar started the new year at 25 March (so what we call 10 February 1695 would by them have been labelled 10 February 1694) and, at the time, lagged the Gregorian calendar by 10 days (e.g. 30 June in Europe would be 20 June in England). I have used Julian dates throughout, except that I start the new year at 1 January. For primary-source documents that employed Gregorian dates (e.g. the diplomatic reports and some letters), I report dates in the same split form to which contemporaries often resorted (e.g. 20/30 June).

Throughout the book I follow contemporary practice and employ the term 'specie' as shorthand for silver and gold coin. I use the term 'price currents' to refer to the several newssheets that specialized in providing London merchants with weekly prices for a broad range of commodities, especially for gold and silver bullion and of guineas, and also exchange-rate quotations. When citing contemporary sources, I have adjusted all spellings to present-day standards. I did however keep to the original spelling for publication titles, to aid in searching for them in on-line catalogues.

Finally, a few terms relating to parliamentary process and the royal administration. The word 'division' refers to a formal, recorded vote. In any division there were 'tellers', MPs responsible for counting the votes for their side. In meetings of the full house there were two tellers per side, but in committee meetings only one. A bill would typically receive first and second reading before the full House. Then, if members thought it worth proceeding upon, it was sent to a committee for more detailed consideration. The committee would report any proposed amendments back to the House, after which a few adjustments might be made before the bill received its third and final reading and the House decided whether to pass it. Both Houses often went into a 'committee of the whole house', which had its own chair distinct from the Speaker, and in which was waived the normal rule that a member could speak to a given question only once. The Commons had two special standing committees of the whole house, one on 'supply' (which recommended to the full house how much money should be granted that year for the military and for the court) and the other on 'ways and means' (which debated and recommended to the full house the specific measures by which to raise whatever amounts of supply had been decided upon). Contemporaries often spoke of 'court' and 'country' parties within the House of Commons. Court MPs generally sought to approve supply at the levels requested by the government and pushed for effective taxes and quick resolution of financial measures. Country members, by contrast, suspected the court of padding its requests for supply and so aimed to inspect the supporting documentation carefully, restrain grants of supply and ensure that taxes would generate few if any surpluses. They were not displeased that this slowed the parliamentary process down very considerably, for they did not want the court to think it could have its way with parliament. The 'treasury lords' were the four or five individuals named by William to administer royal revenues and expenditures; few, and sometimes none, of them were 'lords' in the traditional sense of the word. Finally, contemporaries used the term 'lords justices' to refer to a group of seven men appointed by the king each summer to govern England while he was away leading the war effort on the continent. Diplomatic observers used the more descriptive term 'regency council'. The lords justices sometimes met alone ('cabinet') and at other times together with the members of privy council ('council'), a larger advisory body that included members both ex officio and appointed by the king.

Notes

1 *Mortgage Wars*, p. 16.
2 Hayton, *History of Parliament*.
3 The most celebrated instance was the 1819 act for the resumption of specie payments.
4 The first clear instance I have seen of this line of argument is in Hawtrey, *Currency and Credit*, pp. 292–93. It has since reappeared in many other scholarly interpretations. See for instance Fay, 'Locke versus Lowndes', pp. 148–50; Shirras and Craig, 'Sir Isaac Newton', p. 226; and Feavearyear, *Pound Sterling*, pp. 135–36.
5 The exception is a study by the intellectual historian Appleby, *Economic Thought and Ideology in Seventeenth-Century England*. Appleby aimed to explain why parliament had chosen Locke over Lowndes; and her answer emphasized issues of politics and distribution. She argued that Locke's approach appealed to the selfish motives of powerful interest groups. It allowed a parliament dominated by landowners to reassert its control over the English economy, which in recent decades had increasingly come under the sway of merchant importers. Merchants wanted the coin raised because it would have increased the purchasing power of ordinary people and so stimulated domestic trade. Parliament favoured retaining the existing standard because it believed this would cause the general price level to fall, benefiting landlords and manufacturers exporting overseas – 'the upper class in general'. While there is some truth to this account, I believe there were other, deeper forces at work.
6 See Kelly's Introduction to Locke, *Locke on Money*, especially pp. 23–35.
7 Kelly accomplished some of this in his Introduction to *Locke on Money*. But his focus was on understanding Locke's economic ideas; his coverage of the recoinage act itself was relatively brief and intended only as context.
8 I draw here upon a contemporary description by one rather dour whig who added another contrast: that tories swore and drank while whigs did not! See Papillon, *Memoirs of Thomas Papillon*, pp. 374–76.
9 Charles Davenant, himself no able speaker and a failed suitor for public office, wrote a long memorial to complain of the practice. See Davenant, 'An essay on public virtue' (circa 1697), in BL, Harley MS 1223, fols. 7–69. A portion of the manuscript is printed in Li, *Great Recoinage*, pp. 200–16.
10 'Maxims of State or Observations on Government by the late Marqs of H---x, 1695. [With] a supplemnt by Mr Charles Mountague 1695', BL, Add. MS 6703, fols. 26–28.

Bibliography

Manuscript sources

British Library
   Add. MS 6703
   Harley MS 1223

Printed primary sources

Great Britain. *Statutes of the Realm*. Edited Alexander Luders and John Raithby. London: G. Eyre and A. Strahan, 1810–22. Accessed online at http://www.british-history.ac.uk/statutes-realm/.

Papillon, A. F. W. *Memoirs of Thomas Papillon of London, Merchant (1623–1702).* Reading: Joseph Beecroft, 1887.

Secondary sources

Appleby, Joyce Oldham. *Economic Thought and Ideology in Seventeenth-Century England.* Princeton: Princeton University Press, 1978.

Burton, Ivor F., P. W. J. Riley and E. Rowlands. *Political Parties in the Reigns of William III and Anne: the Evidence of the Division Lists.* Bulletin of the Institute of Historical Research, special supplement no. 7. London: Athlone Press, 1968.

Fay, C. R. 'Locke versus Lowndes'. *Cambridge Historical Journal* 4 (1932–1934): 143–155.

Feavearyear, Albert. *The Pound Sterling: A History of English Money.* 2nd ed. Oxford: Clarendon Press, 1963.

Hawtrey, Ralph G. *Currency and Credit.* London: Longmans, Green, 1927.

Hayton, David, Eveline Cruickshanks and Stuart Handley (eds.). *The History of Parliament: the House of Commons, 1690–1715.* 4 vols. Cambridge: Cambridge University Press for The History of Parliament Trust, 2002. Available online at http://www.historyofparliamentonline.org/volume/1690–1715.

Horsefield, John Keith. *British Monetary Experiments, 1650–1710.* Cambridge: Harvard University Press, 1960.

Horwitz, Henry. *Parliament, Policy and Politics in the Reign of William III.* Newark: University of Delaware Press, 1977.

Howard, Timothy. *The Mortgage Wars: Inside Fannie Mae, Big-Money Politics and the Collapse of the American Dream.* New York: McGraw-Hill Education, 2014.

Jones, D. W. *War and Economy in the Age of William III and Marlborough.* Oxford: Basil Blackwell, 1988.

Kelly, Patrick Hyde. Introduction to *Locke on Money,* by John Locke, 1–121. Oxford: Clarendon Press, 1991.

Li, Ming-Hsun. *The Great Recoinage of 1696 to 1699.* London: Weidenfeld and Nicolson, 1963.

Macaulay, Thomas B. *The History of England from the Accession of James II.* Boston: Crosby and Nichols, 1862.

Shirras, G. Findlay, and J. H. Craig. 'Sir Isaac Newton and the Currency'. *Economic Journal* 55 (1945): 217–241.

Part I

The institutional and economic context

2 England's wartime system of public finance

My goal in this chapter is to familiarize you with the details of England's system of public finance at the time. I provide only as much information as you will need to follow the story in later chapters.

Military spending, taxes and government borrowing (short- and long-term)

The Nine Years' War led to massive increases in government expenditure. For the core years of 1693–97 the royal administration spent an average of £6.9 million per year.[1] This demanded major adjustments on the revenue side, since before the war government income had been only about £2.1 million per year.[2]

Several new taxes were introduced and efforts were made to increase the take from existing taxes. I explore some of the details in the next section. But revenue still fell well short of expenditure; the crown's average annual income in 1693–97 was only £4.0 million per year.[3] This was in part because parliament stinted the military, every year delivering less than William and his officials requested. It came about too because MPs consistently overestimated (deliberately so, critics alleged) the proceeds of the new taxes they had agreed to appoint.

Parliament did however make deliberate provision for one part of the shortfall: by authorizing the Exchequer to borrow long-term. Over the core years 1693 to 1697 some £4.9 million, about £1 million per year on average, was brought in this way.[4] Some of the loans were perpetual; the government committed only to paying the interest and left itself the option to redeem the principal in better times. Others were designed to return a blend of interest and principal but with the payments amortized over many years – as much as a century. Thus was born Britain's national debt: destined to grow far larger in later years. During our period the administration generally honoured the associated payment obligations in a timely manner.

A second portion of the gap between revenue and expenditure was unintended and handled by the administration in a less tidy and reliable way.[5] Every year, as a matter of course, the Treasury arranged loans to cover the period, usually a year or less, between a given season's military spending and eventual receipt of all the tax revenues earmarked to cover it. Had every tax generated revenues in the amounts expected, short-term loans would have been as reliable an investment asset as their long-term counterparts. But the appointed taxes usually turned out to be less lucrative than hoped. Parliament always compensated for this in some way, typically by assigning the revenues of some new tax to cover the shortfall on previous ones. But it would take many more months for this new revenue to come in and often the new taxes proved deficient in turn. So over time the Treasury ended up holding more and more short-term loans on its books, many of which were taking longer and longer to be repaid. Predictably, this made it harder and more expensive for the Treasury to borrow short term and harder for existing lenders, if they needed cash right away, to resell their loans in the open market. But at least such debts were already officially recorded and carried parliament's guarantee that they would eventually be repaid.

The final part of the revenue shortfall was more haphazard and accommodated in a still less happy way.[6] The various military spending offices (chiefly army, navy and ordnance) paid their suppliers in the first instance with simple paper IOUs: 'debentures' in the case of army and ordnance, 'bills' for the navy. It was a matter for constant negotiation with the Treasury as to when and for what purposes paymasters would be assigned the funds needed to honour their IOUs. There were similar negotiations between paymasters and their various suppliers about when and in what currencies the IOUs would be paid. Because taxes always fell short of their estimated revenues and the armed forces frequently spent somewhat more than had been budgeted for them, payment arrears built up in all branches of the military. Some of these arrears were not settled until years after the war had ended. In the meantime the relevant IOUs were sharply 'discounted' in the open market, meaning they were sold to others for less than the amount the Treasury promised eventually to pay. Discounting was especially problematic for rank-and-file military personnel, who often could not afford to hold IOUs until they were paid in full. Military contractors, by contrast, were able to avoid most of its harmful effects; as discounts escalated, they raised their asking prices accordingly.

Short-term government borrowing

During the war the Treasury regularly confronted a timing problem. Normally the first of the new season's taxes wasn't approved until late December, the last not until sometime in April or May. It would be months before the revenues from a given tax began, and a year or more until they finished, coming in. But military spending had to begin during the winter. Soldiers and horses needed to be shipped to, or maintained in, continental locations well before the campaign commenced in April or May. Ships had to be outfitted with the full set of food supplies and armaments they would need for the coming season. Had England's financial system been working properly, the lag between expenditure and revenue should only have been a problem in the first year of the war. But in large part because parliament kept the military administration on a very tight leash, the lag persisted. Throughout the war military expenditures ran at least several months ahead of the revenues by which they were to be financed. So Treasury had constantly to borrow short term to bridge the gap.

Knowing that short-term borrowing would be necessary, parliament usually built loan clauses into its revenue statutes. The clauses authorized Treasury officials to borrow upon a given tax fund within prescribed limits: usually something close to the total revenue the tax was expected to generate. The loans were received in bits and pieces from a series of different lenders. By law these lenders were to be repaid in the same sequence in which they had brought in their money. The intent was to improve the security of Exchequer loans by ensuring creditors would be paid in good time, rather than constantly put off as better-connected lenders were permitted to jump the payment queue. The Exchequer issued its lenders a wooden proof-of-payment, called a 'tally',[7] and an accompanying paper 'order' on which the repayment terms were specified: the amount of the loan, the specific tax fund from which it was to be repaid, the rate of interest and the tally's position in the repayment sequence for that tax. To keep down the associated management costs, the Treasury accepted short-term loans only in relatively large blocks. Tallies and orders (henceforth 'tallies' for short) were issued in round denominations ranging from £50 to £10 thousand but typically for £500 or £1000 – at a time when most people earned far less than £100 a year. Tallies were made payable to bearer and fully transferable. So lenders could wait for repayment of their principal, with interest, until the relevant tax proceeds had arrived. Or they could sign their tally over to someone else (perhaps in satisfaction of a debt or maybe because they wanted some more liquid asset in exchange) who in turn would await repayment.

Seldom was the Treasury able to borrow up front the full amount that parliament had authorized it to take in upon a given tax. This was in part because some of the corresponding revenues were granted over a number of years, so that the tallies would not be paid off until well into the future. It was also because parliament consistently overestimated the anticipated revenues; once the shortfall was ascertained parliament would remedy it with some new tax. On either count, loans late in the queue might not be repaid for a couple of years or more. So the Treasury took to issuing 'tallies of fictitious loan' for the latter portions of any given tax. In other words, it treated paymasters as having made a 'loan' and issued them tallies late in the payment sequence. This practice entitled paymasters to take receipt of the relevant tax proceeds once they actually arrived or to exchange their tallies for better ones struck on the replacement funds eventually approved by parliament. Should funds turn out to be sufficient after all, paymasters might instead get real lenders to buy the tallies from them, or suppliers to accept them as final payment, once enough of the tax had come in to push them near the front of the payment queue. Lenders had further encouragement from Treasury to take tallies of fictitious loan. For the interest owing upon them was accounted from the date they were issued to the relevant paymaster—income that was made over to whomever eventually agreed to lend money upon them or accept them in payment of debts already incurred.

Often it was no simple matter to find lenders for the various short-term loans required by the Treasury. Some taxes were known to quite reliable; early tallies on these funds went quickly. But others, especially new ones, were more uncertain and investors might have to be tempted with various incentives or have their arms twisted. It was near full-time work for a couple of Treasury staff to find lenders and make sure they were repaid their loans with the appropriate interest and any additional incentives that might have been agreed upon. And even then, on some of the less reliable taxes it was simply impossible to find lenders for the full amount authorized in the borrowing clause.

For this reason, Treasury officials naturally preferred long-term loans over taxes. Long-term loans attracted a different kind of investor: people who didn't need to keep as much working capital around and could afford to part with their money for long periods of time. As long as the loan terms had been designed appropriately, investors of this kind often lined up at the Exchequer for the privilege of snagging their share of a given loan. So the full amount of the loan might arrive within just a few weeks. The Treasury could put this money to work right away to help meet the military's most pressing needs. The first interest, or principal-and-interest, payments on long-term loans weren't due for a year – by which time the relevant tax proceeds should already have begun arriving.

The wide range of taxes and tallies

The Treasury had many different taxes at its disposal to finance the war. Some, the so-called 'ordinary' revenues, had long existed and would continue after the war. They were divided principally into two broad categories: customs (taxes on imported goods) and excise (taxes levied on domestic goods at the point of production). During the course of the war parliament granted a few additional customs and excise taxes (such as those on glass, coal, salt and malt) in theory on a temporary basis. But a much greater part of the additional funding needed for the war came from long-term loans (mainly lotteries, annuities and the Bank of England) and temporary new direct taxes, especially the so-called 'land tax'. The latter was a 20 percent tax on agricultural and urban rents, then the principal income of England's wealthiest individuals. It was often also called a '4s. aid' because landlords were taxed 4 shillings on every pound of annual rental income. The new direct taxes were deliberately approved for only a year at a time (though each usually took a couple of years to be fully received); hence references to first, second, etc. aids – one per fiscal year. Figure 2.1, which draws upon the Exchequer's own annual revenue accounts, shows all those taxes or loans that generated at least £100 thousand in at least one year.[8] Within each category the various taxes and loans are arranged in the order in which they were approved by parliament. The information in Figure 2.1 isn't that important in itself; but it will be helpful background for later discussions. In that connection, note that for some taxes and loans contemporaries had more than one name. Confusingly, for instance, the 'additional 9d. per barrel' excise was sometimes called the 'double excise', even though there was already another tax by that name. In Figure 2.1, I used the names most commonly applied in the Exchequer accounts (though even there the nomenclature varied).

In order properly to understand contemporary pamphlets and manuscripts relating to public finance, it is important to recognize that there were separate sets of tallies for each tax and, within that tax, for each fiscal year. So for instance the tally series for customs duties on East-India goods in 1692–3 was distinct from that for customs duties in 1695–96. Similarly, each of the various 4s. aids had its own tally series. Figure 2.2, again drawing upon the Exchequer's own annual accounts, compares the quantity of tallies struck for each tax to the actual revenues received upon them.[9] Once more, within each category the various taxes are arranged temporally. The figure shows very clearly that some taxes generated considerably less income than contemporaries had expected. For example, in 1694–95 the Exchequer took in loans for over half a million pounds on the new duties on marriages, births and burials. But the tax proved very hard to administer and no actual revenues were received upon it during our period. A similar problem is evident with the new duty on coals, which was in fact revoked during the 1695–96 legislative session. Tallies on funds like these went to very sharp discounts once the revenue shortfall became apparent. By contrast, though lenders on the land tax might have to wait a year for their loan to be repaid, the tax was very reliable year after year. So discounts seldom emerged on land-tax tallies and investors usually queued for the right to lend the first half or two-thirds of the estimated proceeds of a given land tax. And when military paymasters tried to borrow on the strength of any fictitious tallies in their possession, lenders usually wanted tallies on the land tax over any other kind.

The central role of specie

Throughout our entire period, the nation's system of public finance ultimately turned upon silver and gold coin. The following short overview of the system, derived from a careful reading of Treasury records, helps drive the point home.[10]

Let's enter the circle with the military paymasters who needed to purchase supplies and pay their personnel. Perpetually short of funds, they

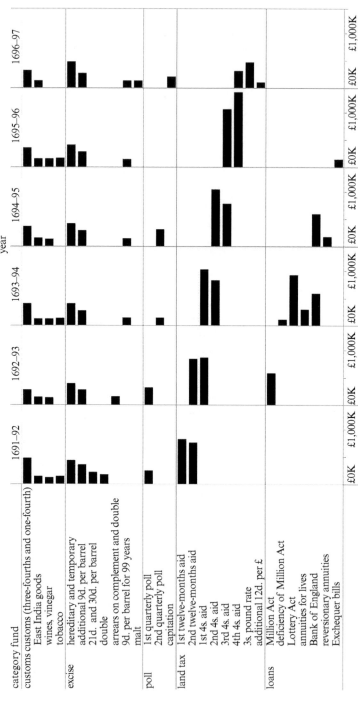

Figure 2.1 Revenues from England's main tax funds, 1691–97.
Source: *CTB*.

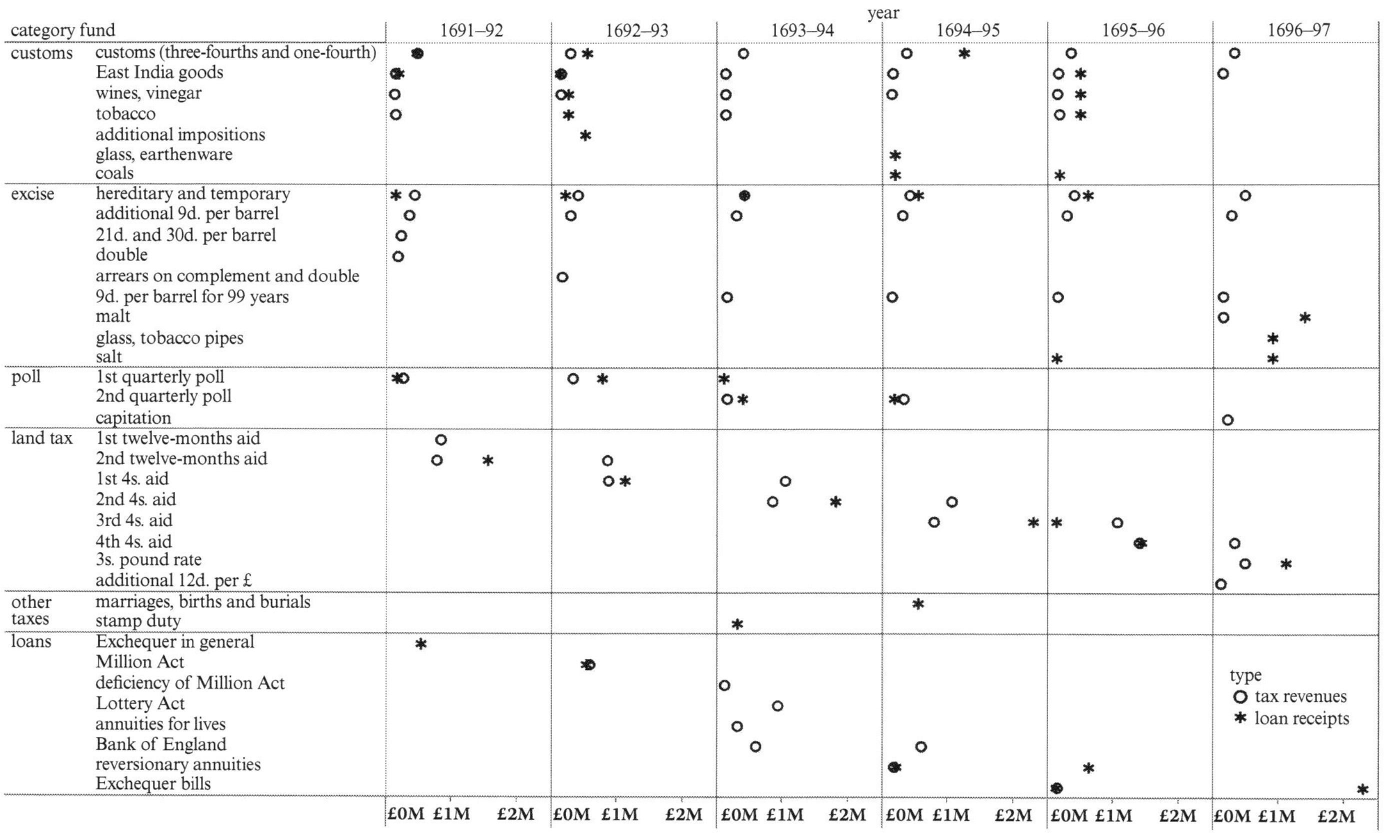

Figure 2.2 Comparison of English revenues and short-term loans by tax fund, 1691–97.
Source: CTB.

tried wherever possible to buy on credit and defer wage payments. But not everyone was willing to deal on credit.[11] And sooner or later even those who had previously agreed to furnish supplies on credit, or to have their wages deferred, demanded final payment. Paymasters tried whenever possible to tender payment in tallies of fictitious loan. But only their largest suppliers could deal in these instruments; other than officers (who were given no choice but to take payment in tallies), most military personnel did not earn enough in a year, and many suppliers operated on too small a scale, to be able to use even the smallest-denomination tallies. And even the large-scale operators, clothing and bread contractors for instance, though they might take tallies on some occasions, at other times pleaded for cash infusions. So the paymasters needed regular and large supplies of coin.

Now let's move one step back in the financial circle. Fortunately for paymasters, the coin they needed was available at the Exchequer. And it was available relatively early in the fiscal year, when a lot of their expenses were being incurred. It came in part from any lotteries, annuity sales or long-term loans approved by parliament. The rest came from short-term loans received in the Exchequer on the strength of borrowing clauses in the most recent revenue statutes. Both kinds of loans were made exclusively in specie; the Exchequer accepted no other currency, in large part because this was the very sort of money the paymasters most needed. The first months of every new calendar year were relatively easy times for Treasury and paymasters alike; as the new loans arrived, coin became available in large quantities and was doled out in healthy amounts to the paymasters. The real administrative grind arrived later in the fiscal year, especially from September onward, as parliamentary supplies began to run short. Then coin was much harder to come by; paymasters received new infusions from the treasury lords only if they could demonstrate very urgent need. This was the time of year when Treasury might authorize paymasters to discount their tallies of fictitious loan in the open market.

Now to close the circle. The Exchequer needed to repay any short-term loans and make annual payments on its long-term borrowing: annuity payments, lottery payouts (which were structured as annuities) and interest or interest-and-principal payments on long-term loans. These payments were always made in specie. But for some relatively small exceptions during the crisis period of 1696–97, the Exchequer dealt in no other currency. This was a second store of specie, distinct from that it received earlier in the year on short- and long-term loans. This second supply of specie the Exchequer obtained from its tax collectors and receivers. There were whole networks of tax collectors spread across the country. Customs and excise were the two main permanent tax bureaucracies. Each had their local collectors and London-based receiver-general or 'cashier' (with an accompanying staff). Customs added a layer of regional receivers between collectors and receiver-general. Revenues were forwarded from collectors through receivers to the relevant cashier or receiver-general, who was responsible in turn for paying them into the Exchequer. During the war years large, temporary bureaucracies were also erected for one-time revenues like land taxes. Each county, and major cities like London, had their own 'receiver-general' who supervised the collectors and receivers appointed by local officials. Receivers-general were responsible for paying land taxes into the Exchequer, though they might use a London-based correspondent for this purpose. Collectors took payment locally in specie. Land-tax and customs collectors typically forwarded the proceeds to regional receivers in this same currency. Receivers, and Excise collectors, had the option of sending so-called inland bills of exchange (a kind of money order) to their agents, or Excise cashier, in London. It is unclear how many used this option. But no matter the medium by which revenues were transmitted to London, they were always paid into the Exchequer in specie. Any inland bills were cashed by their London recipients before the latter made payment to the Exchequer.

So without adequate quantities of specie available beginning (loans and expenditures), middle (taxes) and end (loan repayments), the Treasury's whole system of public finance would have come grinding to a halt. This was to become a central concern in 1695 and 1696 as the quality of the nation's silver coin declined, gold coin became of uncertain value and the prospect of a recoinage (which would mean calling in most of the silver coin all at once) loomed ever larger.

Funding an English army in Flanders

To appreciate the coming story, you'll need to be familiar with one last piece of the government's financial machinery. Since the war was being fought on the continent, a good portion of the funds approved by parliament eventually had to be converted into continental currencies. This wasn't as much of an issue for the navy, which could often equip its ships at home before they set out for the season. But London's army paymaster regularly had to find a way of getting Flemish currency into the hands of the army's deputy paymaster stationed with the troops in Flanders. And England had also committed to providing subsidies to some of its less-affluent allies, money which again had to be provided in local currencies. The leading expert on this subject estimates that in this way England spent overseas an average of £970 thousand per year during the war, climbing to £1.3 million per annum during the key years 1694–96.[12] In a moment I will describe the several means by which this spending was financed. But first I need to introduce the instrument by which the vast majority of funding was transferred to the continent: foreign bills of exchange. (Henceforth I will refer to these only as 'bills of exchange', reserving the term 'inland bills of exchange' for their domestic counterpart.)

Bills of exchange were originally devised by the merchant community to clear overseas debts with as little expense as possible. Say merchant A in London needed to pay a supplier B in Amsterdam. One option would be for merchant A to buy an appropriate amount of some valuable commodity in London and ship it to supplier B. Gold and silver bullion were common choices for this purpose, since they had a high value-to-bulk ratio, were of uniform quality, could not spoil and (for reasons we will explore in a moment) had guaranteed floor prices on the other end. But there was usually an easier and cheaper way to make payment. Merchant A had only to find some other London merchant C who was owed by customer D in Amsterdam at least as much as what merchant A owed to supplier B. Merchant A could then arrange to pay merchant C the English-currency equivalent of what he owed supplier B. Merchant C in turn would give merchant A a piece of paper – the bill of exchange – by which customer D was instructed, by order of merchant C, to pay supplier B the Dutch-currency equivalent of the English money he had just received from merchant A. Handled in this way, no bulky commodities needed to cross the channel in either direction; merchant A's debt was cleared simply by sending the bill of exchange from London to Amsterdam. The two sets of international debts (of A to B and of D to C) were simultaneously cleared by cancelling their local counterparts (A and C in London and B and D in Amsterdam) against one another.

A little bit of terminology will provide a convenient shorthand for later references to, and quotations from contemporary documents concerning, bills of exchange. Merchant C was referred to as the 'drawer'; he was drawing upon customer D's obligation to pay him. Merchant A was the 'remitter'; he would send or 'remit' merchant C's bill of exchange to supplier B in Amsterdam. Supplier B was the 'payee' and customer D the 'payer', for obvious reasons.

For every bill of exchange, drawer and remitter had to agree upon two things: the date by which the bill would be paid overseas and an exchange rate (the number of foreign currency units of account that would be given out by the payer overseas per domestic currency unit of account paid locally by the remitter, or vice versa). The payment date was usually stated as the number of days or weeks after the payee first 'presented' the bill, i.e. informed the payer of his intention to collect.[13] Most often the time between presentation and payment was specified in a unit of measure called the 'usance': a standard that varied from city to city but in Amsterdam and Antwerp was equivalent to one month. On occasion parties would use some custom unit of measure, such as a certain number of days or weeks. Rates of exchange were a matter for negotiation between drawer and remitter, but within certain constraints. One constraint was what other merchants were offering; if one drawer was insisting upon terms too dear, a would-be remitter could always look for a different, less grasping one. The biggest constraint was the possibility of clearing the debt via bullion shipments. There was a definite cost to using bullion, but if drawers demanded more than this, better just to ship bullion instead.

What other merchants were asking or getting for their bills of exchange depended to a great extent, though not exclusively, on the state of trade between the two countries involved. Drawers from city X with debts owed them by people in foreign city Y could expect to realize a better local-currency price for such debts: a) the greater the total quantity of debt owed by persons in city X to persons in city Y (i.e. the more X-city people were demanding bills drawn on debtors in city Y); and b) the lower the amount of debt owed by persons in city Y to persons in city X (i.e. the less X-city people were willing and able to supply bills drawn on debtors in city Y). Demand and supply of debt payable in city Y could be affected by a wide range of circumstances. But foremost among them was the state of trade between the two cities and their surrounding areas; demand was greater if city X imported a lot of goods from city Y and supply was greater if city Y imported a lot of goods from city X.

The possibility of settling international debts via bullion shipments meant that exchange rates usually fluctuated within a relatively narrow band on either side of the ratio between the two cities' official (usually national) mint prices for gold or silver bullion (what economists call the 'mint par'). The mint price is just the number of local monetary units of account coined from a given weight of bullion refined to some official standard of purity. In a world where bullion could be shipped and coined without cost, and purchased always at the local mint price, exchange rates should never have varied from this ratio. Assume for the moment that the coins of cities X and Y were of the same fineness and weight. Merchants in city X could buy gold or silver bullion (which in this hypothetical scenario would always be freely available at the mint price of m local currency units per weight unit), ship it to city Y and have it minted there into foreign coins (which by assumption would generate the mint price n of foreign currency units per weight unit). So the merchants in question would obtain n foreign-currency units for m units of local currency, i.e. the 'mint par' exchange rate between the two cities would be n/m. This exchange rate would obviously change somewhat if the coins of the two cities differed in weight or fineness. Here is a concrete example. The mint prices for sterling (92.5 percent pure) silver bullion in England and the United Provinces were £3.1 per 'pound troy' and about 77.1 'schellingen' per 'mark'.[14] Since a pound troy was a little more than 1.5 times the weight of a Dutch mark, the mint par was about 37.9 schellingen per £. But merchants typically had to pay something more than the mint price to buy silver locally. They also incurred freight and insurance costs when shipping bullion to a foreign destination. So anyone using bullion to pay a foreign debt could only realize an exchange rate somewhat lower than the mint par. In the case of England and the United Provinces, this effective rate was about 36.4 schellingen per £.[15] Most contemporary newspapers reported exchange rates in an accounting unit called 'schellingen banco'. In Amsterdam these were credits on the books of the Amsterdam Exchange

Bank and worth about 1.05 times 'current' or actual coined schellingen. So the estimated mint-par exchange rate in this currency was lower still, about 34.7.[16] Under normal circumstances that would have been the floor for exchange rates on bills drawn in London and payable in Amsterdam; for if anyone offered to exchange schellingen for pounds at a rate lower than this, merchants would just have shipped bullion between the two cities instead. For the same reason there was a ceiling, a little above the mint par, beyond which the exchange rate on bills going in the other direction was unlikely to rise.

Since the point will become relevant a little later on, it bears mentioning that there were typically two mint pars between any two countries: one for silver and another for gold. This is because the ratio between the mint prices of these two metals was seldom the same from one country to the next. Effective exchange rates when shipping gold bullion were also influenced by the fact that gold coins, at least in England, did not circulate at their official mint values and were allowed instead to find their own price in the marketplace. Merchants would take all these factors into account and use the cheaper metal when settling their international debts via bullion. As a result, silver bullion was used when debts were owed from England to the Netherlands and gold when debts ran in the opposite direction. When settling debts from the Netherlands to England, it became even more economical to use gold (and the rates on bills of exchange adjusted accordingly) after the market price of guineas rose very considerably in 1695.

Finally, negotiations on exchange rates were also affected by the length of time between the original purchase date and the eventual payment date. Since the drawer was effectively borrowing short-term from the remitter (receiving local money now for money that would be delivered on the continent at a later date) a longer gap (a higher number of usances) meant a longer loan. For longer loans the remitter expected a better exchange rate: more foreign-currency units received abroad in future per unit of local currency he was paying the drawer today.

Now we can return to the English government's problem of paying for an army fighting on the continent. In order to get Flemish money into the hands of his deputy paymaster in Flanders (Richard Hill), England's army paymaster (Richard, Earl of Ranelagh) had three main options at his disposal – all of them making extensive use of bills of exchange. The first, and in some ways the simplest, was for Hill to draw bills of exchange upon Ranelagh. Specifically, Antwerp merchants would pay Hill, in local currency, for the right to collect English pounds in London from Ranelagh – money their London agents could then use to pay suppliers there. This method was used from time to time, but usually only in exceptional circumstances. A second possibility was to employ an agent in Europe to draw bills of exchange upon Ranelagh in London and provide the cash proceeds to Hill in Antwerp. This was the main method used early on in the war. The Treasury's agent at the time was William Schuylenberg, Ranelagh's counterpart in the Dutch army. A third option was to employ a London-based agent to draw bills upon European debtors and remit those bills to sub-agents in Flanders from whom Hill could then collect the cash proceeds. This is how the Treasury moved most of the army's cash from 1692 onward. In Chapter 5 we will meet some of the London agents the Treasury employed for this purpose. Two of them were 'goldsmith bankers' – a term contemporaries used to refer to those goldsmiths who had turned into private bankers: accepting deposits, issuing paper notes convertible into specie on demand, and making loans.

Notes

1 Jones, *War and Economy*, pp. 70–1.
2 Chandaman, *English Public Revenue*, p. 361.
3 Jones, *War and Economy*, pp. 70–1.
4 Dickson, *Financial Revolution*, pp. 48–9.
5 Dickson, *Financial Revolution*, pp. 341–57.
6 Dickson *Financial Revolution*, pp. 393–95, Ehrman, *Navy in the War*, ch. 11, sect. 3.
7 Tallies were made of wooden sticks some four feet long. After being given a rectangular cross-section, they were cut in half lengthwise using a random series of twists and turns. The lender was issued the 'stock' piece while the Exchequer retained the 'foil', suitably marked to allow for indexed storage. Whenever an order was presented for payment, the corresponding tally stock piece presented by the claimant had first to be matched to the foil in storage to ensure authenticity.
8 The Exchequer accounts are tabulated in *CTB*, vols. IX–XI. I skipped the earliest years of the war since the Exchequer lumped those together in a single account.
9 To generate this figure I had to make one adjustment to the Exchequer's accounts. Occasionally it reported tax receipts or borrowing across a group of taxes rather than for each individually. In such cases I simply divided the figure evenly across the several tax funds in the group.
10 The records in question are printed in *CTB*, vols. IX–XI. The documents frequently give details about the specific currencies in which paymasters were issued funds from the Exchequer. But they rarely mention the currencies in which taxes and loans were paid into the Exchequer. So in the following overview I have had to make a few assumptions on the latter front. But these assumptions are fully consistent with the few references in the *CTB* to the cash media in which tax collectors and receivers transacted their affairs and with the overall structure of the Treasury's system of tax anticipations.
11 So for instance victualling commissioner Thomas Papillon told the king in November 1693 that while he was doing his best to get the fleet provisioned in a timely manner, his work had almost been brought to a stop. '[T]hey had bought what they could by contract and could not now buy in the market without money' (manuscript of 1 Nov. 1693, printed in Papillon, *Memoirs of Thomas Papillon*, p. 397). The victualling officers later reported that on the whole 2/3rds of their suppliers required ready money and would not take payment in tallies (NA, SP 44/274 (hereafter 'Lords Justices Minutes'), 19 Aug. 1695).
12 Jones *War and Economy*, p. 38.
13 Allowing time for payment opened the possibility for drawers to work on credit. They could use the sale proceeds of a bill to purchase goods locally and ship

them to the payer, thereby creating the payer's debt obligation to the drawer only sometime after the bill itself had been drawn.

14 I derived the latter number from a report in Polak, *Historiografie en Economie*, that from 1680 onward Dutch mints supplied 25.1 guilders (the equivalent of ~83.7 schellingen) per Dutch mark of pure silver. I then adjusted that figure downward for the lower fineness of sterling silver.

15 Jones, *War and Economy*, p. 77.

16 Jones, *War and Economy*, p. 123.

Bibliography

Manuscript sources

National Archives, SP 44/274 ('Lords Justices Minutes')

Printed primary sources

Great Britain. Public Record Office. *Calendar of Treasury Books.* Volume IX: *1689–1692*. Edited by William Shaw. London: HMSO, 1931. Accessed online at http://www.british-history.ac.uk/cal-treasury-books/vol9.

Great Britain. Public Record Office. *Calendar of Treasury Books.* Volume X: *January 1693 to March 1696*. Edited by William Shaw. London: HMSO, 1931. Accessed online at http://www.british-history.ac.uk/cal-treasury-books/vol10.

Great Britain. Public Record Office. *Calendar of Treasury Books.* Volume XI: *April 1696 to March 1696–7*. Edited by William Shaw. London: HMSO, 1931. Accessed online at http://www.british-history.ac.uk/cal-treasury-books/vol11.

Papillon, A. F. W. *Memoirs of Thomas Papillon of London, Merchant (1623–1702)*. Reading: Joseph Beecroft, 1887.

Secondary sources

Chandaman, C. D. *The English Public Revenue, 1660–1688*. Oxford: Oxford University Press, 1975.

Dickson, P. G. M. *The Financial Revolution in England: A Study in the Development of Public Credit, 1688–1756*. London: Macmillan Press, 1967.

Ehrman, John. *The Navy in the War of William III, 1689–1697: Its State and Direction*. Cambridge: Cambridge University Press, 1953.

Jones, D. W. *War and Economy in the Age of William III and Marlborough*. Oxford: Basil Blackwell, 1988.

Polak, Menno S. *Historiografie en Economie van de 'Muntchaos': De Muntproductie van de Republiek (1606–1795)*. Amsterdam: NEHA, 1998.

3   The inception of the Bank of England

The Bank of England, as it took shape in 1694, used monetary innovation to align public needs (for war loans long- and short-term) with private opportunities (for an unusually high rate of return to shareholders in the new venture). In this chapter I describe in some detail the Bank's basic design and its early business operations. This will enable us to better appreciate the nature of several other banking projects that came to the fore in the next few years (projects that played a vital role in the politics of the recoinage) and to grasp a key vulnerability in the Bank's operations (one that both the Treasury and the Bank's opponents would soon use to their own ends).

Details of the Bank's path to realization are scant. Most come from accounts probably written by or for William Paterson, whom many consider to be its inventor. As we shall see, he proposed something rather different than the Bank that was instituted in 1694. But we will be better positioned to appreciate the Bank's significance if we start by exploring his basic idea.

Paterson's 'Transferable Fund of Interest'

Paterson was a West Indies merchant with a good working knowledge of European public finance and banking. Drawing upon that experience, in May 1691 he approached the Treasury with a plan for how it might raise some of the funds needed for next year's military campaign. He proposed a large loan contributed in specie by numerous small investors, but with an unusual twist; the state would make no attempt to repay the principal and commit only to paying the interest annually.[1] The idea would be of obvious interest to the Treasury, sparing the need to find a new revenue source with which to repay the principal. Though the individual lenders could not get their money back from the state itself, they would be able to do so by other means. They were to be given paper certificates or 'bills' in the amount of their contribution to the loan. The bills, which would entitle them to collect interest at the rate of 6 percent per annum, were to be transferable. So lenders could recover their principal by offering their bills to some other investor(s), whether for cash or to honour an existing debt. The government was to pay an additional 1 percent to a group of trustees who would manage the scheme. Their principal duty would be to ensure that interest was paid in the requisite amounts to all registered bill holders. Each of them would also be required to set aside some minimum amount of specie (or bills from which specie could be raised), amounting in all to £200 thousand, with which to buy – on demand, at full face value, and with no questions asked – the bills of any of the scheme's investors who wanted to have their money back. The trustees would collect the standard interest rate on any bills so purchased until the latter could be resold to some other investor. (In the version presented to the Commons, they would also be paid an additional 5 percent interest on the specie reserve for the first year.) Paterson called this new and unusual sort of loan a 'transferable fund of perpetual interest' – a phrase that captures his idea quite well.

The treasury lords asked Lowndes, then assistant-secretary, to report on the proposal. He recommended very strongly against it, for several reasons.[2] First, it would be hard to find lenders because they couldn't be guaranteed to recover their principal. While in theory they could sell their bills, there was no guarantee anyone would be prepared to buy. Second, even if lenders proved available, the bills were almost certain to fall to a steep discount. Tallies were already going at a discount even though they paid interest at 8 percent and holders were very likely to get their principal back within a year. These bills were likely to fall to an even deeper discount given that they would pay less interest and the principal might never be recovered. Third, the bills were sure to be paid into the Exchequer on taxes and loans. Even if they held their full face value, to the extent taxes were paid in this medium the Treasury would be deprived of the specie it needed to redeem existing tallies. Nor could this specie be obtained from other lenders; for no one would pay good coin into the Exchequer if there was a chance they would be repaid in such bills.

Reluctant to proceed, the treasury lords advised Paterson that they would consider his scheme only if he first gathered a 'voluntary society of monied men' prepared to declare publicly that they would accept the bills as payment in their own private dealings. But as soon as Paterson delivered on this request, the Treasury raised the stakes further. The society's members would have to commit in advance to lending the whole sum themselves if other investors weren't willing to step forward with the requisite contributions.[3]

Around this time, some of Paterson's associates proposed an important modification: making the bills legal tender.[4] Paterson later claimed to have opposed the very idea.[5] It is unclear in any case exactly how it would have worked. Technically, with a legal-tender currency the loan could have been made just by printing up the requisite currency and giving it to the Exchequer, without any need to attract a body of specie lenders. Or perhaps his associates were counting on the loan having to be contributed in specie and merely wanted the bills, still a kind of loan receipt, to be legally admissible as a means of payment – whether for taxes and later war loans or in paying private debts.

When the proposal came before the Commons early in 1692, the legal-tender idea was rejected outright; the bills had to be accepted voluntarily or not at all. Several MPs argued for setting the whole plan aside, dismissing it as a dishonour and a cheat as well as impracticable. It seems too that the trustees were still to be liable for raising the whole of the loan themselves should subscriptions fall short of the loan amount. Most of Paterson's backers pulled out at this point. He tried to assemble from the remnants a commitment to raise a loan of just £500 thousand. But he claims the Treasury, uninterested in so small a sum, let the project die that year.[6]

Paterson tried his luck again late in 1693. Only a few incidentals had changed, though there was no mention this time of giving the bills legal-tender status. The proposal came before a Commons committee on 5 February 1694 and was summarily rejected. Bonnet reported the principal reason offered against it: that the loan might well fail.[7] No one would want to participate, either because parliament was to have the right to recall the loan at will or because lenders might not be able to recover their principal. Paterson later claimed that others had complained the terms of the loan were too generous, especially for the group that would raise the specie reserve.[8]

A comparison with Godfrey's 'Bank of England'

The project that came before the Commons a few months later and eventually turned into the Bank of England had nothing to do with Paterson. It came rather from a coalition put together by Michael Godfrey and a number of other wealthy London merchants who, shut out by the war from their usual line of business (the wine trade with France), had been trying to make inroads into the East-India trade – nominally still a state-protected monopoly.[9] Paterson later complained that they had stolen his idea and succeeded where he failed only because they had ties to the royal court and a good reputation in parliament.[10] But in fact the new project was quite different from the one he had been flogging. His fund of transferable interest was little more than a standard loan, novel only in being transferable in small pieces and having a set of market makers. But the project led by Godfrey very consciously and publicly paired Paterson's idea of a transferable, permanent loan with the rudiments of a banking operation.

We know the Godfrey project only in its final form as implemented in the act that authorized creation of the Bank of England (5 & 6 W. & M., c. 20).[11] The following short account is a logical reconstruction of the design implicit in that statute. Bank investors were invited to 'subscribe' toward a loan of £1.2 million, i.e. specify some maximum amount of specie that they were willing to contribute toward said loan. Subscribers would have to make an immediate down payment, in specie, of 20 percent of the value of their subscription. In subscribing they were also legally binding themselves to deliver all, or any part, of the remaining 80 percent, again in specie, when and if asked to do so. In principle, therefore, subscribers were taking on an obligation to lend the whole £1.2 million in specie. But from the outset the plan was to ask of them only a *part* of what they had subscribed. The rest would be collected instead from persons who were not themselves subscribers but who were just looking for a reasonably profitable place to park some of their cash for a while. For this purpose it was proposed to use 'bills', but of a different kind than Paterson had envisioned. His were to be certificates of participation in the original loan, authorizing holders to claim their share of the interest being paid by the state on that loan. The Bank's bills, by contrast, were for third-party investors who were lending some spare cash to the Bank itself. Their bills would last only for a limited time (a year as it turned out), after which the investors could opt to be repaid their principal – leaving the Bank to find someone else to replace them. The Bank would then use the specie contributed by bill holders to help fund the £1.2 million loan – collecting interest from the government at 8 percent but paying bill holders at a rate considerably below that. This would give share-holders a very handsome rate of return, since they would have to contribute only a fraction of the loan but would earn interest of 8 percent on the whole amount (less whatever interest was paid to bill holders). Contemporaries must have been well aware of this new wrinkle, since both diplomatic ob-servers, hardly financial experts, commented upon it even before the author-izing statute had passed parliament.[12] The terms of the authorizing statute enabled shareholders to do better still. The Bank was entitled to issue up to £1.2 million in bills. This meant that between specie contributions from shareholders (presumably for something less than the full £1.2 million re-quired for the loan) and bill holders (for up to an additional £1.2 million if all went well), the Bank would have more cash than it needed to finance the government loan. These additional specie resources could also be loaned out to the crown (though by law only on tax funds authorized by parliament for this purpose) at rates well above those being paid to bill holders.

The Godfrey project was both similar to and different from Paterson's scheme. Both were designed to address the problem of how to get people to participate in a loan that had no planned repayment date and could well turn out to be permanent. Both targeted the stores of specie that merchants kept on hand in case they needed to meet some creditor's demand and so which they could not afford to tie up in long-term investments that would be difficult to turn back into ready money. The trick was to let them contribute to a long-term loan while making it easy either to liquidate that contribu-tion or to use it, in place of their original specie holding, as a means of pay-ing their creditors.[13] With Paterson's design, this was achieved exclusively by means of bills, which were shares in the government loan itself, directly transferable to others or capable of being cashed at a moment's notice. In the Godfrey plan, it was managed in part by using a joint-stock design – so that subscribers to the loan could readily sell their shares on the London stock market[14] – and in part by using a different kind of bill to attract investors whose commitment was explicitly short-term and so whose contributions would have to be rolled over annually or replaced with cash from new short-term investors. The latter feature clearly made Godfrey's project a bank, if by that we mean an organization that borrows at one rate of interest in order to re-lend at a higher one. Paterson later claimed he had intended all along to turn his project into a bank, but chose to conceal this potential because the very word tended to inflame parliamentarians.[15] On his own telling he was named a director of the Bank of England only as an afterthought, in grudging recognition that the idea of a transferable fund of interest had come from him.[16] This may have been true. But this doesn't change the fact that his core idea was for something other than a bank – what we might call a simple loan syndicate.

The two projects differed also in one other important respect. It is impossible to know for sure given the fragmentary nature of the materials at our disposal. But it seems that Paterson conceived his bills as a net addition to the national money supply. Though he wanted nothing to do with the idea of legal tender, he did see the bills as a new kind of currency that would supplement gold and silver as a means of payment both in private transactions and at the Exchequer for taxes and loans.[17] This was certainly Lowndes' assumption and the basis for one of his warnings against the scheme. It would also explain why the Treasury was worried about whether the bills would circulate at face value and why Paterson explicitly proposed setting aside a specie reserve to ensure a ready market for them. Otherwise they might impose losses upon the Exchequer, should it happen to receive them at a certain value and be unable to dispose of them again at a price that high. The Godfrey design, by contrast, did not call for its bills to be used in this way. If they circulated at all, they could be used only in private transactions between members of the general public and not at the Exchequer. This would go a long way to explaining why Godfrey's plan succeeded where Paterson's had failed. The risk of Bank bills going to some discount would be borne by the bill holders and the Bank alone and could never compromise the Treasury's operations. It would also explain why the statute by which the Bank was established did not require, indeed made no mention of, a specie reserve. For from the government's point of view it was unimportant whether and to what extent the bills retained their value in the open market. That would be the Bank's own concern.

The Bank in operation

In this section I provide an overview of the Bank's basic business model in its first several years of operation. I draw upon this information in Chapter 5 to explain the growing financial problems that the Bank began to encounter in 1695 in connection with its 'remittance' operations, i.e. the business of supplying funding to the English army in Flanders. I also draw upon it in the final section of this chapter to show that, despite some appearances to the contrary, the Bank remained heavily dependent on specie in its day-to-day operations. This simple fact, which we shall see was also true for all the other banking projects that came to the fore during our period, played a fundamental role in shaping the politics of the recoinage debate and of the ensuing monetary crisis.

Note that the following overview affords the first complete picture ever provided of the Bank's early methods. Until now the accounting information required for this task had not been available. The first volume in the Bank's so-called 'General Ledgers' series commences only in June 1695.[18] This led historians of the Bank to conclude that we were missing records for the Bank's first year, when so many interesting things were happening.[19] It turns out however that a full set of accounts was available all along, hiding in plain sight. I recently discovered them interspersed among the first four volumes of the Bank's record of deposits and withdrawals – the so-called 'Drawing Office Customer Account Ledgers'.[20] I used those ledgers, together with the first General Ledger, to generate a comprehensive transcription of the Bank's accounts for its first several years of operation.

Figures 3.1 and 3.2 provide overviews of the Bank's balance sheet from its inception to the end of 1696.[21] Note that in keeping with the conventions of double-entry accounting, the Bank recorded additions to asset and liability accounts as debits and credits respectively. I have chosen to report all account balances in the form of net debits (debits less credits). Consequently, asset and liability account balances show as positive and negative sums respectively. Figure 3.1 is stacked to show the overall balance of assets and liabilities. Figure 3.2 is unstacked to make it easier to see changes in individual accounts.

Let's begin with the liability accounts. The total value of Bank bills out in circulation, a balance between the amount issued and the amount brought back to the Bank for encashment, is tracked in the account of that name. The notes account does the same for a second type of paper currency issued by the Bank. Notes were issued for the most part as receipts for specie deposited with the Bank. Bearing no interest, they were payable (in specie) at the Bank on demand, in whole or in part (in the latter case, the note would go back into circulation, marked down in value). I will investigate the bill and notes accounts in greater detail in a moment. The account labelled 'stock and cash calls' mainly reports the £720 thousand in specie received from subscribers in the Bank's earliest months. During the monetary crisis of 1696, as its store of specie dwindled almost to zero, the Bank also took in two further instalment payments from its shareholders (one of them as a temporary loan), each for 20 percent of the par value of the stock. Most of the latter intake was probably contributed in the Bank's own notes rather than in specie. But this had the same ultimate effect, by freeing the Bank from having to pay out specie on said notes. In the 'exchanges' account I have fused two accounts, kept separate by the Bank (one a liability and the other an asset), that pertained to a new line of business upon which it embarked

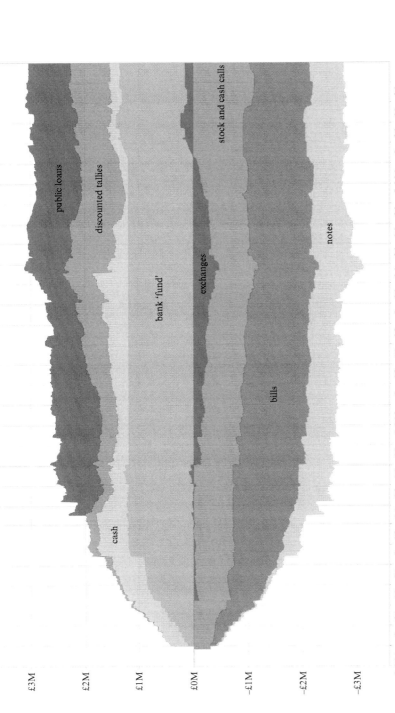

Figure 3.1 Running net debits (stacked) on the Bank of England's main accounts, 1694–96.
Source: Bank Drawing Ledgers and Bank General Ledger 1.

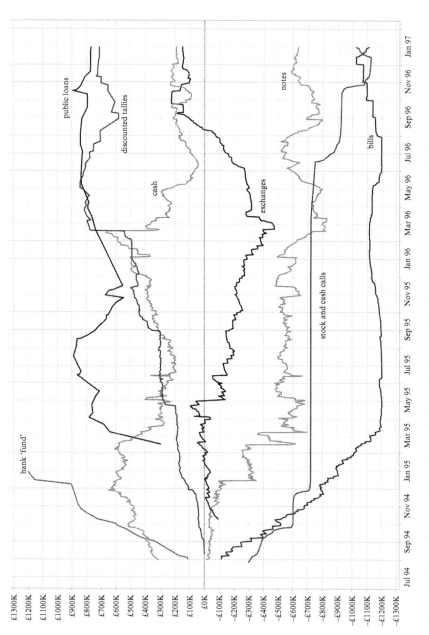

Figure 3.2 Running net debits (unstacked) on the Bank of England's main accounts, 1694–96.
Source: Bank Drawing Ledgers and Bank General Ledger 1.

in late 1694: supplying funds, in Flemish currencies, to the English army in Flanders. I postpone consideration of that account to Chapter 5.

Moving on to the asset accounts, the 'fund' was the Bank's name for its inaugural £1.2 million loan to the crown. Were it not for my having pushed the exchanges account to the bottom of the stack, its graph in Figure 3.1 would have appeared as a perfectly flat line after 1 January 1695, by which date the Bank had paid the whole of the loan into the Exchequer. The cash account was not just, as its name suggests, a record of specie on hand. In some sense it was an accounting construct, a kind of virtual cash drawer through which all assets and liabilities passed as they were purchased/sold or acquired/paid. As such, credits or debits for any given day regularly included things quite distinct from 'cash' in the narrow sense of that word.[22] Still, since for any given day non-'cash' items generally appeared twice in the cash account, once on the credit and another time on the debit side, the daily *balance* on that account usually represented something close to the amount of specie on hand.[23] Figure 3.2 shows that the balance on the cash account was constantly fluctuating, meaning that specie was regularly entering or leaving the Bank. Usually these opposing movements more or less balanced out over the course of a week or a month; but it is also obvious that sometimes they did not. The account labelled 'public loans' tracks money loaned directly to the government, in recognition of which the Bank received Exchequer tallies. The account for 'discounted tallies' tracks tallies that the Bank had bought from others in the secondary market, in effect taking over short-term government loans from the original lenders. The Bank referred to the tallies so obtained as 'discounted' (the other kind it called 'tallies of loan'), but really this was a misnomer. Before the Bank began operations, tallies being resold in the secondary market were almost always discounted. Buyers could demand a discount because sellers were at a disadvantage, trying to swap for ready cash an asset with an uncertain payment date and that many were therefore reluctant to buy. But all this changed once the Bank began buying tallies; the discount at least on the best-quality tallies soon went to zero.[24] Note that while the Bank did also engage in some private lending (both directly and by discounting commercial bills), I left these accounts out of Figures 3.1 and 3.2. For they are so small as to be almost invisible. Virtually all of the Bank's lending was to the government alone.

A few of the accounts require closer examination.

Figure 3.3 shows the running total of debits (issues) and credits (cancellations) on the Bank's various bill accounts.[25] Under the 'Paymasters' label I have aggregated the accounts for five different military officials: Charles Bertie (ordnance), Charles Fox (Irish transports), Richard Ranelagh (army), Edward Russell (navy treasurer) and Anthony Stephens (navy cashier). The fact that the Bank kept such accounts means that some of the earliest bills were issued as obligations against those men, though payable in the Bank on their behalf. But after the first few weeks all bills were issued only against Bank cashiers such as Ince, Mercer and Monteage. Note that Mercer took

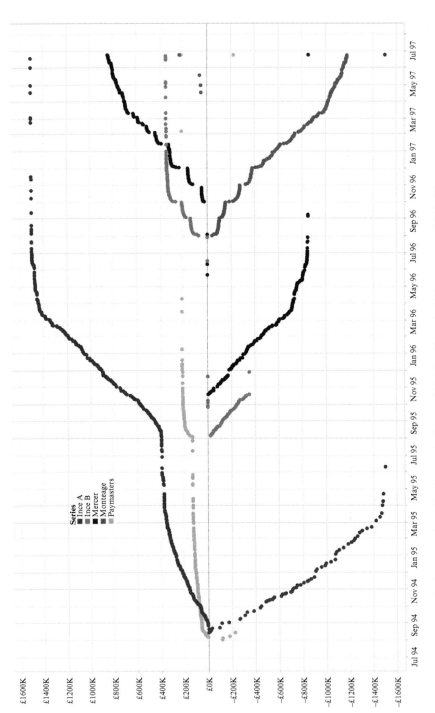

Figure 3.3 Running debits (+) and credits (−) on the Bank of England's main bills accounts, 1694–97.

Source: Bank Drawing Ledgers and Bank General Ledger 1.

the B series of bills over from Ince part way through their annual run. From this Figure we may draw several conclusions. First, about £530 thousand of the bills issued in the Bank's earliest days were made payable on demand. Some of these came back for encashment almost immediately, but many were held for months and a few for as long as a full year. It could be that military paymasters didn't need them right away and cashed them only as occasion demanded. But since the military was always hard pressed, it seems more likely that the paymasters succeeded in getting some of their creditors to take payment in bills and the latter cashed or renewed them at their appointed due dates. In that case, some of the creditors were clearly choosing to hold bills for a time as short-term investments. Second, apart from the bills just mentioned, all others were given maturity dates of one year from the date of issue (or, starting in the second year, for the first day of the corresponding month). They were the equivalent of modern one-year term deposits, except fully transferable. Most bills were presented for payment on their due date, but every year there were some laggards. Third, as the bills that had been made payable on demand were presented to the Bank, the Bank in turn cancelled them and issued out new bills payable a year hence – always keeping the total amount beneath the legislative ceiling of £1.2 million. Finally, there was a pretty stable and reliable demand for Bank bills; they were rolled over or sold to new investors almost as quickly as the previous year's bills were retired.

Figure 3.4 shows the running total of net debits (issues less cancellations) of Bank notes.[26] I have broken out separately the notes issued to military paymasters. Unlike the rest, these were given out not in return for specie deposited with, or assets sold to, the Bank but rather in fulfilment of government loans the Bank had agreed to make.[27] A few particulars are worth noting. First, for the first four months or so the Bank's net note issue was very small, only around £100 thousand. Second, the large surges in net note issues in December 1694 and February and March 1695 were driven almost entirely by loans to the military. Third, the vast majority of the notes issued to the paymasters returned upon the Bank for encashment almost immediately. The only exception was in December 1694; and the slower pace of return in this case probably means only that the navy treasurer was cashing them gradually as he needed specie with which to pay sailors and navy creditors. Fourth, something changed starting around March 1695; though the large quantity of notes issued to the paymasters that month quickly returned upon the Bank, other note issues to private citizens more than compensated. After March, the overall net issue of notes never sank below £450 thousand and before the monetary panic that began in May 1696 was hovering around £750 thousand.

Finally, Figures 3.5 through 3.7 establish the nature of the Bank's involvement in additional, short-term, lending to the state. Figures 3.5 and 3.6 show the various tax funds upon which the Bank loaned short-term to the Exchequer, the first directly and the second indirectly through the secondary market for Exchequer tallies. Together they may give the impression that with a few exceptions (e.g. reversionary annuities) the Bank liked to buy tallies and then

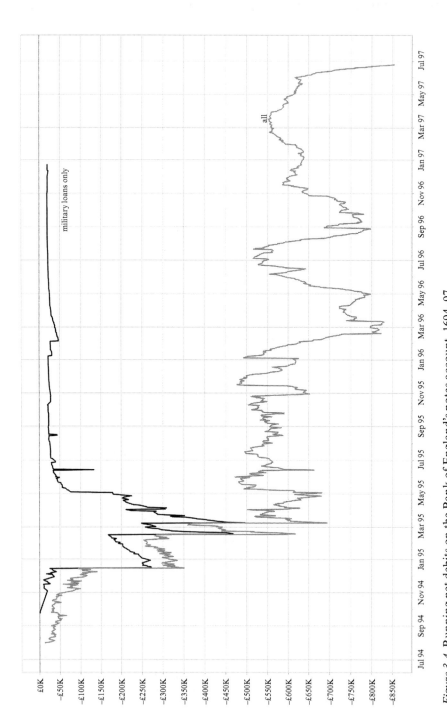

Figure 3.4 Running net debits on the Bank of England's notes account, 1694–97.
Source: Bank Drawing Ledgers and Bank General Ledger 1.

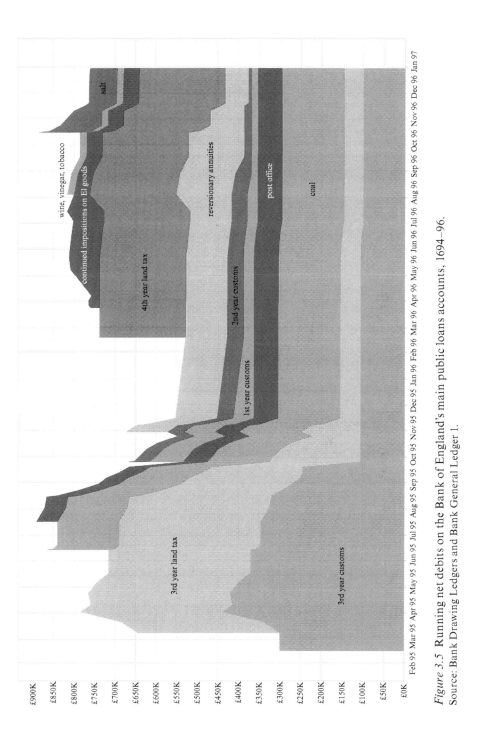

Figure 3.5 Running net debits on the Bank of England's main public loans accounts, 1694–96.
Source: Bank Drawing Ledgers and Bank General Ledger 1.

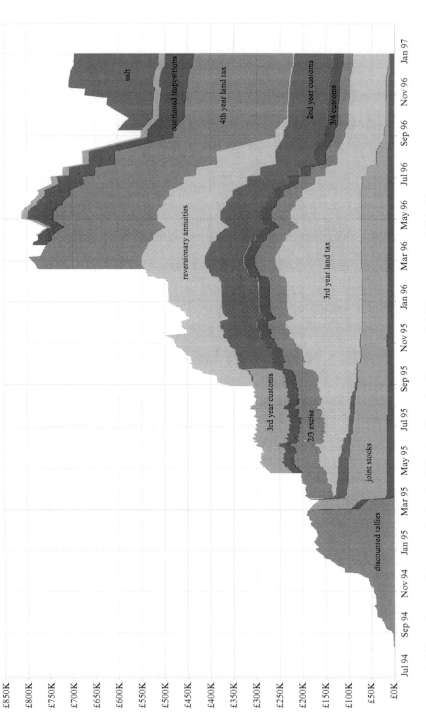

Figure 3.6 Running net debits on the Bank of England's main discounted tallies accounts, 1694–96.
Source: Bank Drawing Ledgers and Bank General Ledger 1.

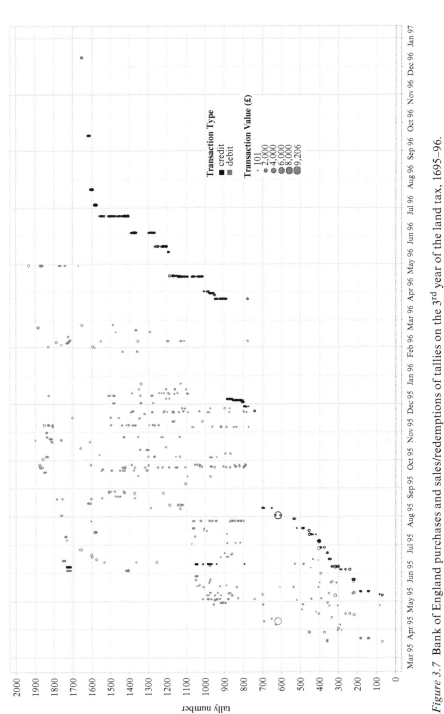

Figure 3.7 Bank of England purchases and sales/redemptions of tallies on the 3rd year of the land tax, 1695–96.

Source: Bank Drawing Ledgers and Bank General Ledger 1.

hold them for relatively long periods of time. But this is misleading for two reasons. First, within each category of tally, investments were usually being rolled over every few months. Figure 3.7 illustrates the pattern for one tax fund: the third year of the land tax. Debit and credit transactions refer to tally purchases and sales or redemptions respectively. At first the Bank was buying up only those tallies estimated to be a few months away from coming due for payment. Once the Exchequer paid those tallies off, the Bank might reinvest the funds, buying later tallies in the same series.[28] But the same Figure also shows that tallies purchased from June 1695 onward started to take a lot longer to come due for payment. This relates to the second reason the graphs are misleading; they reflect behaviour into which the Bank was forced and which it almost certainly would not have chosen if left to its own devices. Beginning in summer 1695, growing uncertainty about clipped money slowed tax receipts. Then, after January 1696, additional delays resulted when the Exchequer was required by law to melt down all taxes received in clipped coin before paying the proceeds out to tally holders. The Bank, like many other investors, got caught in this squeeze and ended up having to hold many tallies for far longer than it wanted or had anticipated. Its preferred behaviour, as illustrated for instance by its investments in the third year of the customs and of the land tax, would have been to hold tallies only for a few months before taking repayment and then, as long as its overall cash position was still healthy, reinvesting the proceeds in other tax funds or in later tallies of the same series.

The importance of specie to the Bank's operations

From the foregoing overview, especially Figure 3.2, it is clear that the Bank paid the bulk of its founding loan into the Exchequer in its own bills and notes. We can be quite precise about this: £777.7 was contributed in bills and £306.7K in notes.[29] At first glance this makes it seem that the Bank departed from the design implicit in its authorizing statute, which called for lending to the government in specie that was borrowed in part from shareholders and for the rest from bill holders. But paying the loan in the first instance in bills and notes was just a procedural shortcut to this same final outcome. The Treasury gave the bills and notes to its paymasters. The bulk of the notes came back upon the Bank for encashment almost immediately, meaning they were ultimately financed by specie raised from shareholders or by selling bills to third-party investors. Granted, many of the bills paid into the Exchequer stayed out in circulation for months, some for an entire year. But to the extent they did so, the paymasters' creditors were foregoing their right to claim final payment from the Treasury and in effect lending the corresponding amount of specie to the Bank (which would otherwise have had to sell bills to some third party and transfer that cash to the paymasters to enable them to pay their creditors).

Consequently, taking the state of the Bank at the first 'general balance' (i.e. reconciliation) on 15 March 1695, and setting aside for now its dealing in foreign bills of exchange, its actual operation conformed quite closely to the loan-intermediary model set out in the statute. Commitments for the whole £1.2 million had been received within 12 days of the subscription books being opened on 21 June 1694. The Bank chose to call in only 60 percent of the sum subscribed. Members of the general public took up enough bills to cover the remaining £480 thousand of the loan and about £720 thousand more. The latter specie influx gave the Bank capacity for some additional lending: hence the £826 thousand in Exchequer tallies it was holding by that date. The only real departure, early on, from the design implicit in the statute was the decision to use notes rather than bills for paying some part of the loan. This was probably, at least at first, an arrangement of convenience rather than a major design change. If, some months into its existence, the Bank had already built up a large store of cash from selling bills to third-party investors, there was no point in paying later loan instalments with bills; the paymasters could be paid in notes, which they would present for encashment as soon as they needed actual specie.

Had the Bank stuck to the basic loan-intermediary model, it would have had relatively little need for a specie reserve – almost none at all if existing holders regularly rolled their bills over when they came due or if the Bank could find buyers for new bills as fast as the previous year's bills were encashed. But in March 1695 the Bank began innovating in a way that gave it the capacity for creating new money (rather than just borrowing and relending specie)[30] but also demanded that it start keeping a relatively large specie reserve. Specifically, in that month the Bank began issuing large quantities of notes to private individuals, notes that remained out in circulation rather than, as before, coming back almost immediately for encashment. Some part of this may have been the result simply of people depositing specie and agreeing to hold Bank notes in their stead. But it may also have been due in part to the Bank using its notes to create money *ex nihilo*. Specifically, it may have begun printing notes and using them to buy financial assets from other investors: Exchequer tallies, bills of exchange (used to fund the English army in Flanders) and commercial bills. The Bank's records weren't kept in a way that would allow us to distinguish between the several possible sources of note issue. But whatever the causes of the sudden surge in notes in circulation, the Bank now needed to hold back a relatively large specie reserve against the possibility that a large proportion of its notes would suddenly be presented for encashment all at once.

Maintaining a good-sized specie reserve was no easy task for the Bank because large quantities of notes returned for encashment on a regular basis. Figure 3.8 suggests that on an average day some 10 percent of the total amount in circulation was presented for payment at the Bank.[31] Presumably this was because Bank notes were a very limited-purpose kind of money. As far as the Exchequer was concerned, they were entirely one-way money, accepted there when the Bank agreed to make a new war loan but never to be taken back again, whether in payment of taxes or from third-party lenders

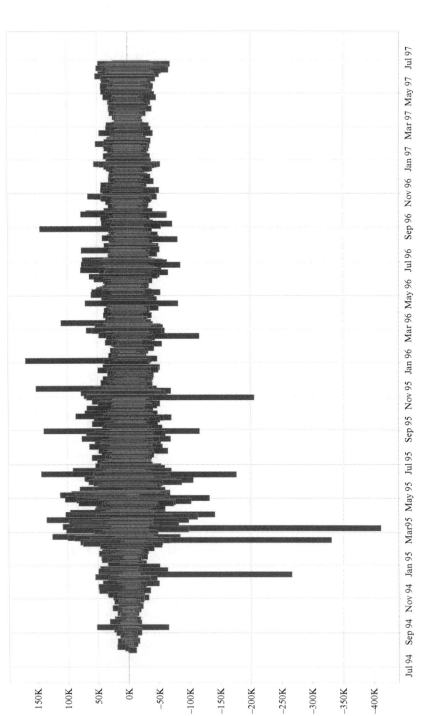

Figure 3.8 Daily issues (−£) and cancellations (+£) of bank notes, 1694–96.
Source: Bank Drawing Ledgers and Bank General Ledger 1.

who may have amassed their own store of Bank notes.[32] As far as the Treasury's records permit us to judge, it seems the Exchequer continued to transact its business principally in specie even after the Bank came on the scene. There are no references during our period to the Exchequer taking in Bank notes upon taxes or new loans and using them to pay principal or interest on existing Bank loans. Tax receivers continue sending their money up to London in specie under armed guard.[33] And in June 1695 they complained that, with silver coin then in disrepute, the only way they could their taxes in was to agree to take gold guineas at high prices – a dilemma that would not have existed had Bank bills and notes, or indeed any paper currencies, been accepted in payment of taxes.[34] So anyone needing to pay their taxes or interested in lending to the Exchequer could not use Bank notes directly for this purpose and would first need to convert that currency into specie at the Bank. The same would hold true for any merchants or manufacturers needing to pay their employees and small-scale creditors, for the same reason as with military paymasters.

One way the Bank could hope to offset the daily exodus of specie was by regularly attracting other individuals willing to deposit specie and take notes in their place. But there was relatively little the Bank could do on this front. Indeed, it was only for accidental reasons that people had suddenly became at all willing to hold Bank notes in relatively large quantities. As we shall see in Chapter 4, a Commons committee report released in late March 1695 created great uncertainty about the future value of clipped coin. This, together with the poor state of the silver coin then in circulation and the ubiquity of counterfeit money, made the general public eager to deposit specie with the Bank and take notes instead, or to hold onto, rather than encash, notes taken from the Bank in payment of tallies and discounted commercial bills, or from military paymasters in payment of their debts.[35] For while they might have worried about notes falling to a discount of some kind, they were surely unlikely to lose as much as half their face value – a prospect faced by anyone holding clipped silver coin. Though the Bank could have tried to interest more people in swapping coin for notes by offering some modest rate of interest on the latter, this would have been difficult for practical reasons. Since most notes were for odd and relatively small amounts, calculating the interest due would have been time-consuming and not worth the trouble. Nor would it have been possible to begin paying interest on notes already in circulation without calling them all in and marking them with a date at which interest eligibility would commence. In its early years the Bank used interest-bearing notes only once (again during the monetary crisis of 1696) and this on issues that were new (so they could easily be marked with start and maturity dates), of large denomination (greater than £50), and payable only in whole (so that the interest owing could be tracked and paid more easily). So for the most part there was little the Bank could do to actively control the quantity of incoming specie deposits; they were limited to whatever the general public was willing to bring forward. For the same reason, they would have to restrict the quantity of notes issued for buying other assets (as contrasted with notes issued in receipt of specie deposits) to a level they knew could be accommodated given the current rates at which existing notes tended to be presented for payment and at which new specie deposits were arriving.

This left three main ways in which the Bank could actively control the size of its specie reserve.[36] One was by trying to persuade people to keep the bulk of their working cash with the Bank. They offered certain advantages to those who complied, such as the right to exchange goldsmith notes for Bank notes or to discount at preferred interest rates.[37] They complained to the Treasury whenever they thought paymasters were drawing down their war-loan balances prematurely for their own private purposes and asked that the paymasters be directed to keep that cash in the Bank instead.[38] In May 1696, as cash reserves began to fall very dramatically, the directors claimed that they had always kept large quantities of their own cash with the Bank and urged all shareholders to follow their example.[39] A second method was to resist constant pressure from the Treasury for new short-term loans. Even if these were financed in the first instance by issuing notes to military pay-masters, the Bank had to worry that large quantities of these notes would come back upon it for payment in specie, draining its reserve. The minutes of both institutions reveal constant strife over the question whether the Bank could afford to lend more. The directors' protests that they were already at their limits, though treated with suspicion by William in particular,[40] are borne out by the evidence of the general ledgers. Finally, the directors tried to ensure that large quantities of specie would normally be flowing from the Exchequer into the Bank's coffers on a regular basis. In this connection the inaugural loan to the government was a big help. The Bank collected interest on this loan from the Exchequer, always in specie, on a weekly basis. By law it was entitled to claim whatever had come in upon the relevant tax fund – in this case a tax on ships in proportion to their tonnage (for short, contemporaries called it the 'tonnage tax') – during the past week. And for the rest the Bank took care to invest only in very short-term kinds of loans. It bought tallies with relatively near-term and well-distributed repayment dates, so that it could claim repayment from the Exchequer, again in specie, on a regular basis. This allowed the directors to respond to any unantici-pated decline in the Bank's specie reserves by simply holding this cash back for a time rather than immediately re-investing it in new short-term loans.

The latter two methods were not always reliable. The Treasury had con-siderable bargaining power with the Bank and so, as we shall see, was able to force it into lending more at times quite inopportune for the Bank itself. The Treasury also had a lot of control over the timing and pace of interest payments on the Bank's foundational loan. Finally, the tax revenues from which Exchequer tallies were ultimately to be repaid did not always come in as quickly as expected or in the necessary amounts, and the Treasury was sometimes able to force the Bank to take tallies associated with relatively unreliable and uncertain tax funds. For all of these reasons the Bank was sometimes left vulnerable to unanticipated surges in the pace at which its notes were being presented for payment – an Achilles' heel that its opponents would attack several times over during the recoinage debate and ensuing monetary crisis.

Notes

1 I am drawing here upon the manuscript, 'Proposal for Settling a Transferable Fund of Perpetuall Interest (National Library of Scotland, Adv. MS 31.1.7, fols. 79–80). It is undated and no author is named. But in title and content it conforms very closely to the sort of scheme that Paterson claimed, in *Some Account*, pp. 1–2 and *Brief Account*, pp. 4–5, to have presented to parliament around this time. Since the manuscript collection in question was probably gathered by Montagu, I will refer to it henceforth as the 'Montagu Papers'.

   Some Account has not previously been attributed to Paterson, probably because the author is denoted as 'J. S.'. But the writing style is just like that of *Brief Account*, which is usually ascribed to him. And the author occasionally speaks in the first person of events that only Paterson himself could have witnessed. The initials 'J.S.' were very likely an inside joke. One of Paterson's critics had humorously suggested that the latter work was written by 'Jerry Squirt': a character in a contemporary comedy who would 'carp and quibble, pun and play the fool with every thing that came before him' (Chamberlen, *Some Useful Reflections*, p. 3). So in signing *Some Account* with the initials 'J.S.', Paterson may have been thumbing his nose at Chamberlen.
2 Lowndes' report, written late in 1691, is preserved in Montagu Papers, fols. 75–77. It makes no mention of the original author. But the proposal it describes is identical to the Paterson project I have just described.
3 Paterson, *Some Account*, p. 2.
4 I am drawing here from the short accounts offered in *CJ*, 18 Jan. 1692, and Luttrell, *Parliamentary Diary*, p. 140. A manuscript entitled 'Proposed, That the Parliament Doe Establish a Fund or Foundation of Currant Property for Advanceing the Sum of Four Millions to the Use of the Publick (Montagu Papers, fols. 79–80) may be a statement of the views of this group. The proposal reads like a version of Paterson's scheme, with the added wrinkle that the bills 'be made current by act of Parliament'.
5 Paterson, *Brief Account*, p. 5.
6 Paterson, *Some account*, p. 2.
7 Geheimes Staatsarchiv, Preußischer Kulturbesitz, Berlin, I. HA Geheimer Rat, Rep. 11, Nr. 1792–1811 (henceforth 'Bonnet Reports'), 6/16 Feb. 1694.
8 Paterson, *Some Account*, p. 4.
9 See Jones, 'London Merchants', and Henry Horwitz, 'East India Trade'.
10 Paterson, *Some Account*, pp. 4–5.
11 A short manuscript entitled 'A Proposal for Raising £1200000 by Bank Tickets' (in Montagu Papers, fol. 86) may have been an early version. If so, then parliament or Treasury must have insisted upon a major change somewhere along the way. The 'Proposal' called for the whole £1.2 million loan to the paid into the Exchequer in 'tickets', with the bank raising only £400 thousand as a 'stock' to be reserved for cashing the tickets on demand.
12 See Bonnet Reports, 20/30 Apr. 1694, and BL, Add. MS. 17677 (henceforth l'Hermitage Reports), 17/27 and 20/30 Apr. and 24 Apr. / 4 May 1694.

13 Thomas Paine made the same observation, almost a century later, about the Philadelphia-based Bank of North America. One of its principal conveniences was that 'it gives a kind of life to what would otherwise be dead money'. All merchants needed to keep some amount of 'remnant money' by them for everyday purposes, money with which they could do nothing useful. 'By collecting those scattered sums together, which is done by means of the bank, they become capable of being used, and the quantity of circulating cash is doubled' (*Dissertations on Government,* p. 35).

14 See Murphy, *Origins of English Financial Markets,* for an accessible account of how this market worked during our period.

15 Paterson, *Brief Account,* pp. 2–6. Paterson had good reason to overstate his case, given the Treasury's standard practice of rewarding the creators of public-finance projects that made it through the parliamentary maze.

16 Paterson, *Some Account,* p. 5.

17 So for instance he advocated for his project on the grounds that it would not only be an easy way of raising a war loan but would also supply a new kind of money: 'the convenience, security and advantage of such [a] fund for great payments in and about the cities of London & Westminster would exceedingly facilitate the circulation of money & consequently give great life and vigour to trade, industry and improvements' ('Proposal for Settling a Transferable Fund of Perpetual Interest', Montagu Papers, fol. 87r). In presenting the project to the Commons in 1692, the First Lord of the Treasury proposed that the crown be obliged to take the bills in taxes and other public payments (Luttrell, *Parliamentary Diary,* p. 140).

18 See BEA, ADM7/1 (henceforth 'General Ledger 1').

19 Horsefield, for instance, wrote that 'unfortunately there is no surviving record' before the first general ledger (*British Monetary Experiments,* p. 129).

20 I am referring specifically to BEA, C98/2512-2515 (hereafter 'Drawing Ledgers').

21 Note that I have left out a few minor accounts (e.g. interest, profits and loss and dividends) in order to let the main outlines of the Bank's business model emerge more clearly.

22 Consider for instance the Bank's loan of £250 thousand to the Treasury on 15 Dec. 1694. The loan was deposited that same day to the account of the navy's treasurer, Admiral Edward Russell. No actual specie ever changed hands; the Bank simply credited Russell with a fictional deposit of £250 thousand and counted itself as having loaned this sum to the Treasury. Nevertheless, the Treasury's loan and Russell's 'deposit' were entered on the Bank's books that day as a credit and debit respectively to the cash account.

23 On most days the cash account would also have included a certain, relatively small, quantity of goldsmith notes. The Bank had a retinue of 'out-tellers' whose job it was to collect payment on bills of exchange coming due (they were 'out' tellers because to collect they went to the places of business of the persons or firms upon whom the bill was drawn). Judging from the Bank's minutes, the tellers sometimes took payment, at least partially, in goldsmith notes. It's not at all clear to what extent the tellers then took these notes to goldsmiths to demand payment in specie or kept them as money and used them to pay the Bank's own creditors. The minutes in question, specifically those of its 'Court [viz. Board] of Directors', may be found in BEA, G4/1 and G4/2 (hereafter 'Bank Minutes').

24 The Drawing Office Ledgers don't show this directly. But Bank officials often claimed this had been the case. See for instance Godfrey, *Short Account,* p. 2.

25 For these accounts I extended the transcription to the end of 1697 since they are so compact that it was easy to do so.

26 Again I extended this series to the end of 1697 because it was easy to do so.

27 The accounts in question, for Bertie, Ranelagh, Russell and Stephens (all in the first volume of the Bank Drawing Ledgers) show that the notes were issued mostly in denominations of £100, with a few for £50, and were sequentially numbered. In most cases the ledger records the number of each note as it was returned for payment. Notes before 1 Jan. 1695 were issued in fulfilment of the original £1.2 million loan and after that date for additional, short-term loans.

28 Figure 3.7 also shows that on one occasion (7 June 1695) the Bank resold some of these tallies rather than holding them to maturity.

29 I derived these figures by noting the days on which loan payments were made (as listed in the Bank's account of the loan on folio 21 of the first Drawing-office Ledger) and then watching how the bill and note accounts moved on those same days. Using this same technique, it is clear that a further £90.6K of the loan was 'paid' by holding that much money back to cover costs that the Bank incurred on the Treasury's behalf in raising funds for the English army in Flanders. This means that only £25K of the loan was contributed in actual specie.

30 There was a kind of money creation happening even if the Bank had remained nothing but a loan intermediary. This was the extent, namely, to which holders of Bank bills and notes used those currencies as means of payment in transactions with their own creditors. But this was money creation only from the perspective of the system as a whole, the benefits of which could not be directly captured by the Bank. By contrast, the kind of money creation I describe in this paragraph would have generated profits that went straight to the Bank's own bottom line.

31 Note that the Figure somewhat overstates the Bank's encashment problem. The biggest note cancellations were usually associated with loan repayments from the Treasury. Presumably the Bank notes in question had been received by customs or excise cashiers and not yet cashed for deposit in the Exchequer, or were still on hand with military paymasters (who had received earlier loans in this currency and not yet used the notes).

32 The likely reason for this was the fear expressed by Lowndes about Paterson's earlier proposal: that if taxes were paid in the new paper bills, the Exchequer would be deprived of the specie it needed to repay earlier loans (Montagu Papers, fol. 76v). This sort of thinking seems to have been widespread at the time. For when putting forward his own paper-currency proposal in 1694, Mint master Neale sought to defend himself against the 'great objection': 'a supposition that the king will be paid his revenue all in this credit' (*Proposal*, p. 3).

33 See for instance *CTB*, 23 Mar. 1695;19 Sep. 1695; 15 Feb. 1696; 21 Feb. 1696; 23 Mar. 1696.

34 See *CTB*, 3 July 1695.

35 In 1696, one very knowledgeable observer maintained that once the silver coin became of uncertain value, 'credit performed all the offices of money; ... all great dealings were transacted by tallies, bank bills and goldsmith notes'. He warned that recoining the money 'will make many people willing to be their own cashiers, which must in a manner put an end to the banking goldsmiths. And for the same reason little running cash will be carried to the Bank of England' (Davenant, *Two Manuscripts*, pp. 68–69).

36 Three other options – to raise the interest rate the Bank was paying on its bills, call in more money from shareholders, or reduce or withhold dividend payments – were all quite unappealing. Since they would have significantly decreased profits and/or Bank stock prices, they were employed only during the crisis months of summer 1696.

37 Bank Minutes, 24 Oct. 1694 and 16 Jan. 1695.

38 For instance, upon complaint from Bank directors that George Doddington, a victualling commissioner, was withdrawing money faster than his official occasions required, the treasury lords instructed him 'to leave all public money in their hands till the service requires it' (*CTB*, Minutes, 9 July 1695).
39 Bank Minutes, 13 May 1696.
40 See for instance *CTB*, Minutes, 12 and 17 Apr. 1695.

Bibliography

Manuscript sources

Bank of England Archive
    ADM7/1–2 ('Bank General Ledger 1' and 'Bank General Ledger 2')
    C98/2512–2517 ('Bank Drawing Ledgers')
    G4/1–2 ('Bank Minutes')
British Library
    Add. MS. 17677 OO-QQ ('l'Hermitage Reports')
Geheimes Staatsarchiv, Preußischer Kulturbesitz, Berlin
    I. HA Geheimer Rat, Rep. 11, Nr. 1792–1811 ('Bonnet Reports')
National Library of Scotland, Edinburgh
    Adv. MS 31.1.7 ('Montagu Papers')

Printed primary sources

[Chamberlen, Hugh]. *Some Useful Reflections Upon a Pamphlet Called A Brief Account of the Intended Bank of England.* [London: s.n., 1694].
Davenant, Charles. *Two Manuscripts by Charles Davenant.* Edited by Abbott Payson Usher. Baltimore: Johns Hopkins University Press, 1942.
[Godfrey, Michael]. *A Short Account of the Bank of England.* [London: s.n., 1695].
Great Britain. *Statutes of the Realm.* Edited Alexander Luders and John Raithby. London: G. Eyre and A. Strahan, 1810–22. Accessed online at http://www.british-history.ac.uk/statutes-realm/.
Great Britain. Parliament. House of Commons. *Journals of the House of Commons.* London: House of Commons, 1803. Accessed online at http://www.british-history.ac.uk/commons-jrnl/.
Great Britain. Public Record Office. *Calendar of Treasury Books.* Volume X: *January 1693 to March 1696.* Edited by William Shaw. London: HMSO, 1931. Accessed online at http://www.british-history.ac.uk/cal-treasury-books/vol10.
Luttrell, Narcissus. *The Parliamentary Diary of Narcissus Luttrell, 1691–1693.* Ed. Henry J. Horwitz. Oxford: Clarendon Press, 1972.
[Neale, Thomas.]. *A Proposal for Raising a Million on a Fund of Interest...* [London: s.n.], 1694.
Paine, Thomas. *Dissertations on Government, the Affairs of the Bank, and Paper Money.* Philadelphia: Charles Cist, 1786.
[Paterson, William]. *A Brief Account of the Intended Bank of England.* [London: s.n., 1694].
[Paterson, William]. *Some Account of the Transactions of Mr. William Paterson in Relation to the Bank of England, and the Orphans Fund: in a Letter to a Friend.* London: [s.n.], 1695.

Secondary sources

Horsefield, John Keith. *British Monetary Experiments, 1650–1710*. Cambridge: Harvard University Press, 1960.

Horwitz, Henry. 'The East India Trade, the Politicians and the Constitution: 1689–1702'. *Journal of British Studies* 17, no. 2 (1978): 1–18.

Jones, D. W. 'London Merchants and the Crisis of the 1690s'. In *Crisis and Order in English Towns, 1500–1700*, edited by Peter Clarke and Paul Slack, 311–55. London: Routledge & Kegan Paul, 1972.

Murphy, Anne. *The Origins of English Financial Markets: Investment and Speculation Before the South Sea Bubble*. Cambridge: Cambridge University Press, 2009.

4 Parliamentary measures against clipping and bullion exports, 1689–95

In this chapter I provide a short overview of earlier parliamentary debates on the sorry state of England's coin. This background information will prove helpful when it comes time to interpret the debates of 1695–96. For many of the arguments that featured in those debates had been around for years, shaped by political conflicts that lingered on into the recoinage debate. But it will also provide a helpful contrast, making it easier for you to see what was different and even downright unusual about the later debate. The contrasts will provide some important clues when it later comes time to try to sort out the underlying politics.

The want of money, 1690–94

Clipping had been eating away at England's silver coin long before the war began. Already in 1682 Sir William Petty, an independent scholar and founding member of the Royal Society, was drawing attention to the problem and, to keep it from getting worse, urging the administration to recoin all hammered money.[1] And in 1683, Sir Dudley North, a merchant and soon to be MP and treasury lord, warned the Commons that clipping, if left unchecked, must end in 'some great disorder of the people'.[2] So it isn't too surprising that parliament raised the issue early on in King William's new regime. In May 1689 the Commons struck a committee 'to consider of the great abases committed in the impairing the coins of the kingdom, and how the same may be prevented' and many key administrative officials were named to the body.[3] The administration of the day seemed to take the problem seriously, since the committee was staffed with many high-level crown officials.[4]

But the committee never reported back to the House and for the next several years neither government nor parliament paid much attention to the issue of clipping. The coinage-related bills that began appearing annually in 1690 focused instead on a different problem: what contemporaries referred to as a 'want of money'. The phrase referred to the widespread public perception that money generally, and full-weight silver coin in particular, was far less abundant in England than it should be.

Contemporaries traced the problem to a couple of sources. One was the fact that certain merchants were exporting bullion in large quantities. Contemporaries pointed in particular to the trades to the East Indies and Turkey, both of which used bullion exports extensively. Critics alleged that by this means England was being deprived of the new coin into which such bullion would otherwise have been minted. This thesis was popular with advocates of the English woollen-textiles industry, especially clothiers, merchants specializing in English cloth exports and those gentry whose rents depended on wool prices. Cloth-industry supporters regularly attributed declining sales and/or prices to the fact that the East India and Levant Companies were using bullion rather than English cloth to finance the imports they brought back to England. The East India Company came in for a special measure of blame since a good part of its imports were Indian-manufactured cotton and silk textiles – thereby depriving clothiers of a portion of their domestic market too. (The Levant Company fared better since its merchants continued exporting some English cloth and the only silk they brought back to England was raw – suitable for use by domestic weavers.) This line of criticism had a long history. Thomas Mun, himself a director of the East India Company, sought to respond to it in his book, *England's Treasure by Forraign Trade* (1628). He argued that the Company's bullion exports worked on balance to increase the national 'treasure' or store of specie, because the imports thereby obtained could be re-exported for even more money. But the tradition nevertheless remained very much alive, as evidenced in Restoration-era works like Hodges' *True and Onely Causes of the Great Want of Moneys in These Kingdoms* (1666), Haines' *Prevention of Poverty, or a Discourse of the Causes of the Decay of Trade, Fall of Lands and Want of Money* (1674) and Petyt's *Brittania Languens: Or a Discourse of Trade: Shewing the Grounds and Reasons of the Increase and Decay of Land Rents, National Wealth and Strength* (1680).

A second thesis was that certain London-based precious-metals dealers were melting English coin and exporting it to take advantage of higher bullion prices abroad. It was common knowledge that other governments had tried to attract foreign bullion to their mints by offering a higher price for it. Specifically, they had arranged to increase the local money unit-of-account value of a given weight of silver or gold bullion. So, for instance, between 1636 and 1679 France increased the official value of a 'marc' of fine silver from 24.5 to 29.6 'livres'.[5] Similarly over the course of the seventeenth century the mint price of a 'mark' of fine gold in Spain had risen from 880 to 1292 'reals'.[6] By contrast in England the unit-of-account value of a pound troy of sterling silver hadn't budged since 1551, when it had been set at 60 shillings.[7]

On either line of interpretation, the appropriate response to the scarcity of coin was some kind of legislative action. One option was to make it illegal to export bullion of any kind. Even cloth-industry supporters recognized this as a fairly extreme measure. So a second tack was to tighten existing prohibitions against exporting 'English' bullion, i.e. against melting English coin for export as bullion. It was very easy of course for merchants to claim that their bullion was of foreign, not domestic, origin. The trick was to find some way of falsifying their claims. Finally, there had long been calls for government somehow to raise the unit-of-account value of silver bullion in England. Many contemporaries referred to this as 'raising the coin' (though others disliked the label). There were three basic means for achieving it. One was to lower the weight of any new coins being minted. Another was to increase their alloy content. So for instance the anonymous author of *The Use and Abuses of Money* (1671) advocated changing the alloy proportion of English silver coin from 7.5 to 25 percent. And Haines proposed that 'to raise and preserve the plenty of money' the king should call in all the money and coin it anew at three-quarters of its present weight.[8] Finally, because English coins bore no stated denominations, it was an option simply to raise their official values, declaring the crown (and lesser silver coins *pro rata*) to be worth a greater number of shillings.

There was strong support in parliament, during the years immediately following the Revolution, for taking some kind of action to increase, or at least protect the existing, supply of coin. Once a year, for the next five sessions, the Commons was presented with legislative proposals. A 'Bill to discourage the exportation of bullion, and to encourage the importation, and to the converting thereof into the current coin of this realm' was read on 19 May 1690. No copy has survived and we know nothing of its contents. It never reached second reading because William ended the session just four days later. Early in the following session, on 13 October 1690, a bill with almost the same title received first reading.[9] One clause called for the Mint to raise the mint price of sterling silver from 62s. to 65s. per pound. In effect this would have lowered the weight of new English silver coin by about 5 percent. A second clause proposed that all bullion be deemed domestic by default; anyone hoping to export some would have to prove it was of foreign origin. The bill passed the Commons on 17 November. The Lords, after second reading, decided to remove the clause for raising the mint price. The bill later died in committee. A measure of the same title returned the next session, receiving first reading in the Commons on 23 December 1691. No documentation has survived. Four times in January 1692 the bill was scheduled for, but never actually received, debate in committee. In the end it simply disappeared from the agenda. In the next session, the Commons was presented on 8 December 1692 with a 'Bill to prevent the exportation of gold and silver and melting down the coin of this realm'. This too was a measure for lightening the silver coin by about 5 percent. Three weeks later the House divided on the question whether to send it to committee. Though the motion was carried by the narrow margin of 137 to 126, the inaugural committee meeting was repeatedly postponed and still had not taken place before the session ended in mid-March 1693. Finally, in the 1693–94 session, a 'bill for preventing the exportation of English bullion' was presented on

10 January 1694. This bill seems to have focused only on direct, physical measures for preventing exports. For there is no mention of it in Locke's correspondence with his London 'College' (as his friends John Freke and MP Edward Clarke styled themselves) and during that session only a single, rather offbeat pamphlet called for raising the coin.[10] This is also the focus of a draft set of clauses 'touching the exportation of bullion' offered by MP William Culliford in 1694,[11] probably in connection with this bill. Culliford simply resurrected a portion of the 1690–91 bill: declaring all bullion English by default and requiring prospective exporters to prove otherwise. In any event, the measure was rejected after third reading on 4 April 1694.

Post-revolutionary proponents of raising the coin pointed to the fact that while the Mint gave 62s. for a pound of silver bullion, the market price was one or two shillings higher. The 'working goldsmiths' (the term for those who manufactured in gold as contrasted with those goldsmiths who had turned to banking) whose petition prompted the first coinage bill of the new regime attributed the high price of gold to market manipulation by merchants, especially certain Portuguese Jews trading in precious metals.[12] The parliamentary committee charged with investigating their complaint agreed that much of the export trade was handled by 'jews, who do any thing for their profit'.[13] The committee also noted the recent decision by Louis XIV to raise the official value of French silver coin by 10 percent.[14] Later that year a petitioner claimed to have identified a similar reason for bullion exports.[15] Half of a large bullion stash he had discovered aboard an outbound ship consisted of silver 75 percent pure. MPs would have recognized the implication immediately. The Dutch made a special trade coin, the 'lion dollar' (named for its embossed image), from silver of this purity. Contemporaries weren't quite sure how, but they were certain Holland profited somehow by minting lion dollars.[16] And one writer alleged the coins were being sold to the French, who supplied them in turn to their ally Turkey.[17] On this line of interpretation, banning bullion exports couldn't help; the law would somehow always be evaded. The only way to keep good English coin from being melted was, as Mint Master Thomas Neale put it, 'to make the standard of England such that an ounce of silver coined may be worth as much as 'tis uncoined'.[18] At least one MP pointed to the case of clipped coin as proof that such a strategy could work.[19] Though it continued circulating at the same 'tale' (face value) as full-weight money, its lower metallic content protected it from being melted for export, so that it stayed in circulation.

Proposals for raising the coin were consistently attacked by merchants associated with bullion-related trades. So for instance on 3 December 1690, the day the Lords had scheduled for first reading of the new parliament's second coinage bill, the House was visited by a deputation of merchants that included at least four members of the Levant Company. Their leaders, James and John Houblon (the latter soon to be mayor of London and Governor of the Bank of England), offered an impressive array of arguments against the coinage bill.[20] The same sort of reasoning featured in books published at the time by other merchants related to the East India and Turkey trades, such as Sir Josiah Child's *Discourse About Trade* and North's *Discourses upon Trade*, and by scholars renowned for their understanding of trade, such as Abraham Hill's *Letter About Raising the Value of Coin* and Locke's *Some Considerations of ... Raising the Value of Money*. Coin was being melted for export not because it was worth more as bullion but on account of the war. The navy was buying more supplies from the Baltic and the government had to feed and pay the English soldiers fighting in Flanders. These additional expenses could not all be financed by an increase in English commodity exports, especially since the war had disrupted many existing markets in Europe.[21] Bullion shipments were perhaps the only way to cover the resulting payments imbalance. Local bullion prices had risen above the mint price only because it was illegal to export or melt English coin; higher prices were the premium demanded by suppliers prepared to break the law. If England wanted to keep its coin from being melted, the law against exporting domestic coin should be rescinded. Raising the coin wouldn't stop melting. The strategy hadn't worked in those countries that had tried it. Raising the coin didn't actually make it more valuable. Foreigners would continue to value coin by its metallic content, not the denomination. Hence the very month that France raised its silver coin, the external value of the French *livre* fell in foreign-exchange markets.[22] And domestic prices would soon rise by the amount the coin was raised, so that even the real domestic purchasing power of the coin would be no greater than before. The only effect would be to deprive landlords, creditors and the king of 5 percent of the purchasing power associated with their rents, loans and taxes respectively. Nor would raising the coin halt bullion exports. Three years previously Spain had reduced the weight of its silver 'pieces of eight' by 20 percent. Yet Spanish coin was still being melted for export, even though this was a capital offense there. If England raised the mint price of bullion, the market price would soon rise above it again. The campaign for raising the coin was being waged by parties who knew all this but hoped to use it as an occasion to line their own pockets. Goldsmith bankers picked out and set aside any full-weight coin their customers deposited. The moment the mint price rose, they would melt this heavy money down and bring it to the Mint to be coined anew – realizing for themselves the resulting increase in face value. The Mint Master was supporting the measure because he knew it would increase coining and so his income.

Many of those opposed to raising the coin warned that parliament should stop trying to correct the want of money (which would persist as long as the war did) and concentrate instead on the real problem: clipping. In his presentation to the Lords, James Houblon cited the example of Portugal.[23] By 1686 their money had lost about a third of its normal weight to clippers. Their king deliberately chose to do nothing about the problem, reasoning that clipped money would be safe from melting and export. Far from trying to correct the problem, he issued an edict compelling everyone to accept it at face value. But just a few months later everyone began refusing it. Since no other money was available, all commercial activity ground to a halt. The king was obliged to set up mints all across the kingdom to recoin the money as quickly as possible. North prophesied that if the currency of clipped money in England weren't stopped now, hammered coin would continue shrinking until people came suddenly to refuse it – making for a much worse problem. '[W]e are all shoving the evil-day as far off as may be, but it will certainly come at last'.[24] Locke wrote to similar effect in 1692. If the problem weren't 'speedily stopped ... [it will] quickly, I fear, break out into open ill effects and at one blow deprive us of a great part (perhaps near ¼) of our money'.[25] Locke added that the dearth of heavy silver coin was owing in large part to England's practice of accepting clipped money at face value. The cases of France and Holland had shown that whenever a country introduced into circulation coins having a lower silver content per unit of account, those of better quality quickly disappeared into hoard.[26] Both North and Locke recommended a royal decree compelling clipped coin to circulate at its value by weight, not tale.

The problem of clipping, 1694–95

Not until the session of 1693–94 did clipping finally reappear on the Commons' agenda. Burnet later claimed that the king had been pushing that session for the administration to take decisive action against clipping.[27] Specifically, William wanted to issue a proclamation by which clipped coin would be demonetized overnight. In effect it would become just so much silver bullion, valued by the ounce at the current mint price rather than by its denomination. This would have stopped clipping in an instant since, in reducing the weight of silver coins, clippers would have been reducing their value in the same proportion. Burnet alleged that Sir Edward Seymour, then a Treasury Lord, eventually persuaded William to leave the problem alone.[28] Seymour's clinching argument was that leaving clipped coin in circulation would make taxes and loans come into the Exchequer more quickly; clipped silver would become a kind of hot potato that no one wanted to be left holding if and when it was demonetized. So the only effort that session to halt clipping came from Culliford, at this point a backbench MP. On 22 December 1693 he introduced a bill 'for better discovery of clippers'.[29] Culliford proposed merely to fine anyone possessing bullion that wasn't officially stamped as being of foreign origin. The measure was rejected in the Lords at the committee stage after someone pointed out that silver bullion would simply be turned into coin instead (given that hammered money was easy to imitate).

Meanwhile clipping was continuing apace, causing hammered coin to shrink at an alarming rate. One contemporary reports that samples of the money arriving in the Exchequer in July 1694 weighed on average only 60.1 percent of the Mint standard, compared to 66.7 percent a year earlier and 84 percent in 1689.[30]

Perhaps for this reason, by the 1694–95 session of parliament the administration had finally decided to act. The court signalled its resolve by inviting the Reverend William Fleetwood, chaplain to William and Mary, to preach against clipping before the mayor and aldermen of London. Delivered on 16 December 1694, the sermon was published two days later under the imprimatur of the Bishop of London.[31] Early in the new year the Treasury entertained a concrete proposal from a freelance projector, the merchant Lewis Gervaize, for repairing the silver coin.[32] And the administration was well represented on a select Commons committee appointed a few days later 'to receive proposals how to prevent clipping of the coin ... and the exportation of silver'.[33] Among its sixty-four members were the Chancellor of the Exchequer (Montagu) and one other Treasury lord (John Smith), the brother (and in many ways the proxy in the lower house) of First Treasury Lord Sidney Godolphin (Charles Godolphin, himself a customs commissioner), as well as commissioners for ordnance and victualling.

As it turned out, however, the administration took no active lead in the matter that session and left the Commons committee to its own devices. Committee member Clarke several times complained of this in letters to Locke. He wrote that Chancellor Montagu in particular, when pressed to take a stand, confessed to feeling 'like a monkey thrown into the water which always claps his paws or hands to his eyes and sinks to the bottom'.[34] The administration probably became distracted by a sudden, unexpected development: the death of Queen Mary on 28 December from smallpox. William seems to have been genuinely grief-stricken and retired from the political scene for some weeks. Then on 25 January, some former tory ministers, led by the Earl of Nottingham, mounted a blistering attack on William's current administration. In a speech in the Lords that day, Nottingham was highly critical of recent government policy, including the decision to create the Bank of England and failure to act on the deteriorating state of the silver coin. His diatribe initiated months of open warfare between the old and new administrations, culminating later that session in charges that the tories had accepted bribes from the East India Company and in a bill for impeaching their leader, the Duke of Leeds. Montagu led the whig attack and so, understandably, may not have had much time for or interest in the state of the coin.[35] So in the work of the Commons committee for preventing clipping, we have our best opportunity to observe the natural state of parliamentary opinion on the question.

The committee was odd from the outset in that it was simultaneously assigned the task of preventing silver exports – a problem that many merchants and their supporters saw as very distinct from the clipping issue. Indeed, it seems MPs expected the committee's work to be more about bullion exports than about clipping. For its composition suggests a looming battle between the proponents of the domestic woollen cloth industry on the one hand and merchants involved in bullion-export-related trades on the other. On the one side were thirteen members who had long been pushing the cause of the clothing trade – most of them on record as being opposed to the wearing of East Indian textiles.[36] On the other side were the current governor and deputy-governor and one former governor of the East India Company (Sirs John Fleet, Thomas Cook and Joseph Herne respectively), several vocal Company supporters (Thomas Littleton, John Perry, Sir Thomas Clarges and Francis Gwyn), a Company stockholder and creditor (Sir John Banks), one current member of the Levant Company (Sir Thomas Vernon) and three MPs who had tried to keep the clothing trade free of protective measures proposed by established insiders (Sir Francis Masham, Anthony Bowyer and Richard Howe). This tension was evident in the committee's final recommendations to the House, presented two months later.

The projectors offering legislative proposals to the committee largely ignored the bullion-exports issue and concentrated their attention instead on clipping.[37] Eighteen of the twenty-one submissions made to the committee spoke to this problem; only nine addressed bullion exports – and most of these simply as a short aside. Of the eighteen proposals that addressed the clipping problem, fourteen called for a recoinage and one of the other four was a second proposal from someone who had recommended a recoinage in his other submission.

For those projectors recommending a recoinage, the central problem was how to finance the losses that would be suffered once clipped coin was demonetized (as everyone agreed must eventually happen). For this purpose, six projectors proposed appointing some sort of public tax, three recommended raising the coin and one advised a mixture of the two. Only two projectors proposed raising the coin solely on the grounds that it would stop melting and exports. Note too that when projectors made multiple proposals, the second design differed from the first only in making taxes, rather than raising the coin, the means for financing clipping-related losses.[38]

We know very little about the state of opinion within the Commons committee itself. But the few bits of information available suggest that the big question was whether or not to raise the coin. This is implied by what committee member Clarke and his colleague Freke (not himself an MP) chose to report to Locke about the committee's work. They described it as a committee to prevent clipping and tried to get the members to focus on this task. But Clarke feared the most likely outcome would be a proposal for 'the diminishing of our coin', as he preferred to call it.[39] Freke portrayed Clarke's main contribution to the committee as a motion to preserve the current weight and fineness of England's silver coin – which Clarke was sure would suffice to defeat any subsequent effort to raise the denomination of the coin.[40] And to get the Commons into the right frame of mind for receiving the committee's report, Clarke elected to publish Locke's *Short Observations* – a critique of Neale's 1693 proposal for raising the coin (Locke had written it two years earlier but chose not to publish it after the bill failed of its own accord). The question of raising the coin was also front and centre in the one surviving report of the committee's internal discussions.[41] Here, unlike in the projectors' submissions, everyone seemed to approach raising the coin as a strategy for preventing bullion exports. One member explicitly argued that bullion was worth more abroad than in England. Another asserted that bullion exports were indeed at the root of the country's want of money and counselled lowering the weight of English silver coin. The other four speakers took the opposing view. One acknowledged that merchants were exporting bullion to take advantage of better prices abroad. But he thought raising the coin would only make matters worse; imports would become more expensive, forcing England to export even more bullion to finance a worsening balance of trade. Two speakers asserted that coin would be melted as long as England had an army in Flanders and it was illegal to export specie. And two traced the scarcity of heavy coin instead to the clipping trade, one of them proposing that the correct fix was not raising coin but demonetizing clipped money.

The committee reported its findings to the House, on 12 March 1695, by way of a set of fifteen resolutions. No one would have been surprised at its opening resolution: that the best method for preventing further clipping was to turn all hammered silver coin into milled money. But the next several resolutions, taken together, were perhaps unusual. Two of them amounted to a recommendation that the losses from clipping be financed by a tax; holders of clipped coin would get back the same weight of new milled coin and a transferable, interest-bearing 'bill' for the remainder. The committee also proposed that all silver coin be raised 10 percent in denomination: the crown to 5s. 6d. and the rest *pro rata*. All those who had made presentations to the committee saw taxation and raising the coin as alternative means to the same end: financing the losses from clipping. On this reading, there was no point in pursuing both measures. Obviously a majority of the committee disagreed. Their most likely reasoning was that bullion was indeed worth more abroad and that something had to be done, once all the silver money was restored to its full weight, to keep the new money from being melted for export. The next six resolutions proposed direct, technical measures for halting clipping and need not concern us here. Only the final two resolutions addressed bullion exports. In that connection the committee proposed putting the onus on prospective exporters to prove their bullion was indeed of foreign origin, and imposing a heavy penalty upon any who tried to counterfeit the official stamp certifying its foreign origin. Implicitly, it would remain legal to export foreign bullion.

The House made no immediate decision on the committee's report and simply set aside a day (16 March) for the full House to consider it. In a highly unusual development, however, the entire slate of resolutions was immediately published in the daily printed *Votes* of the House. The *Votes* only ever published resolutions once they been approved by the Commons as a whole and never at the committee stage. Freke and Clarke explained to Locke that this was the work of House Speaker Sir John Trevor. He was angry with the court because Chancellor Montagu had used the East India Company bribery scandal to finagle his impending dismissal as Speaker. Trevor 'was resolved to give it [the Government] a cast of his office at parting as a testimony of his affection'.[42] He probably expected releasing news that the House was contemplating raising the coin would put downward pressure on the external value of the English pound and perhaps make it more difficult for the crown to raise short-term loans (because of fears that any coin made over to the Exchequer would be repaid in a lighter money). Certainly by 19 March (the next available reporting date after the *Votes* were published) the exchange rates on Amsterdam and Antwerp had fallen to 31.1 and 30.9 schellingen banco per £, down from the levels of 32.5 and 32.2, respectively, at which they had been holding steady during January and February.[43]

In the end, however, the Commons decided to forego a recoinage that session. After several postponements, the clipping-committee report was at last debated by a committee of the whole on 10 April. The House also referred to this same committee an alternative bill from the Lords, one that offered only direct, technical (and ultimately ineffective) measures for preventing clipping. Two days later the committee of the whole reported, and the House approved, a resolution to grant a new tax to cover the cost of a recoinage and the losses from clipping. But in the end both the resolution and the whole clipping-committee report were quietly dropped. Instead the House turned to the Lords' bill, which was debated for several days, passed by the Commons with some amendments on 25 April and made law on 3 May as 6 & 7 Will. 3, c. 17. The new statute tightened the penalties against clipping and introduced a measure to prevent English bullion exports. It also granted the crown a half-year exemption from the law prohibiting exports of domestic silver bullion – on condition the exports were limited to 700 thousand ounces and used only for paying the English army in Flanders.

So when in the next session parliament finally decided upon a method for putting an end to clipping, two well-established but fundamentally opposing accounts of England's monetary troubles would end up competing with one another. The one, associated very closely to the domestic clothing trade and associated merchant interests, emphasized the want of coin and sought an end to bullion exports: in part by tightening penalties against them and especially by raising the coin. The other, linked to merchant companies whose trades required bullion exports, thought the core problem was clipping, denied that raising the coin would be of any help and recommended demonetizing clipped coin as the best way to restore the health of the nation's monetary system. Somewhere between these two extremes lay the relatively technical position of the Treasury and projectors in public finance. The latter group seemed perfectly prepared to contemplate raising the coin, but only as one of two possible solutions to the vexed problem of financing the losses from clipping. One of the great peculiarities of the 1695–96 session was that suddenly the Treasury seemed to have come around to the view of the clothing merchants and was advocating raising the coin as a way to stop it from being melted for export. This dramatic turnabout gives us our first clue that in the later debate all may not have been as it seemed.

Notes

1 Petty, *Sir William Petty.*
2 North, 'Representation', p. 304.
3 *CJ*, 1 May 1689.
4 In order of their being named to the committee they were: Henry Goodricke (head of Ordnance and at this time also the administration's chief manager in the Commons), Sir Robert Clayton (Customs Commissioner), Thomas Done (auditor of imprests – money officially allocated to royal officials), Sir Henry Capel (until recently a Treasury Lord), Thomas Papillon (Victualling Commissioner), William Wogan (King's Serjeant-at-Law-legal counsel for the crown), Sir John Knatchbull (Privy Seal Commissioner), John Elwill (receiver-general of taxes for counties Devon and Exeter and a military contractor), William Harbord (army paymaster for Ireland) and John Somers (Solicitor General). The committee also included several wealthy financiers who had loaned extensively to the crown: Sir John Cutler, Sir Robert Clayton and Sir John Banks.
5 Calculated from de Wailly, *Mémoire sur les Variations*; Denise, 'Refontes des Monnaies'; Charlet, *Monnaies des Rois de France*; and the original French monetary ordinances (available online at http://www.ordonnances.org/).
6 Shaw, *History of Currency*, pp. 422, 334–35.
7 In practice it had risen a little, to 62 shillings, in 1666 after the crown began covering the cost of minting coin.
8 Haines, *Prevention of Poverty*, p. 15.
9 A draft is printed in RCHM, *Manuscripts of the House of Lords, 1690–1691*, pp. 179–80.
10 Hodges, *Humble Proposal.*
11 Somerset Record Office, Sandford MS DD/SF 2708.
12 'The Design of Working Goldsmiths in their Address to the Honble the House of Commons', BL, Harley MS 1243, fol. 193v.
13 *CJ*, 8 May 1690.
14 By a royal decree of 3/13 Dec. 1689, the declared value of the gold *louis d'or* was raised from 11.25 *livres* to 12.5 *livres* (an increase of 11.1 percent) and that of the silver *écu* from 60 to 66 *sous*. See Vuitry, *Désordres des Finances*, pp. 141–44; Dieudonné, *Monnaies Royales Françaises*, pp. 178–9, 351; and Mayhew, *Coinage in France*, p. 137.
15 *CJ*, 22 Oct. 1690.
16 During a Commons committee debate in early 1695, Sir Thomas Vernon claimed that London Jews were earning a return of 18 percent by exporting English silver to Holland and having it coined into lion dollars (Codrington Library, All Souls College, MS 152(5) [hereafter 'Codrington MSS'], fols. 146–147r). George Gathorne made the same claim in his committee submission, though he put the profit rate at 30 percent (Codrington MSS, fols. 123–125).
17 *Consequences of Tolerating Gold and Silver to be Exported.*
18 Neale, letter of 10 Apr. 1690 to an unnamed MP (probably Paul Foley), BL, Harley MS 1243, fol. 194.
19 Charles Hutchinson, cited in Luttrell, *Parliamentary Diary*, p. 343.
20 See James Houblon's submission to the Lords, printed in RCHM, *Manuscripts of the House of Lords 1690–91*, pp. 205–6, and an earlier draft, 'Observations on ye Bill Intituled A Bill to Prevent the Exportation of Bullion & to Incourage the Bringing in Forreigne Silver' (BL, Sloane MS 79, fols. 24–26).
21 Jones ('London Merchants', p. 322), maintains that there was indeed a small increase in exports, as well as a small decrease in imports. But presumably the two together were still not sufficient to fill the financing gap. Jones adds that some

part of the burden was covered by foreign capital coming to London to finance ongoing participation in the existing export trades (p. 326).

22 Unfortunately, Houblon reported only the absolute value of the new, lower exchange rate, not the proportion by which it fell.

23 BL Sloane MS 79, fol. 25r.

24 North, *Discourses upon Trade*, p. 19.

25 Locke, *Some Considerations*, pp. 159–60.

26 Locke, *Short Observations*, pp. 140, 158–59.

27 Burnet, *History*, pp. 4:252–3.

28 The episode Burnet describes must have happened before April 1694, since Seymour left the Treasury that month.

29 *CJ*, 22 Dec. 1693.

30 Hopton Haynes, 'Brief Memoires Relating to the Silver & Gold Coins of England', BL, Lansdowne MS 801, fol. 73.

31 Fleetwood, *Sermon Against Clipping*.

32 *CTB*, Minutes, 4 Jan. 1695.

33 *CJ*, 8 Jan. 1695.

34 de Beer, *Correspondence*, p. 295.

35 See Horwitz, *Parliament*, pp. 145–52.

36 John Sanford, Sir John Guise, Charles Hutchinson, Sir William Cook, Samuel Fuller, William Cooke, Sir John Kaye, Thomas Blofield, Sir Richard Onslow, Sir John Morton, Ralph Hawtrey, William Bromley and Sir Matthew Andrews.

37 Two copies of their written submissions have been preserved: Codrington MSS, fols. 100–48; and BL, Add. MS 18759 (henceforth 'Mint Papers'). The fact that both collections contain the very same set of manuscripts suggests they are complete.

38 de Cosera and Stampe wrote two proposals each. Neale offered two alternatives in his single submission.

39 de Beer, *Correspondence*, p. 279.

40 de Beer, *Correspondence*, p. 292.

41 Codrington MSS, fols. 146–147r. There's a small chance this was a record of a debate in the full House since it included remarks by John Dutton Colt, who was not named to the committee. But the rest of those on record were so named and Commons committee memberships were often fairly fluid.

42 de Beer, *Correspondence*, p. 292.

43 *Collection for the Improvement of Husbandry and Trade* (henceforth 'Houghton, Collection').

Bibliography

Manuscript sources

British Library
   Add. MS 18759 ('Mint Papers')
   Harley MS 1243
   Lansdowne MS 801
   Sloane MS 79
Codrington Library, All Souls College, Oxford University
   MS 152(5) ('Codrington MSS')
Somerset Record Office
   Sandford MS DD/SF 2708

Printed primary sources

Burnet, Gilbert. *History of His Own Time: With Notes by the Earls of Dartmouth and Hardwicke, Speaker Onslow, and Dean Swift: To Which Are Added Other Annotations.* Vol. 4. Ed. Martin Joseph Routh. Oxford: University Press, 1833.

[Child, Josiah]. *A Discourse About Trade Wherein the Reduction of Interest in Money to 4l. per Centum Is Recommended.* London: A. Sowle, 1690.

The Consequences of Tolerating Gold and Silver to be Exported Out of This Kingdom Discovered. [London: s.n., 1692?].

De Beer, E. S. (ed.). *The Correspondence of John Locke.* Vol. 5. Oxford: Clarendon Press, 1979.

Fleetwood, William. *A Sermon Against Clipping, Preach'd Before the Right Honourable the Lord Mayor and Court of Aldermen, at Guildhall Chappel on Decemb. 16 1694.* London: J. Whitlock, 1694.

Great Britain. Parliament. House of Commons. *Journals of the House of Commons.* London: House of Commons, 1803. Accessed online at http://www.british-history.ac.uk/commons-jrnl/.

Great Britain. Public Record Office. *Calendar of Treasury Books.* Volume X: *January 1693 to March 1696.* Edited by William Shaw. London: HMSO, 1931. Accessed online at http://www.british-history.ac.uk/cal-treasury-books/vol10.

Great Britain. Royal Commission on Historical Manuscripts. *The Manuscripts of the House of Lords, 1690–1691.* Historical Manuscripts Commission, 13th report, Appendix, Part V. London: HMSO, 1892.

H[aines], R[ichard]. *Prevention of Poverty, or a Discourse of the Causes of the Decay of Trade, Fall of Lands and Want of Money.* London: Nathaniel Brooke, 1674.

Hill, Abraham. *A Letter About Raising the Value of Coin.* London: Randal Taylor, 1690.

[Hodges, John]. *True and Onely Causes of the Great Want of Moneys in These Kingdoms.* London: printed by P. L. for I. H., 1666.

Hodges, William. *An Humble Proposal to Their Most Excellent Majesties, King William and Queen Mary, and to the Two Most Honourable Houses, the Lords and Commons, Assembled in Parliament.* [London: s.n.], 1693.

[Locke, John]. *Short Observations on a Printed Paper Intituled, For Encouraging the Coining Silver Money in England and After for Keeping It Here.* London: A. and J. Churchill, 1695.

[Locke, John]. *Some Considerations of the Consequences of the Lowering of Interest, and Raising the Value of Money: In a Letter Sent to a Member of Parliament.* London: Awnsham and John Churchill, [1692].

Luttrell, Narcissus. *The Parliamentary Diary of Narcissus Luttrell, 1691–1693.* Ed. Henry J. Horwitz. Oxford: Clarendon Press, 1972.

Mun, Thomas. *England's Treasure by Forraign Trade.* London: Thomas Clark, 1628.

North, Dudley. *Discourses Upon Trade, Principally Directed to the Cases of the Interest, Coynage, Clipping, and Increase of Money.* London: Thomas Basset, 1691.

North, Dudley. 'A Representation Intended to be Layd Before the Parliament in the Year 1683 Concerning the Bad Condition of the Mony Current in England and the Meanes to Remedy It'. Printed in Richard Grassby, *The English Gentleman in Trade: The Life and Works of Sir Dudley North* (Oxford: Clarendon Press, 1994), pp. 304–7.

Petty, William. *Sir William Petty, His Quantulumcunque Concerning Money: To the Lord Marquess of Halyfax, Anno 1682.* London: Awnsham & John Churchill, 1695.

[Petyt, William]. *Brittania Languens: Or a Discourse of Trade: Shewing the Grounds and Reasons of the Increase and Decay of Land Rents, National Wealth and Strength.* London: Thomas Dring, 1680.

The Use and Abuses of Money, and the Improvements of It, by Two Propositions for Regulating our Coin. London: Allen Bancks and Charles Harper, 1671.

Contemporary periodicals

Collection for the Improvement of Husbandry and Trade. Ed. John Houghton. London. ('Houghton, *Collection*').

Secondary sources

Charlet, Christian. *Monnaies des Rois de France: de Louis XIII a Louis XVI, 1640–1793.* Paris: Maison Florange, 1996.

de Wailly, Natalis. *Mémoire sur les Variations de la Livre Tournois Depuis le Règne de Saint Louis jusqu'à l'Établissement de la Monnaie Décimale.* Paris: Imprimerie Impériale, 1857.

Denise. H. 'Des Refontes des Monnaies sous l'Ancien Regime'. *Gazette Numismatique Française* 12 (1906): 48–178, 393–405.

Dieudonné, Adolphe. *Manuel de Numismatique Française.* Paris: August Picard, 1916.

Horwitz, Henry. *Parliament, Policy and Politics in the Reign of William III.* Newark: University of Delaware Press, 1977.

Jones, D. W. 'London Merchants and the Crisis of the 1690s'. In *Crisis and Order in English Towns, 1500–1700*, edited by Peter Clarke and Paul Slack, 311–55. London: Routledge & Kegan Paul, 1972.

Mayhew, Nicholas J. *Coinage in France from the Dark Ages to Napoleon.* London: Seaby, 1988.

Shaw, William A. Shaw. *The History of Currency, 1252 to 1894.* New York: Putnam, 1896.

Vuitry, Ad. *Le Désordre des Finances et les Excès de la Spéculation à la Fin du Règne de Louis XIV et au Commencement du Règne de Louis XV.* Paris: Michel Lévy Frères, 1885.

5   The growing problem of war remittances

In this chapter I explore the Bank's role in financing the English army in Flanders. (This is the line of business summarized in the 'exchanges' account in Figures 3.1 and 3.2.)[1] I show that the Bank repeatedly encountered unforeseen difficulties that turned contracts it had hoped would be profitable into money-losing operations. I explore the several means by which the Bank adjusted to these unhappy developments, especially an intriguing decision to try to reproduce on the continent the loan-intermediary strategy that had proved so successful for it in London. The chapter also affords an opportunity to examine the inner workings of foreign-exchange markets and the impact of changing domestic monetary conditions on the Bank's bottom line and the Treasury's fiscal operations. The developments of these months would prove crucial in shaping the government's thinking about when and how to repair the silver coin.

The Bank's first remittance contract, 1694–95

Just a few months after it began operations, the Bank took over the business of army remittances, i.e. providing funds in the local currencies needed to pay the English soldiers fighting in Flanders. It seems this move was forced upon it by the Treasury, which saw an opportunity to save itself some money.[2] For the past several years the Treasury had contracted out its remittance operations, six months at a time, to two tory goldsmiths, Sir Josiah Herne and Sir Stephen Evance. A new contract was due to begin in October 1694. As negotiations got under way in late September, the Treasury clearly tried to play the Bank off against Herne and Evance to get a better deal for itself. Treasury minutes are usually cryptic at the best of times. But the bargaining seems to have shaken out as follows.[3] The exchange rate on the previous six-month contract had been 10.1 guilders per £. Herne and Evance offered the same rate again and were quibbling only about the means by which they were to be paid. The Treasury wanted them, among other things, to take £100 thousand in tallies on the poll tax. The partners countered that they would accept just £50 thousand of such tallies and only those next in line for repayment after the £400 thousand already issued on that fund.

Representatives for the Bank were called in later the same day and told that if Herne and Evance got the contract, the Treasury planned to repay them in part with specie collected via the tonnage tax – the source of interest payments on the Bank's original £1.2 million loan to the government.[4] The directors responded to this threat by offering to remit the money themselves on three conditions: a) the tonnage-tax revenues would be used to pay interest already owing to the Bank; b) the Treasury would convert the poll-tax tallies into specie and provide that money too to the Bank; and c) the rest of the money needed to finance the remittances would be drawn not from a new loan by the Bank but from the £1.2 million loan it had already agreed to make. After some further negotiating the directors offered to remit about £236 thousand (enough to fund the army for about 10 weeks) at a rate of 10.3 guilders per £. They were prepared to remit more, but only if the Treasury came up with some additional cash. The Treasury accepted this offer only on the understanding that the Bank would continue handling army remittances once the current tranche of funding had been used up. Herne and Evance were promptly informed that their services were no longer required.

The Bank had delivered the agreed-upon amount by the end of December (see Figure 5.1). The two sides must have quietly decided to carry on for a few weeks more under the terms of the October agreement. For a further £38 thousand and £56 thousand in credits were sent over in January and February respectively at the same exchange rate. Only in March 1695 did the two sides begin negotiating a new agreement.

Figure 5.1 gives the impression that in its first few months the Bank did not perform as well as had the Herne-Evance partnership. For the average monthly remittance fell from what it had been over the previous year. This was no reflection upon the Bank however; the problem rather was that the Treasury had temporarily run out of funds for the army. Ranelagh wrote Hill in October that once the money sent by the Bank earlier that month had been exhausted, he didn't expect to be able to send any more. He also instructed Hill not to draw any more bills of exchange upon him, because he would not have any cash with which to honour them. Ranelagh's only hope was that the king would somehow rescue the situation when he returned from the continent.[5] William was back in London by 10 November.[6] He must have ordered the Treasury to take corrective action. For just five days later another large tranche of funding was approved for the army, part of it diverted from the Bank's existing loan and part to be raised by way of loans on credit of the Exchequer in general.[7] In effect the king had authorized the Treasury to borrow short-term in anticipation of new funding that would soon be approved by parliament. Similar disbursements to the army followed in late November and mid-December.[8] Hill must also have been authorized to begin drawing again upon Ranelagh. For on 19 November he started once more to sell bills of exchange to Antwerp merchants.[9] Since the bills were drawn at two or three usances, Ranelagh could expect to have received the requisite cash (probably from Exchequer loans on the land tax

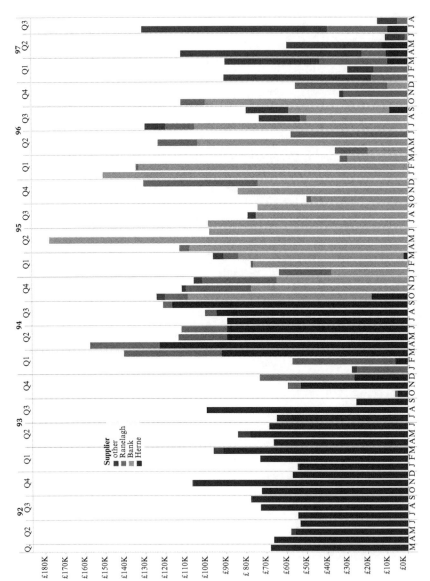

Figure 5.1 Receipt of funds by Deputy Paymaster Richard Hill in Flanders, 1692–97.

Source: Hill Account Book.

for 1695) before they came due. Between new Bank remittances and Hill's drafts, by the end of January funding for the army in Flanders was fully up to date.[10] Presumably this happy state of affairs continued into February, for further large remittances from the Bank were forthcoming that month (see Figure 5.1). The Treasury must have been reasonably pleased with the Bank's performance, for late that month it sought a new agreement by which the Bank would continue in its new role.

At this time the Bank had a fairly simple process for getting Flemish currency into the hands of Hill in Flanders. It began by taking in English currency from Ranelagh, or using its own money and charging a corresponding sum to Ranelagh's account with the Bank. In return Ranelagh was given 'letters of credit' that he immediately dispatched to Hill in Flanders. The latter documents authorized Hill to collect specified sums of Flemish currency from the Bank's agent in Antwerp: at this time one Jacob de Coninck, a banker in his own right. The Bank then had to reimburse de Coninck somehow for the cash he was providing to Hill in Antwerp. This it did by using English money to buy bills of exchange from London-based merchants who were owed money by debtors on the continent. The Bank remitted the bills to de Coninck, whose employees were responsible for presenting them to the local payers when they came due.[11] de Coninck was compensated for his efforts (and the short-term loan he was in effect offering the Bank) by way of brokerage charges and a commission on the bills remitted him. The Bank made its money, in theory, by the difference between the exchange rate it charged Ranelagh on his letters of credit and the exchange rate (net of commission and brokerage charges) that it paid on the bills of exchange it was remitting to de Coninck.

Figure 5.2, derived from de Coninck's account with the Bank, provides a handy overview of the Bank's early remittance operations. Letters of credit were sent over to Hill in fairly large amounts at the contractually-fixed exchange rate of 10.3 guilders, or about 31.7 schellingen banco, per English pound. The Bank bought locally, and remitted to de Coninck, a large number of relatively small bills of exchange, negotiated at various exchange rates (and usances). Figure 5.2 shows that the Bank was getting a considerably better rate on the bills it purchased than it was giving Ranelagh on his letters of credit. Keep in mind however that the exchange rates reported in the Bank's ledgers and shown in Figure 5.2 reflect the cash amounts received by de Coninck upon collection. The effective exchange rates actually realized by the Bank would have been lower than this. For de Coninck's commission and brokerage fees weren't included in the Bank's records for individual bills; they were deducted at financial year-end in a single large transaction. His average total charge was around 2.3 percent of the value of the bills remitted.[12] By comparison the average differential between the exchange rates the Bank was giving for bills of exchange and the rate it was getting from the Treasury started at 2.4 percent in October and fell to 1.8 percent by the end of January. So net of de Coninck's expenses the Bank at first would barely

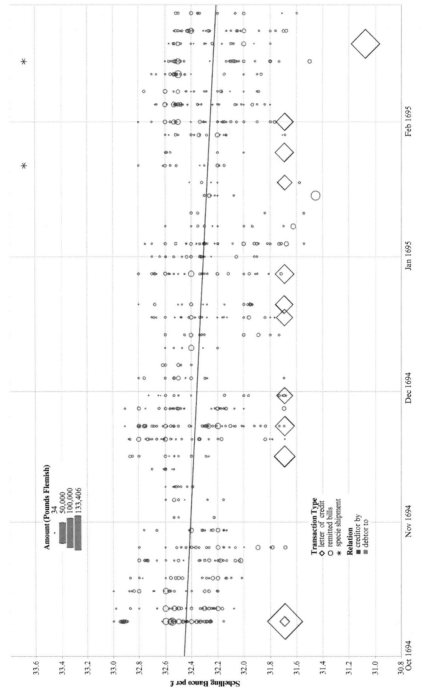

Figure 5.2 De Coninck's transactions with the Bank of England, by exchange rate, Oct. 1694–Feb. 1695.
Source: Bank General Ledger 2.

have been breaking even, and later was actually losing money, on its remittance operations. This probably explains why in January and February the Bank used a couple of specie shipments (always risky, especially in time of war): to try to get a better exchange rate for itself. The fact that the Bank almost immediately began losing money on its remittance operations shaped the course of negotiations on the next remittance contract.

A new remittance contract and a new exchange-rate shock, March–April 1695

In late February 1695 the two sides began discussing the terms of a new agreement. The Bank's initial offer was to remit £90 thousand per month for three months at 10.1 guilders (about 31.1 schellingen banco), on condition the lower exchange rate was also applied retroactively to all but the first £90 thousand of its previous remittances.[13] Mordecai Abbott (secretary to Ranelagh) later explained that the Bank had requested the adjustment to compensate for losses on its previous remittances.[14] The Treasury quietly acceded on the rate issue and even to the Bank's request for applying a lower rate retroactively.[15] It countered only with a demand that the remittance target be raised to £100 thousand per month. In payment the Treasury offered not specie, as the Bank would certainly have preferred, but the next best thing: early tallies on the new land tax recently approved by Parliament. In effect the Bank would be lending the cost of the remittances until these tallies came due for repayment. On 8 March the two sides formally accepted the Treasury's latest terms, back-dating the start of the contract to 20 February – one day after the Bank's most recent letter of credit.[16] The agreement was only for three months.

The new contract promised to make the remittance business profitable for the Bank again. With the new exchange retroactively applied, the Bank would be making an average commission rate, net of de Coninck's implied fee, of 1.7 percent. And even in February, at exchange rates that both parties surely thought were abnormally low and destined not to last, the Bank would still be realizing an average commission rate of 1.2 percent. All looked reasonably good for the moment.

But just days after the new contract was finalized, the London-Antwerp exchange rate fell sharply. A price current put it at 30.9 schellingen banco on 19 March, down from 32.0 during the week the new contract was finalized.[17] (The external value of the pound fell generally, not just in trading with Antwerp. So for instance over the same period the exchange rate on Amsterdam declined from 32.3 to 31.1 schellingen banco.) Worse still from the Bank's perspective, the exchange rate remained at the new, lower level until mid-May (when it started falling even further). The impact on the Bank's remittance operations is clearly visible in Figure 5.3.[18] In a letter to Hill of 15 March, Abbott warned that 'the Bank complains already that they lose by your new contract'.[19] Indeed, at the new market rate for bills of exchange on

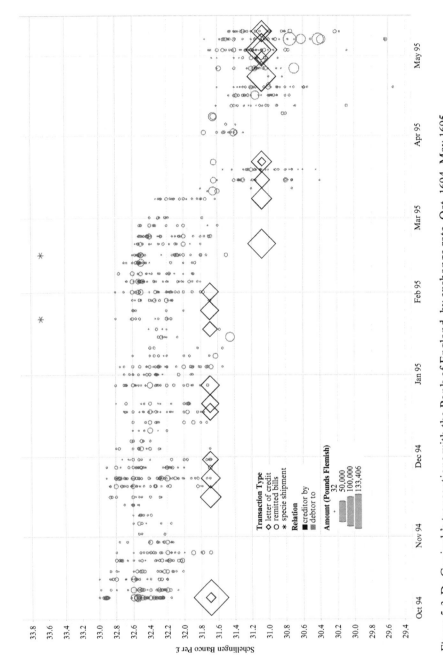

Figure 5.3 De Coninck's transactions with the Bank of England, by exchange rate, Oct. 1694–May 1695.
Source: Bank General Ledger 2.

average the Bank was barely breaking even on its remittance operations –
even before de Coninck's charges were deducted.

When he wrote Hill, Abbott expected the Bank to go on sending letters
of credit despite the recent drop in the exchange rate. After all, they were
tied by the contract to a three-month term. But the Bank's initial response
was to refrain from buying bills of exchange for remittance to de Coninck.[20] This resulted in a growing overdraft with de Coninck, as indicated
in Figure 5.4. The solution was temporary at best, presumably reflecting a
hope on the Bank's part that the exchange rate would soon recover. Even so
it must have put a tremendous strain on de Coninck. For on 25 March news
arrived in London that he had refused to honour the Bank's most recent
letters of credit.

The Bank dealt with the problem in two main ways. First they tried to get
money directly into Hill's hands as soon as possible by means that didn't put
any further pressure on de Coninck. Specifically, they arranged to borrow
short-term, on their own personal credit, from bankers and merchants on
the continent. They did so by drawing bills of exchange upon their lenders
and then remitting the bills to Hill in Antwerp. The bills were drawn at 2, 3
and even 4 usances, so that the directors would have as much time as possible to repay their creditors (hoping no doubt that exchange rates would
improve in the meantime). Hill discounted the bills locally and debited the
Bank for the resulting interest charges.

Second, the Bank worked to reduce its overdraft with de Coninck so
that he would resume payment on the letters of credit already sent. This
they achieved by sending over no further letters of credit for a time (Hill's
needs were covered instead by the bills the Bank had sent him directly) and
continuing to supply funding to him. Funding was provided in part by the
usual means of buying bills of exchange in London drawn upon continental
debtors and then sending the bills to de Coninck. But given the present lowness of the London-Antwerp exchange rate, the Bank would have used this
method as sparingly as possible. It began trying instead to send money to
de Coninck indirectly by way of an agent in Amsterdam: the banker Henry
Meulenaer. Amsterdam being a larger, busier commercial centre, it was a
little easier and cheaper to buy bills on other European centres and remit
them to Meulenaer. It was then Meulenaer's responsibility to discount the
bills locally and pass the proceeds along to de Coninck in Antwerp. This
would also have worked in the Bank's favour by taking some pressure off the
London-Antwerp exchange rate. It took a while for this second strategy to
work. On 17 April, Ranelagh informed the treasury lords that as of 8 April
Hill still hadn't received any money from de Coninck on the Bank's outstanding letters of credit. William summoned the directors the next day and
complained most bitterly. They replied that the next letters from Flanders
would show the letters of credit had already been honoured.[21]

Hard-pressed as it already was by the declining exchange rate, the Bank
now found itself coming under additional pressure. For on 8 April, Ranelagh

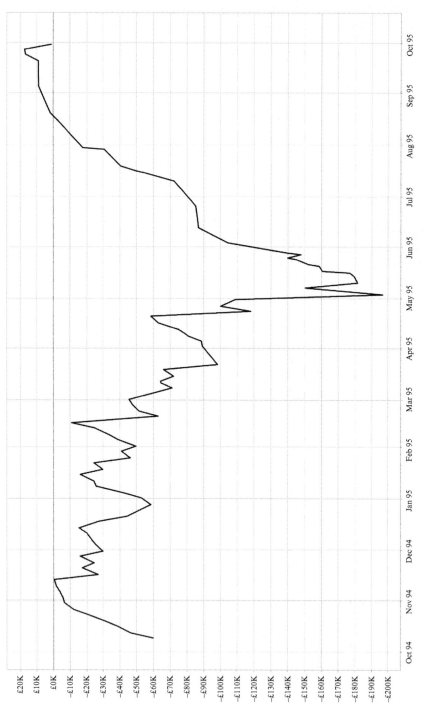

Figure 5.4 Running net debits on the Bank of England's account with de Coninck, 1694–95.
Source: Bank General Ledger 2.

having already exhausted the Bank's March loan of £300 thousand, the Treasury asked to borrow another £200 thousand or so and have the Bank remit this money at £60 thousand per week for the army in Flanders.[22] The treasury lords proposed payment in tallies on a branch of the customs revenue. This was good security, since the tax in question was well-established and known to produce well above £300 thousand per year. But the Treasury was offering tallies on the second and third years of the tax, which would not come due for payment until sometime in 1696 and 1697 respectively. Not wanting to commit the Bank to so long a loan, the directors declined the Treasury's offer. On 12 April they learned the king was 'dissatisfied with their answer' and wanted them to reconsider. Three days later the directors resolved to lend only as much as could be repaid from the second year of the tax, and this only on condition that parliament pass a clause raising the current £1.2 million ceiling on the issue of Bank bills. If that clause could not be obtained, the Bank wasn't prepared to fund new letters of credit by way of a loan. Instead it wanted payment in specie, suggesting for this purpose cash currently being raised by the Treasury from the sale of annuities. On 17 April William concluded the Bank's terms were 'too hard' and ordered that the funds be borrowed elsewhere. The next day the Treasury lowered its loan request to £77 thousand, payment still to be in tallies on the second year of the customs. Abbott wrote Hill on the 19th that he had hoped to send a letter of credit on de Coninck for £60 thousand that very day, but terms had been finalized too late in the day for this to be possible. But as it turned out, the Bank was not yet done negotiating. It subsequently demanded, and got: a) immediate receipt of the rebate it had been promised months ago for timely payment of the first quarter of its £1.2 million; and b) a discount on the customs tallies in which it was to be paid for the new loan. '[I]f we are put to these streights already,' complained Abbott to Hill, 'what shall we do before the end of the campaign which is but now beginning'.[23] Only on 27 April was Abbott finally able to send out a new letter of credit. William must have been greatly angered. For that same day he transferred his shares in the Bank to Treasury Secretary William Lowndes.[24]

In the next few weeks the treasury lords succeeded in raising cash from other short-term lenders.[25] So in the final month of the remittance contract scheduled to end on 19 May, the Bank was obliged to furnish letters of credit for a further £250 thousand (see Figure 5.1). Figure 5.3 shows that the exchange rate on Antwerp remained low throughout this period, so that again the Bank was already losing money on its remittance operations even before deducting de Coninck's commission.

Alternative measures: permission money and the Antwerp Agency

When the exchange rate on Antwerp first declined in March 1695, Hill seemed to think the new situation likely to last and advised the Treasury that it would no longer be possible to fund the army in the usual way.[26] The Treasury was soon presented with two proposals for entirely different ways of getting the job done.

The first came from William, who was at the Treasury when Hill's letter arrived. He suggested requesting authorization from the Duke of Bavaria, ruler of the Spanish Netherlands, for coining Flemish 'permission money' at the Mint in London. This was a special debased silver currency in which the duke's soldiers were being paid. If he could get the duke to agree, William proposed that the Bank purchase £75 thousand of silver bullion locally. This would generate the equivalent of £100 thousand in Flemish coin that could then be shipped to Antwerp and used to pay England's troops. On 8 May the king reported having obtained the necessary approval.[27]

It seems the Bank at least tried to follow up on the idea. The next day the directors recommended that samples be obtained of the various coins then current in Flanders.[28] According to a Treasury minute of 9 April, the Bank was about to send £10 thousand in bullion into the Mint to be coined into Flemish money. And on 26 April the Bank appointed a committee to procure bullion for the same purpose.[29] But there is no clear sign in the Bank's General Ledger of coin ever being shipped from London to Antwerp.

The second proposal was broached by the Bank directors themselves. It would eventually become known as the 'Antwerp Agency'. At first the idea was described only in very vague terms. Meeting with the Treasury the day after it had received Hill's advice that new methods would need to be considered, Bank directors suggested they might 'use their own credit in supplying the army'.[30] The next day a similar and equally cryptic description was recorded in the Bank's minutes; the remittance committee was given authority 'to make use of the credit of the Bank & their own credit for furnishing the money for supplying the public services and remittances into foreign parts'.[31] Only from a later description can we begin to make out the gist of what was being proposed. At a Treasury meeting on 19 April William asked 'that some of the directors of the Bank should be sent … into Flanders to settle a credit and borrow money there on that credit'.[32] And when the Bank appointed a committee of directors to run the Agency, it deputed them 'to receive and pay money and to give notes for the same'.[33] The basic idea, in other words, was to try to borrow the necessary funds in Flanders itself by taking specie deposits and issuing interest-bearing notes for the same.[34] Presumably the notes were to be made payable on demand, to give depositors confidence they could always have their specie back whenever necessary. The trick would be to maintain a specie reserve large enough that the Agency could always honour the normal run of demand for notes to be repaid, generating the confidence needed to attract and hold deposits. The Agency could then pay this money over to Hill, confident that the bulk of its notes would remain out in circulation and/or be held as short-term investments. This interpretation is confirmed by l'Hermitage, who wrote The Hague to explain that the directors hoped their circulating bank bills, bearing interest, would take the place of current money, and that with £150 thousand in bills of exchange the directors have carried over, and a million guilders that must come from Amsterdam, they think they can do without bills of exchange for six months, and that during this time the exchange rate will rise.[35]

As long as the exchange rate rose enough any time within the next six months, the Bank could fund remittances more cheaply this way than by buying bills of exchange.[36]

The directors resolved on 19 April to proceed with the idea and three days later approved a specific plan. A few of them would be sent to Antwerp in shifts and paid the same charges currently being allowed to de Coninck (whose services would no longer be required). According to one contemporary, the directors unanimously asserted that 'the advantage ... by this undertaking ... [was] so great, so certain and unquestionable' that shareholders need have no worries.[37] In mid-May the Bank appointed the first set of directors to administer the Agency;[38] the three men in question (Godfrey, William Scawen and Robert Raworth) departed London for Antwerp late that month.[39]

There are clear signs of the experiment having been attempted. On 19 June Hill was issued twenty Agency notes for 200 pounds Flemish each, on 11 July another ten in the same denomination and twenty for 100 pounds Flemish each and on 18 July a final 1000 pounds Flemish in total in unspecified denominations.[40] Like with the Bank's original loan to the Exchequer, it seems the directors were offering payment directly in their own notes.[41] Presumably they were counting upon Hill cashing the notes right away. Or maybe they hoped he might get several of his creditors to accept them in payment and hold them as short-term investments, in lieu of demanding payment in specie. Unfortunately the Agency's records haven't survived. So it is impossible to know when the notes in question returned there for encashment. Nor do we know more generally how many notes the Agency issued in total.

But we can tell by other means that the experiment failed. First, it proved impossible to acquire a specie reserve of sufficient size. When the first Antwerp directors sailed for the continent on 31 May, they took with them £128 thousand in bills of exchange that, as l'Hermitage had noted, were earmarked to fund a specie reserve.[42] But the directors thought the reserve needed to be still larger. In mid-May Montagu asked the Earl of Portland (William's closest confidant and then with him in the Low Countries) to persuade Schuylenberg to lend the Bank a further £50 thousand for this purpose.[43] Montagu, Godolphin and Godfrey repeatedly emphasized to Portland and Secretary of War William Blathwayt (also then with William in Flanders) the vital importance of this loan.[44] '[I]n truth', Montagu asserted, 'if that attempt fail there is an end of the war ...; I am satisfied that while there is such a fleet in the streights and such an army in Flanders nothing but such a credit as the Bank hope to find can mend the exchange'.[45] William did arrange for Schuylenberg to send £50 thousand to Antwerp. But on 22 June the Antwerp directors complained to Blathwayt that the money had been delivered to Hill, who in turn had paid it out to the army. They asked Blathwayt to try again and persuade William this time to lend them 700 to 800 thousand guilders (£80 thousand at the contracted exchange rate). They warned that without some such assistance 'we can't see it possible to supply the army'.[46] William was unable to assist on this occasion.[47] With his help the Bank did eventually receive two large loans in September. But by then the money was needed just to keep the army afloat; all thought of a specie reserve had vanished.

The second piece of evidence that the note-issuing experiment failed is the fact that the Antwerp directors wrote home in mid-June requesting permission to try circulating their notes in Amsterdam instead.[48] This suggests that there wasn't enough of a market for the notes in Antwerp. Perhaps the Agency's directors thought the larger mercantile community in Amsterdam, and the Bank's links with several large mercantile houses there, would help. If the request had been approved, presumably the Agency would have used the proceeds from note issues in Amsterdam to buy bills upon Antwerp (thereby still avoiding the troubled London-Antwerp and London-Amsterdam exchanges). Unfortunately for the Antwerp directors, their proposal was declined. The home office worried that it would be difficult for three directors to manage business in two distant centres at once and that jealousies from the banking community in Amsterdam (much better-established than that in Antwerp) would disrupt their efforts.

A summer of disappointments

Negotiations on a new remittance contract began in mid-May 1695 – the existing one being set to expire on 19 May. A few weeks earlier the Bank had resolved internally to offer a six-month term at a fixed rate of 9.9 guilders per £.[49] Though the minutes of neither Bank nor Treasury report anything more on the subject for the next fortnight, informal discussions must have been under way. For on 4 May the crown issued a warrant that authorized the Bank to export 200 thousand ounces of English silver bullion and a further 500 thousand ounces if it agreed to a new remittance contract.[50] The two sides finally got down to terms on 9 May. William (who often attended Treasury meetings when he was in London) proposed a six-month agreement at a fixed rate of 10 guilders. The Bank wanted a whole year at that rate. On 11 May the Treasury agreed to the longer term, but got an option to convert after one month to a floating rate with a 2 percent management fee.[51]

In the following week Evance and Herne tried to wrest the remittance business away from the Bank. On 13 May they offered a rate of 10.75 guilders on condition the bullion-export right was transferred to them. But they were prepared to commit to this rate only for the next £200 thousand of remittances – enough to fund the army for just two months. The Treasury wanted a fixed rate for a term of at least six months. Evance and Herne upped their bid a few days later to 10.9 guilders. Since this was very near the mint par with Antwerp, it seems their goal was not to make money but only to keep the Bank from securing the next agreement. The Treasury continued to insist upon a longer commitment, asserting the export right was worth far less on its own than if assigned to a party undertaking a long-term contract.[52] Evance and Herne declined a longer term on the plea that the Bank had sufficient power in the market for bills of exchange to impose losses on any prospective competitor.[53] So the Treasury's agreement with the Bank remained in place.

The course of negotiations between Bank and Treasury suggests both parties hoped the London-Antwerp exchange rate would rise in the next year but were trying to insure themselves against the possibility it did not. The Treasury's request for an option to convert to a fluctuating rate after one month shows it harboured some hope the rate would rise very soon. In dangling the bullion-export right before the Bank, however, the Treasury was trying to offer the Bank some insurance (in a manner almost costless to itself). At the current market price of 5s. 7d. per ounce, 700 thousand ounces of bullion was equivalent to about £195 thousand. So the warrant was in effect affording the Bank an opportunity to finance about two months' worth of the remittances at a rate likely to be near the London-Amsterdam mint par of 34.7 schellingen banco[54] – much better than the 30.9 schellingen banco being quoted in early May in the market for London bills of exchange on Antwerp.[55] In accepting an agreement at 10 guilders, the government was implicitly acknowledging that things might get no better and could even get worse. The fact that the Bank agreed to a fixed rate of 10 guilders implies it was prepared for the possibility of rates getting no better than they were in early May but expected them eventually to rise. Ten guilders was equivalent to 30.8 schellingen banco, a rate that would have meant losses for the Bank after the Antwerp Agency's management fee was deducted. But we must also factor in the potential impact of the bullion-export right. Had that right been used to the full under the circumstances prevailing in early May, the Bank could only have expected to earn an overall return at best of about 0.7 percent per pound remitted.[56] This was significantly less than the 2 percent management fee it had offered the Treasury as an alternative. So the Bank must have thought circumstances were going to turn in its favour during the coming year. The same assumption is implied by its request to extend the agreement from six months to one year. This would allow the Bank to lock in the gains from any improvements in the exchange rate during the second half of the year.

Unfortunately for the Bank and the government alike, far from remaining stable or even improving, market exchange rates began declining the very week the new agreement was finalized. On 14 May the London-Antwerp exchange rate stood at 30.1 schellingen banco, down from the level of 30.9

at which it had held steady the previous eight weeks.[57] The rate declined still further to 29.7 in late May and to 27 by mid-August; for the rest of the calendar year it fluctuated in a narrow band around 28.

Several explanations were offered at the time for why exchange rates had fallen. Upon an earlier decline in March, for instance, Hill had speculated that merchants were trying to hedge against the possibility clipped coin would soon be demonetized.[58] And Locke's College had pointed to the untimely publication of the Commons resolution to raise the coin. But the Bank attributed the problem exclusively to the high and rising price of gold guineas. They had been trading at 25s. for the whole of March and April. But the very week that the new remittance contract was concluded they suddenly jumped to 28s. 4d. A week later they were at 29s. and three weeks after that at 30s. Gold bullion, which could be coined into guineas at the Mint without charge and in just a few weeks, had likewise jumped in price: from £4.6 per ounce in April to £4.9 on 14 May and £5.2 a week later.[59] On the Bank's reading, this had made arbitrage traders keen to buy gold bullion and guineas on the continent (where their prices had not risen) and import them to England: an operation that could in principle be repeated endlessly. To obtain the funds needed to pay their suppliers on the continent, arbitrage traders were now purchasing large quantities of bills of exchange at London. This in turn was putting strong downward pressure on the London-Antwerp and London-Amsterdam exchange rates.[60]

L'Hermitage may have been relaying the Bank's own suspicions when he reported that London's goldsmith bankers were behind the sudden jump in the price of guineas. In a report of 21 June, he asserted they were angry that the upstart Bank of England had stolen away so much of the profitable business of public finance and so had resolved to do it all possible harm. Ten of them had combined to inflate the market price of guineas. On l'Hermitage's telling they hoped the Bank would accept guineas at the higher rates; the consortium would then work to lower the market price again, causing large losses for the Bank. The Bank, having foreseen what was intended for it, refused to accept guineas at all. But this benefited the goldsmith bankers by other means; all those who were refused the right to deposit guineas with the Bank turned to the goldsmith bankers instead – driving up their cash reserves and lending capacity.

There may be some truth to the story. Members of the general public certainly had good reason to offer higher prices (i.e. a greater number of clipped silver coins) for guineas than before. In a private report written in July for one treasury lord, Locke argued this very point.[61] Were clipped silver demonetized overnight (as many were now expecting), guineas would probably return to their normal market price (at the time around 21s. 6d.). In that case the proportionate loss of wealth would be smaller for those holding guineas acquired even at 30s. (~28 percent) than for anyone holding clipped silver coin (on average one half). Under these circumstances it would not have been very hard for goldsmith bankers to manufacture a rise in the price of guineas. Thereafter they need only have committed to the fairly low-risk strategy of accepting and paying out guineas at whatever price the market was prepared to support. For its part, the Bank immediately ordered its cashiers to pay away all but 5,000 of the guineas they were holding at the time.[62] A month later they were instructed neither to receive nor pay guineas at any price.[63] And two weeks after that the Antwerp directors proposed trying to engineer a rise in the price of guineas overseas; they thought an investment of £8 to £10 thousand would be enough to get the job done.[64] L'Hermitage's account, however, missed the main mechanism by which the goldsmith bankers would have hoped to do the Bank harm: through the impact on the London-Antwerp exchange rate. The timing of the jump in prices, just a day or two after the Bank entered upon a new fixed-rate contract, does raise suspicions.

The Bank tried in two ways to extricate itself from its unhappy new situation. First, it asked to have the new remittance contract adjusted or cancelled. Second, the Bank repeatedly petitioned the crown to take action to lower the price of guineas. Neither approach was to prove successful.

Despite its best efforts, the Treasury would not agree to let the Bank out of its contract. The directors warned of catastrophic consequences. 'I cannot tell what will become of us', one director wrote Godolphin in late May.[65] They claimed their losses would run as high as £100 thousand: enough to wipe out the whole of the annual interest payment on their founding loan of £1.2 million.[66] And after reading the first letters coming back from the Antwerp directors (from which presumably they learned that the idea of circulating Agency notes wasn't going to work), the London directors informed the Treasury that it would simply be impossible to keep to their contract.[67] Neither bullion nor bills of exchange could be had in London, even though the Bank was offering very good prices.[68] But the Treasury remained unmoved. In mid-June they informed the Bank that it was 'his majesty's pleasure' to forego the option to convert to a floating exchange rate. The Bank would have to go on remitting at 10 guilders per £ for the remainder of the contract.[69]

Nor could the Bank persuade the government to take any action on the high price of guineas. The directors thought it might suffice to instruct the Exchequer to stop taking guineas at high rates.[70] Alternatively, they wanted the lords justices to issue a proclamation fixing the value of guineas at 25s. or less.[71] Treasury officials rejected both expedients. They claimed the Exchequer had tried refusing guineas at high prices but this: a) had done nothing to lower their price in the City; and b) was discouraging lending at the Exchequer and receipt of taxes generally.[72] The treasury lords couldn't resist adding that the Exchequer wouldn't have to take guineas from the general public at all were the Bank more forthcoming with loans.[73] To the lords justices the Treasury argued that instructing tax receivers to take guineas at some set price wouldn't help; speculators would only try to raise the price still higher.[74] In the end the crown took no direct action. Instead London tax receivers were instructed to discourage their collectors from paying in guineas and make them believe that in future guineas would be altogether refused at the Exchequer. The lords justices also ordered customs officials to take any inbound guinea shipments to the Mint for inspection and Mint officials to report the names of any merchants importing guineas that had obviously been coined elsewhere.[75] Neither measure had any apparent effect on the market price of guineas. But tax collectors now began to complain to the lords justices that they had taken in large quantities of guineas from taxpayers at 30s. and the Exchequer was now refusing to receive them at that price.[76] So in early August the lords justices held a special cabinet meeting, inviting the input of several high-level interested parties: a customs commissioner (himself a wealthy financier), two remittance contractors (Herne and the governor of the Bank of England) and another prominent goldsmith banker.[77] The lords justices must have contemplated fixing an official value on guineas, since later that month they invited legal opinions on the question.[78] But in the end they took no further action.

So the Bank was left to cope as best it could. It chose not to pursue one obvious option: simply to default on the new contract. As Figure 5.1 shows, from May to July Hill continued receiving letters of credit from the Bank at a pace sufficient to cover the cost of £93.3 thousand per month for subsisting the army in Flanders (the large additional receipts in May were to pay forage contractors). Even in August and September, when exchange rates had fallen yet further, the Bank was still providing him with a relatively healthy £75 thousand per month.[79]

Instead the Bank pursued alternate ways of getting money to their directors in Antwerp. There was of course the hope that the Agency might succeed in circulating notes abroad, enabling the Bank for a while to borrow the necessary funding at a relatively low interest rate. We have already seen that this experiment failed. And the very decision to put the Agency in place created another problem for the Bank: how to pay off the overdraft it had been running with de Coninck. Figures 5.5 and 5.6 together show how this task was handled. At first the Bank continued remitting bills of exchange directly to de Coninck in Antwerp. But this practice was stopped in late May, perhaps because it was putting the London-Antwerp exchange rate under too much downward pressure. Instead in late May and June the Bank sent several large shipments of bullion to Meulenaer in Amsterdam, who in turn remitted bills of exchange (and sent some specie) to de Coninck in Antwerp. The Antwerp directors cleared the rest of the overdraft with de Coninck in July and August by passing along some of the bills of exchange they had brought over from London in May and others the Bank sent them in late July.[80]

A second coping strategy was to stop buying bills of exchange in London for as long as possible, in hopes the London-Antwerp exchange rate might recover in the meantime. As Figure 5.6 shows, the Bank remitted no bills to the Antwerp directors for almost their first two months overseas.

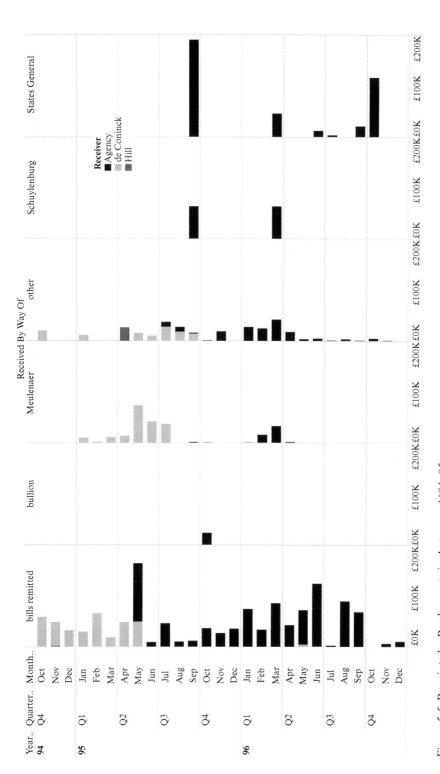

Figure 5.5 Receipts by Bank agents in Antwerp, 1694–95.
Source: Bank General Ledger 2.

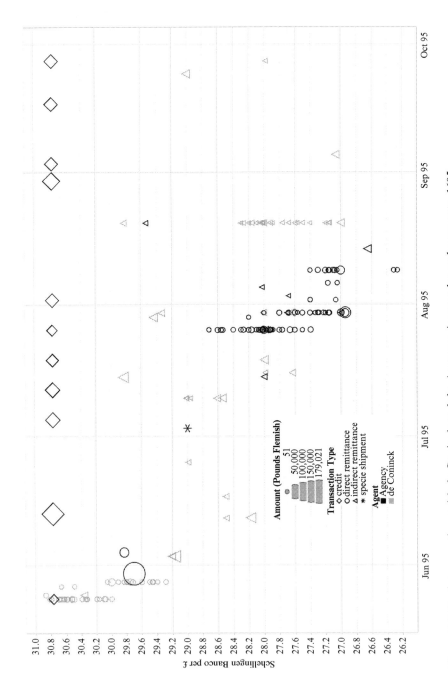

Figure 5.6 Bank transactions with de Coninck and the Antwerp Agency, by exchange rate, 1695.
Source: Bank General Ledger 2.

Unfortunately for the Bank, far from improving, exchange rates actually worsened as time went on.

The strategy upon which the Agency finally settled, then, was to borrow money by way of a conventional loan from some large lender(s). Though more expensive than borrowing by means of low-interest Agency notes, this would still have been cheaper than buying bills of exchange at the ever-lower rates to which they were sinking in London. The Antwerp directors first approached Fonseca, a wealthy bread contractor for the English troops in Flanders. But he informed them that a local statute prohibited any but merchants from lending at interest in Flanders. Godfrey wrote Blathwayt on 6 July to ask William to get the Duke of Bavaria to waive the law in Fonseca's case. Nothing could have come of this request, for over a month later the Antwerp directors were still reminding Blathwayt of it.[81] The Antwerp directors turned their attention next to the Dutch Netherlands. They visited The Hague in early July to request a loan from the States General. Unfortunately for them, the deputies were on vacation and would not be sitting again until mid-August.[82] Their visit to William's camp in mid-July was no doubt connected with their efforts to find a loan on the continent. Unfortunately, while they were attending him in the trenches before the besieged town of Namur, Godfrey was felled by a French cannon ball. This was a blow for Bank and Treasury alike. Montagu feared that without Godfrey, of all the Agency directors the one with the greatest reputation in Antwerp, the remittance situation was now beyond retrieval. 'The badness of our money [and] the slowness of our trade is such as makes it impracticable to answer the demands for fleet and army by anything but credit; and credit once baffled is not [to] be restored'.[83] The Bank directors at London may also have given up hope. Or perhaps the remaining Antwerp directors had finally exhausted their original store of bills and were just trying buy some more time for a loan to be arranged. Either way, around this time the Bank finally relented and began again to buy bills of exchange at London. Figure 5.6 shows the very large losses they suffered on this account.

Not until early September did the Antwerp directors finally succeed in obtaining a loan. When the States General resumed meeting in mid-August, the request for a £200 thousand loan to the Bank was first on their agenda.[84] It was approved very quickly, for on 22 August the directors asked William to confirm to the States General that he was guaranteeing payment of the interest. In the same letter they also asked William to approve an instruction to Schuylenberg to lend them a further £67 thousand. The two loans arrived on 5 and 6 September.[85] Godolphin wrote William on the latter date to report that the London-Antwerp exchange rates had risen 3 percent in the previous week.[86] This he attributed in part to news of the loan agreement but even more so to the most signal English military victory of the war: William's retaking of the fortress of Namur (the French forces there surrendered in the final days of August). Once more the Bank stopped buying bills of exchange at London (see Figure 5.6). And for a time warnings of imminent financial disaster disappeared from Treasury officials' letters to Blathwayt.

Summary

The business of funding the English army in Flanders opened some fault lines in the relationship between Treasury and Bank. They expected the two remittance agreements negotiated in 1695 to prove mutually beneficial. But both agreements immediately came under pressure from declining rates in the London market for bills of exchange on Antwerp and Amsterdam, imposing large losses on the Bank. Given the mechanisms available for transferring funds internationally there was little the Bank could do at first but to: a) slow the pace at which it was remitting bills of exchange; b) diminish the pace at which it was sending over letters of credit (above all by declining to lend the crown the funds the Treasury hoped to borrow for the army); or c) borrow overseas the funding needed for the army in Flanders. All three approaches had problems. The first led de Coninck for a time to stop paying out on the Bank's letters of credit. The second angered William enough that he sold his shares in the Bank. And the third was only a temporary solution, buying the Bank two or three months' time at best. By late April, exchange rates continuing low, Treasury and Bank agreed that they had to find some other way of funding the army. Hence was born the Antwerp Agency and the bold idea of borrowing abroad for a longer period, and more cheaply, by issuing a new paper currency in Flanders. Unfortunately for both parties, this experiment failed: in part because they were too hard-pressed to raise an adequate specie reserve and for the rest because Antwerp wasn't as receptive to lending short term on Agency notes as London had been to lending via Bank bills. And then exchange rates fell even further – this time for an identifiable reason: the high price of guineas. The Bank thought the government could correct this problem, either by exercising the Exchequer's considerable power in matters of coin or by an outright official decree. The Treasury was steadfast in advising against either course of action. Though publicly it argued that neither strategy could work, in practice it was surely thinking above all about the positive impact that high guinea prices would have on the volume and pace of tax revenues. So the Bank was left with no alternative but to borrow for a time in Europe by way of a conventional loan. This was an expensive solution and again could help only in the short term; £270 thousand was not enough to fund the army even until the end of the calendar year. So as summer turned to fall, the Bank would have continued hoping for the government to take some decisive action to lower the price of guineas. Should this lead to higher exchange rates, losses during the early months of the new remittance contract would be offset by sizeable gains during the later months. The Treasury's practical interests were rather different. As long as it believed the Bank's losses from its remittance contract wouldn't prove fatal to the institution as a whole, the Treasury could afford not to worry much about the exchange-rate problem. In fact, it rather favoured a high price for guineas since the resulting monetary uncertainty might speed the flow of taxes and loans into the Exchequer. On the other hand, as the silver coin continued to deteriorate, Treasury officials had to worry about the currency of clipped silver coming to a sudden halt and the price of guineas suffering a dramatic decline. So they were to approach the coming parliamentary session with very different aims than those of the Bank – whose interests, we shall see, were left to languish. Money was not buying the Bank's directors a whole lot of power.

Notes

1 Of the two accounts I fused together there, the Bank used one to track the funds that it had promised to supply for the army in Flanders (liabilities) and the other recording the foreign bills of exchange it purchased to furnish the corresponding amounts of cash abroad (assets). In principle the two should have offset one another, leaving the balance on the 'exchanges' account always near zero. But in practice, after the London-Antwerp exchange rate fell in 1695, making foreign bills of exchange more expensive, the Bank deliberately fell behind in its purchases of the latter (trying to fund the army by other means instead, mostly by loans from foreign bankers). So for the better part of our period the Bank was running a deficit on this composite account. Note that the Bank did not bring its army remittances business fully into the general ledgers. It kept off the books, in a separate ledger (BEA, ADM7/2, hereafter 'Bank General Ledger 2'), accounts of money it was borrowing from the Dutch army paymaster and States General.

2 There may have been another factor at work. His biographer claims that Godolphin pushed to move the contract, being good friends with two of the Bank's directors: Henry Furnese and Theodore Janssen (Sundstrom, *Sidney Godolphin*, p. 69).

3 BL, Lansdowne MS 1215 (hereafter 'Treasury Minutes re Flanders').

4 Technically this would have been legal. For the statute by which the Bank was created had directed that only half the tonnage tax be used to finance interest payments on the loan – but hadn't said which half or in what order (5–6 W. & M., c. 20, §41).

5 Undated letter enclosed in letter of Hill to Blathwayt, 23 Oct. 1694, Bodleian Library, MS Eng. Hist. d.146 (henceforth 'Hill Letters'), fol. 211.

6 Luttrell, *Brief Historical Relation*, p. 3:398.

7 Tallies on credit of the Exchequer in general were tied to no particular tax fund and so were less secure, having no dedicated revenue source from which they were eventually to be paid. But typically they came with a verbal promise of being converted into tallies on the first tax fund granted in the next session of parliament (usually the land tax).

8 *CTB*, Orders, etc., 29 Nov. and 18 and 20 Dec. 1694.

9 Shropshire Archives, Attingham Collection, X112/1A/1 (henceforth 'Hill Account Book').

10 Letters of Abbott to Hill, 25 and 29 Jan. 1695, Shropshire Archive, Attingham Collection, 112/1/2/1 (henceforth 'Abbott Letters').

11 Bank General Ledger 2 contains a complete list of the commercial bills the Bank sent its agents in Antwerp and various other European cities between 1694 and 1700. The list stipulates the drawers and payers, the due date, the amount due in foreign currency and the sum paid for it in English currency. Most of the bills were payable in cities other than Antwerp. de Coninck would have dispatched such bills in turn for collection by his agents in the relevant centres (who likewise charged their own commissions).
12 On 30 Sep. 1695, the Bank charged itself with a loss of £16.2 thousand on for 'discount of bills and loss by exchange' on de Coninck's account going back to Oct. 1694. During that time the Bank had sent de Coninck a total of £698 thousand, almost all of it in bills of exchange.
13 Bank Minutes, 27 Feb. 1695.
14 Abbott Letters, 2 Apr. 1695.
15 This adjustment was made directly in the de Coninck account for the most recent remittance. For earlier transactions it was handled instead by a separate entry in the Bank's profit-and-loss account. That's why in Figure 5.3 the exchange rate is lower only for the letter of credit sent on 19 Feb. 1695.
16 Treasury Minutes re Flanders, fol. 87r.
17 Houghton, *Collection*.
18 The several bill purchases entered at rates of 30.3 schellingen probably reflect clerical errors by Bank staff. They relate to bills drawn upon centres outside the Netherlands and so required Bank staff to convert between three different currencies. The Bank didn't use full double-entry bookkeeping to ensure the accuracy of any non-sterling entries (something it never failed to do for pound sterling amounts).
19 Abbott Letters, fol. 464.
20 While this may have surprised Abbott, Hill was probably expecting it. About eighteen months earlier Hill had predicted to Blathwayt that, given the lowness of the exchange rate at that time, 'Sr Joseph & his brethren [then the remittance contractors] will make no haste to send me credit' (Hill Letters, 1 Oct. 1693).
21 Treasury Minutes re Flanders, fols. 90v, 91r.
22 Treasury Minutes re Flanders, fol. 89r.
23 Abbott Letters, fol. 473.
24 *CTB*, Minutes.
25 *CTB*, Entry Book, April 1695.
26 Treasury Minutes re Flanders, fol. 88r.
27 *CTB*, Minutes.
28 Treasury Minutes re Flanders.
29 Bank Minutes.
30 Treasury Minutes re Flanders, 26 Mar. 1695.
31 Bank Minutes, 27 Mar. 1695.
32 Bank Minutes, 19 Mar. 1695.
33 Bank Minutes, 15 May 1695.
34 Previous Bank historians missed this feature of the Agency. Richards (*Early History*, pp. 179–80) and Acres (*Bank of England*, ch. 9) summarize the available documentation but make no mention of any plan to circulate bills. Clapham thought the Agency was just an in-house replacement for de Coninck (*Bank of England*, p. 26).
35 L'Hermitage Reports, 21 June/1 July 1695.
36 The going interest rate on loans in the Netherlands was 3 percent. Let us suppose that the Agency offered that rate on its bills and chose to keep a specie reserve equal to 20 percent of its total borrowing. In that case the total interest cost for borrowing six months' worth of remittances (£540 thousand) would have been

£5.7 thousand. (To get this result I assumed the Agency borrowed gradually, only as much as it needed to finance the current month, rather than the whole six months' worth up front. I also assumed that the Bank borrowed £108 thousand per month (£90 thousand for the army plus a 20 percent reserve) and that there would be no compounding of interest. For the Bank to make that money back later on, the London-Antwerp exchange rate only needed to rise, from its current level of 31.1, to 31.4 schellingen banco. This of course ignores the Agency's administrative costs, which were sure to be considerable. And it is possible the Bank had to pay more than 3 percent interest to obtain actual specie.

37 *Looking-Glass*, p. 1.
38 Letter of Montagu to Blathwayt, 17 May 1695, University of Nottingham, MS Pw A 935.
39 Letter of Godolphin to Portland, 21 May 1695, University of Nottingham, MS Pw A 473.
40 Shropshire Archives, Attingham Collection, X112/1A/2 (Hill's Ledger for 1694–96). At prevailing exchange rates, one pound Flemish was worth about £0.7. There are two further mentions of Agency notes in Hill's accounts. On 17 Oct. 1696 Hill gave James Bruce (manager of his Antwerp office) three 'banque bills', each for 200 pounds Flemish, which it seems Bruce cashed at the Agency. Ten days later the Agency issued Bruce another ten bills for 200 pounds Flemish each (Shropshire Archives, Attingham Collection, X112/1A/25 [Hill's Cash Book for 1696–97]).
41 The notes covered only a small part of what the Agency owed Hill. At the contracted exchange rate, the notes amounted in all to £5850 – a mere 1.6 percent of the letters of credit issued on the Agency that summer.
42 Bank General Ledger 2, fol. 160.
43 Letter of 17 May 1695, University of Nottingham, MS Pw A 935.
44 Letter of Godolphin to Portland, 21 May 1695, University of Nottingham, MS Pw A 473; letter of Godfrey to Blathwayt, 28 May 1695, University of Nottingham, MS Pw V 59 [hereafter 'Letters to Blathwayt']; letter of Montagu to Blathwayt, 11/21 June 1695, Letters to Blathwayt.
45 Letter to Portland, 11/21 June 1695, University of Nottingham, MS Pw A 936.
46 Letters to Blathwayt, 2 July 1695.
47 He does seem to have tried. A letter of 4 Aug. 1695 from the Antwerp directors to Blathwayt refers to William having ordered Dutch officials to promote an Agency loan in that country (Letters to Blathwayt).
48 Bank Minutes, 26 June 1695.
49 Bank Minutes, 22 Apr. 1695.
50 *CTB*, Entry Book.
51 *CTB*, Minutes.
52 This implies the export right was designed to serve as a lever with which to extract better rates than would otherwise by offered by those selling bills of exchange. This might explain why the Bank never actually used the vast majority of the export right; the whole point was to hold it in reserve as a bargaining chip.
53 *CTB*, Minutes., 18 May 1695.
54 In order to realize the mint par, the Bank would have needed to buy silver bullion at the English Mint prices of 5s. 2d. per ounce. This might have been possible since 'English bullion' was a synonym for melted coin. In other words, to raise bullion supplies the Bank would be permitted to melt any full-weight silver coin in its possession. The effective exchange rate attainable would have fallen to the extent the Bank could not obtain bullion this way and had to buy it instead at current market prices.
55 Houghton, *Collection*.

56 If the Bank was able to acquire all 700 thousand ounces at the current market price of 5s. 7d. and have it minted in Amsterdam (as it did with a small bullion shipment sent to Meulenaer in mid-May), it would have attained an exchange rate of about 33.4 schellingen banco per £ on £195.4 thousand worth of English bullion. (This uses the mint par rate of 36.4 schellingen banco calculated by Jones (*War and Economy*, p. 77), but adjusted to a market price of 5s. 7d. instead of the 5s. 4½d. he used). Given that the monthly charge for the army in Flanders at this time was £99.3 thousand, were the rate on bills of exchange to have remained at 31.1 for the full year of the contract, the Bank would have realized a weighted average exchange rate of ~31.5 schellingen banco (ignoring the cost of shipping specie from Amsterdam to Antwerp). This was only 2.3 percent better than its contracted rate of 30.8, from which we must deduct the 2 percent charge the Bank agreed to allow the Antwerp directors (only on that portion remitted by way of bills of exchange).

57 Houghton, *Collection*.

58 Treasury Minutes re Flanders, 25 Mar 1695.

59 Houghton, *Collection*.

60 Bank Minutes, 18 and 20 June 1695; *CTB*, Minutes, 3 July 1695.

61 Locke, 'Guineas'.

62 Bank Minutes, 15 May 1695.

63 Bank Minutes, 12 June 1695.

64 Bank Minutes, 26 June 1695.

65 Letters to Blathwayt, 28 May 1695.

66 Letters to Blathwayt, 22 June 1695.

67 Bank Minutes, 18 and 20 June 1695.

68 Letters to Blathwayt, 22 June 1695.

69 *CTB*, Minutes, 12 June 1695.

70 *CTB*, Minutes, 11 June 1695.

71 Letters to Blathwayt, 22 June, 2 and 6 July 1695; Lords Justices Minutes, 2 Aug. 1695.

72 The Treasury was receiving petitions from its tax collectors that unless they were permitted to take guineas at 29s. or 30s., they would be unable to get their taxes in on time, or perhaps at all.

73 *CTB*, Minutes, 5 and 11 June 1695.

74 *CTB*, Entry Book, 3 July 1695. On this point the Treasury seems to have misconstrued the Bank's request (perhaps deliberately). The directors had wanted, not an instruction to the king's receivers on the rate at which they should take guineas, but rather a royal decree fixing their value – just as crowns were officially set at 5 shillings and other silver coins *pro rata*.

75 BL, Add. MS 72566–67 (hereafter 'Cabinet Minutes'), 18 July 1695; letter of Trumbull to Blathwayt, 19 July 1695, in RCHM, *Downshire Manuscripts*, p. 511; *CTB*, Minutes, 19 and 26 July; *CTB*, Entry Book, 19 July.

76 Luttrell, *Brief Historical Relation*, p. 3:510.

77 Cabinet Minutes, 6 Aug. 1695.

78 Luttrell, *Brief Historical Relation*, p. 3:514.

79 While the overall volume was reasonably good, it seems Hill was unhappy with the pace at which funding was arriving. For on 19 July Abbott wrote Hill that Ranelagh 'is sorry the gentlemen of the Bank do not supply you with the value [of their letters of credit] sooner, for it is a miserable case to have an army in the field & to be besieging towns without subsistence and money for conveyancing' (Abbott Letters, fol. 487).

80 Bank General Ledger 2.

81 Letters to Blathwayt, 14/24 Aug. 1695.

82 Letters to Blathwayt, 14/24 Aug. 1695.
83 Letters to Blathwayt, 30 July 1695.
84 Letters to Blathwayt, 20 Aug. 1695.
85 Bank General Ledger 2.
86 Letter to William, 6 Sep. 1695, University of Nottingham, MS Pw A 475. This is confirmed by Houghton, *Collection*. On 20 Aug. the rates on Amsterdam and Antwerp stood at 27.3 and 27 schellingen banco respectively. Unfortunately, Houghton gave no quotations for the week of 27 Aug. But he reported them respectively at 28.1 and 27.8 on 3 Sep. and at 28.25 and 28 a week later.

Bibliography

Manuscript sources

Bank of England Archive
    ADM7/1-2 ('Bank General Ledger 1' and 'Bank General Ledger 2')
    G4/1-2 ('Bank Minutes')
Bodleian Library, Oxford University
    MS Eng. Hist. d.146 ('Hill Letters')
British Library
    Add. MS. 17677 OO-QQ ('l'Hermitage Reports')
    Add. MS 72566–67 ('Cabinet Minutes')
    Lansdowne MS 1215 ('Treasury Minutes re Flanders')
National Archives
    SP 44/274 ('Lords Justices Minutes')
Shropshire Archives (Attingham Collection)
    X112/1/2/1 ('Abbott Letters')
    X112/1A/1 ('Hill Account Book')
    X112/1A/2
    X112/1A/25
University of Nottingham
    MS Pw A 473–76
    MS Pw A 935–36
    MS Pw V 59 ('Letters to Blathwayt')

Printed primary sources

Great Britain. Public Record Office. *Calendar of Treasury Books.* Volume X: *January 1693 to March 1696.* Edited by William Shaw. London: HMSO, 1931. Accessed online at http://www.british-history.ac.uk/cal-treasury-books/vol10.
Great Britain. Royal Commission on Historical Manuscripts. *Report on the Manuscripts of the Marquess of Downshire Preserved at Easthampstead Park, Berks.* Vol. 1: *Papers of Sir William Trumbull.* London: HMSO, 1924.
Locke, John. 'Guineas.' Unpublished manuscript of 3 July 1695. Printed in Locke, *Locke on Money*, edited by Patrick Kelly (Oxford: Clarendon Press, 1991), pp. 363–64.
A Looking-Glass for the Members of the Bank of England: Or, Naked Truth Presented to Their View in a Clear Light. [London: s.n., 1697].

Luttrell, Narcissus. *A Brief Historical Relation of State Affairs from September 1678 to April 1714.* 6 vols. Oxford: Oxford University Press, 1857.

Contemporary periodicals

Collection for the Improvement of Husbandry and Trade. Ed. John Houghton. London. ('Houghton, *Collection*').

Secondary sources

Acres, W. Marston. *The Bank of England from Within, 1694–1900.* London: Bank of England, 1931.
Clapham, John. *The Bank of England: A History.* Vol. 1: *1694–1797.* Cambridge: Cambridge University Press, 1944; reprint ed., Cambridge: Cambridge University Press, 1958.
Jones, D. W. *War and Economy in the Age of William III and Marlborough.* Oxford: Basil Blackwell, 1988.
Richards, Richard D. *The Early History of Banking in England.* P. S. King, 1929; reprint ed., New York: Augustus M. Kelley, 1965.
Sundstrom, Roy. *Sidney Godolphin: Servant of the State.* Newark: University of Delaware Press, 1992.

6   Land-bank projects, 1694–95

In the session of parliament immediately following its creation, the Bank came in for heavy criticism. In Commons and Lords alike there were loud complaints that it had done the nation considerable harm.[1] Though nothing specific came of them, these attacks at least seem to have dissuaded the court party from proposing any new Bank loans that session.[2] Instead, as we have already seen, the Bank was confined to using its existing credit resources to finance war remittances and tallies. This left the field clear for projectors to propose other banking schemes to the parliament. But their task was now more difficult; they had two new obstacles to overcome. First, a plausible case could be made that parliament had implicitly promised the Bank it would be the only institution of its kind. So the legal and moral grounds for creating yet another bank by statute were doubtful. Second, and more importantly, many in London were now very aware that the grant of a bank charter had conferred exceptionally large profits upon a select group of investors. This made MPs guard the possibility of a new charter with a great deal of jealousy, determined to watch carefully over the division of any new spoils.

Anyone pushing a proposal for some new bank had to find ways of surmounting these obstacles. Numerous designs were floated, some more likely than others to succeed. In this chapter I focus in particular on the three most prominent instances of a particular class of banking project: those based on agricultural rents – what contemporaries referred to as land banks. I have chosen this focus for several reasons. First, competition among the three land-bank projectors spawned several waves of vituperative pamphlets from which we may glean some of the stresses and strains at work behind the scenes. Second, out of all the banking designs on offer in the remaining years of the war, it was a land-bank project that eventually succeeded in winning parliamentary approval. Finally, land banks both promised sizeable rewards to those left out of the division of spoils when the Bank was created and at the same time threatened to create a whole new set of distributional issues.

I will focus on the three land-bank projects that received the most attention in parliament during the Nine Years' War. The first two were similar at base so I group them together. The third was very different. But its greater plausibility forced the other two projectors to alter their designs to be more like this one. Eventually two of the three combined forces to back the land-bank project that parliament finally approved.

The initial land-bank projects of Chamberlen and Briscoe

First off the mark was Hugh Chamberlen, or Doctor Chamberlen as he styled himself. A renowned midwife and for a while physician to Charles II, Chamberlen had been pushing banking schemes of one kind or another since the 1660s.[3] At first he concentrated on 'lumbards', which would issue a paper currency secured by some store of durable commodities. But after the revolution he focused on designs whose security was based on some stream of future revenues. In every year of the war from 1690 onwards, he urged upon the Commons several variations on this theme.[4] From 1691 onward the proposed income stream was future land rents. He reports that during the 1691–92 session one such design was favourably received in the Commons – though the session ended before it could be enacted.[5] And the House ways-and-means committee declared that a version presented to them during the 1693–94 session 'is practicable and will tend to the benefit of the nation'.[6]

After 1690, Chamberlen always began his banking projects from the premise of a large group of landowners who had each committed to pay some portion of their rents annually, over a long period of time, into a central 'Office of Land Credit'. He intentionally left some slack in the system. Landowners were to pledge an annual rental income of £150 for 150 years. But out of this envelope of future income they would only need to pay the Office £100 per year in any 100 of the 150 years.[7] On the strength of each such pledge, made legally binding by act of parliament, the Office would be authorized to issue up front an amount of currency equal to the full nominal value of the rents to be received in future – £10 thousand per landowner. Of this currency he proposed to issue £20 million in all. This implied a ceiling on land subscriptions of £300 thousand in annual rental values – by contemporary estimates, roughly a tenth of England's total rental income at the time. The new currency would be minted in the form of special brass 'tickets' designed to be impossible to counterfeit. The tickets were not to be redeemable for specie upon demand. Rather Chamberlen proposed only that parliament declare them money, i.e. legal tender of payment, and that participating landowners be required to make their annual payments to the Office exclusively in such tickets, which would be destroyed as they came in.

Chamberlen was sure the Office's tickets would soon become money, every bit as good as gold or silver specie. People would take them in payment because they could be confident others would do so in turn. For behind it all there would always be a large set of landowners willing to receive them in payment of rent – since they needed to make their annual payments to the Office in this currency. If a landowner ever fell behind in his payments, the

Office had legal title to appropriate as much of his pledged estate as was needed to make good its losses. It was a misconception, Chamberlen insisted, that people accepted goldsmith notes only because they could be turned into coin on demand. People cashed such notes only because they were large-denomination instruments, not suitable for everyday transactions. Chamberlen's tickets would be produced in denominations as low as £5, which would help a little. But they would continue to serve mostly for large payments like taxes and rents, freeing up gold and silver coin for life's small occasions.

Until late in the game, Chamberlen's various land-bank proposals differed only in the formula for parcelling out new tickets. In some designs landowners were allocated a share of 40, in others of 60, percent. A further 20 to 40 percent was earmarked for a new joint-stock fishing company that would pay substantial dividends to the Office's land subscribers. Chamberlen promised to buy agricultural estates with this money and use that stream of rents to fund the fishery's annual operating costs. Chamberlen was strategic in choosing to create a fishing company. This trade had largely been lost to the Dutch and the French in recent decades; so few domestic interests would be threatened by new investment in the area. In some designs 20 percent of the tickets were offered as an interest-free war loan to the crown. And in every version 20 percent would go to the Office to cover its administrative costs – which Chamberlen unapologetically insisted would be large. Employees would be needed to verify land titles, collect from defaulting subscribers and mint, verify and destroy brass tickets. He also consistently called for the creation of supervisory 'commissioners' in large numbers. The latter were to be chosen by parliament and would receive large annual salaries. In one early version Chamberlen promised 'above three hundred new employments fit for noblemen and gentlemen'.[8]

John Briscoe proposed a new land-bank project to the Commons during the 1694–95 session. We know little about him other than that a few years earlier he was involved in a new joint-stock corporation and had been brought into Chamberlen's confidence as someone who might be helpful to the cause.[9] The Doctor later complained that Briscoe had deliberately betrayed him. Briscoe had advised Chamberlen against putting the details of his plan in print or applying to the royal court for support. Yet all the while Briscoe had been working on a book-length description of his own design, one that he dedicated to the king.[10] The book in question, *A Discourse on the Late Funds of the Million-Act, Lottery-Act and Bank of England*, first appeared in fall 1694. A second, somewhat longer edition was published later that year and a third (three times the length of the first) in 1696.[11] The design was worked into a bill presented to the Commons by MP William Brockman near the end of the 1694–95 session.[12] Though it passed second reading and was sent to committee, the bill was not reported out before the session ended a month later.[13] That fall Briscoe implemented a modified version that could work without benefit of a statute (more on this later). And he was for some time a partner in the land-bank project that parliament eventually approved during the 1695–96 session.

Like Chamberlen, Briscoe proposed that landowners 'settle' their estates with his land bank. Commissioners or 'trustees' would investigate their claims and register them in special books kept for this purpose, open to public viewing, in the principal cities of the counties in which those lands were situated. If after six months no claim had been entered against an estate, the commissioners would issue out 'bills of credit,' in denominations from £5 to £100, in an amount equal to the normal sale value of the settled estates. By convention this was twenty times their annual rental income. There was to be no specie reserve; the bills could not be cashed on demand. Instead they were to be declared legal tender by parliament. Subscribers would have two options for using the bills issued on security of their estates: to lend them to the government for the war or keep them for their own use – perhaps to pay off an existing mortgage. In the first case, the crown would pay the bank 3.5 percent interest on its subscribers' loans. The bank would hold back 1 percent for expenses and pass the rest on to the subscribers who had loaned their bills. Landowners choosing this option would also be excused from paying the land tax on whatever portion of their annual rents they loaned to the crown. The war loan could be perpetual or gradually repaid over a period, of the crown's choosing, between 10 and 100 years. If any principal was repaid, the bank would cancel a corresponding quantity of bills. If on the other hand subscribers chose to keep the bills for themselves, they would be charged interest at 0.5 percent per annum and asked to repay the principal over a period, again of their choosing, between 10 and 50 years. The bank would cancel bills equal in value to any principal payments received from subscribing landowners. It seems Briscoe was aiming for a total issue of £5 million. There were to be 20 commissioners, chosen by the king (4), lords (6) and commons (10), and each earning salaries of £1 thousand per annum. A further 25 'directors' were to be elected by the subscribers every three years; Briscoe was silent about the rate at which they were to be compensated.

The land-bank designs of both Chamberlen and Briscoe, had they worked as intended, would have radically altered the distribution of wealth in favour of landowners. But they were designed to have very different effects, suggesting they were targeted at quite distinct audiences. The contrast sheds some light on the politics of money in post-revolutionary England.

On Chamberlen's plan, land subscribers would still nominally have remained borrowers; indeed, for the Office's large cash payouts to, and annual payments from, subscribers he sometimes used the terminology of 'loan' and 'interest'. But at other times he was clear the goal was to free landowners of any debts and transform them into lenders in their own right. Standard practice was to issue mortgages for a maximum of three-quarters of the sale value of an estate. From land with a rental value of £150 per annum gentry should therefore have been able to raise a mortgage of £2.3 thousand. A typical interest rate on mortgage loans at the time was 6 percent. If the mortgage were amortized over 30 years with semi-annual payments, annual principal and interest payments would have come to £173 per year – more than the entire rental income of that estate. The same stream of rents pledged to the Office for 150 years would have delivered £4 thousand in disposable cash plus a further £2 thousand in the stock of a fishery corporation that Chamberlen claimed would pay dividends at rates between 5 and 10 percent. So landowners could have paid off their mortgages and still have almost a further £2 thousand of disposable cash. If dividends on the fishery stock could be maintained even at the modest rate of 5 percent per annum, they would have covered landowners' annual payments to the Office. So landowners could also have expected to recover the use of the rental incomes from their estates. In other words, it was something of a ruse to portray land subscribers as the Office's borrowers. In fact they were being released from all debt, with the full value of their estates restored to them and a large cash infusion as a bonus.

This is why in his various broadsides and pamphlets Chamberlen's rhetoric always turned on the sad state of indebted landowners. The war, especially land taxes, had significantly diminished the incomes of landed men at a time when many had already mortgaged large parts of their rent rolls to finance the lavish spending demanded of them by courtly fashion. At the same time, the war was enriching merchants and financiers, many of whom were earning handsome rates of interest on their loans to the crown. Now that the war had made specie scarce for all, these same monied men were turning the screws on those landowners to whom they had loaned money, to the point even of evicting them from their estates. Chamberlen's land-bank project would lower interest and 'bring usurers and monied men to more conscionable terms'.[14]

Briscoe's design, by contrast, aimed principally to confer upon non-indebted landowners the same ability to lend to the crown that monied men already possessed. But in order to achieve this in a way that landed men would find attractive, he made use of a subtle sleight of hand – so subtle in fact that perhaps he himself was unaware of it. Landowners were to 'settle' their estates as security for some corresponding amount of bills to be issued by the bank. But since the bills were to be legal tender they needed no security; it was not as if bill holders could come to the bank and demand that some estate be sold off to generate the specie they wanted in exchange for their bills. Nor in most cases could the bank itself ever lay claim to an estate. This threat existed only for those who decided to keep the bills issued on their estate for their own uses rather than lend those bills to the king. But given the terms proposed, this was sure to be a small proportion of participating owners; and they would be asked to pay interest of only 0.5 percent per annum – a small fraction of the normal rental value of their estates. Lands were to remain the property of those who settled them on the bank; subscribers would continue to collect the rents for themselves and could still sell their estates to someone else.[15] Really all that a landowner would be surrendering in 'settling' an estate with Briscoe's bank was the right to mortgage it to someone else. But this was hardly a sacrifice since any other lender would demand 6 percent interest while Briscoe was offering loans at 0.5 percent. Settling one's lands with the bank in fact conferred a boon, not an obligation. As a fictional interlocutor in one of Briscoe's dialogues responded when an acquaintance asked how long it would take to regain full title to his property: 'To what purpose should you desire to clear your estate, unless you had rather have 80*l.* or 100*l.* per annum than 160*l.* per annum[?]'.[16] Briscoe's design called for a cumbersome, six-month process of verifying title to any estates proposed for settlement in the bank. Chamberlen found this a weakness. But really it was a clever public-relations device, making it seem as though subscribers were giving away something real, when in fact they were to have their cake and be able to eat it too. Briscoe made a virtue of the fact that his bank was offering war loans at a much lower interest rate than that currently being paid by the government. But really this was almost required by his design. Whereas monied men making a war loan had to surrender some actual property to the Exchequer (in the form of gold or silver coin), with Briscoe's proposed bank landowners would have secured the right to interest payments from the crown without having to give up anything in return. In principle they could have made such a loan interest-free or at whatever minimal rate was needed to cover the bank's operating costs. If Briscoe asked interest of just 2.5 percent for the bank's war loans, this was only to make his terms look reasonable and even altruistic – when in fact his project aimed to create purchasing power out of thin air and confer it upon landowners.

Briscoe's rhetoric, consequently, concentrated not on the sad plight of indebted landowners but on a rather different problem: the high rate of interest being granted on war loans. This, he alleged, would soon ruin the nation's foreign trade. For no one would want to invest in merchant ventures when they could have such high rates of return from a much more secure investment. For the same reason it would lower the value of real estate; investors would be much less willing to buy land, an asset that usually paid a return of only 4 percent. Briscoe made much of the fact that during the war landowners were slowly conceding wealth and status to monied men. The latter, to the extent they invested in war loans, were exempt from taxation on the resulting interest income, while landowners were being forced to pay a fifth of their incomes in taxes. The wealth owned by landowners was of more real value to the nation (being based upon commodities useful in themselves) than the inert metals from which monied men were deriving their war-time advantages. What landed men needed was some way of transforming their particular kind of wealth into a currency that they too might lend out. This was the very possibility his bank was designed to deliver.

If Chamberlen and Briscoe were offering landed men such choice plums, why did the Commons, filled as it was with gentry landowners, not immediately strike a deal with one or the other of them? Contemporaries made little or no use of the objection most likely to be urged today: the prospect of inflation. A few critics complained that the nation would be saddled with more tickets or bills than it knew what to do with.[17] But both projectors argued that many productive resources were currently under-employed and that a large infusion of credit was just what the nation needed at this time. Contemporaries had other reasons for being sceptical. Paterson claimed Chamberlen's scheme was dismissed by parliamentarians as extreme, even delusional: 'imagin[ing] inestimable value from innumerable years to come'.[18] Some may indeed have felt this way; yet the project was deemed 'practicable' by a Commons committee. Probably the biggest obstacle was that both projects required their currencies to be made legal tender. This concern was prominent in the lists of probable objections that Brockman drew up in preparation for the committee debate on Briscoe's bill. Chamberlen constantly sought to defend himself against this criticism in his many pamphlets. Even Paterson had mentioned it as a stumbling block for his own earlier project; some MPs thought his bills were to be made legal tender and were adamantly opposed to any element of compulsion.[19] A close reading of Brockman's and Chamberlen's responses suggests contemporaries objected not to legal-tender status per se but to the prospect of creditors being forced to take payment in a currency that had no intrinsic value. The real worry in other words was the possibility that the new currencies might lose some or all of their value, losses that a legal-tender clause would permit bill holders to impose upon others.[20] MPs seem to have felt an obligation to protect creditors from being cheated in this way. And they would have worried too about the financial implications for the war effort should these experimental monies go to a heavy discount. Another problem was that such money could not be used for overseas payments[21] or to pay workmen, soldiers or sailors – the latter a very pressing consideration for the Treasury and its suppliers.[22] Finally, the very creativity of these schemes worked against them. They offered in effect to hand out large entitlements created *ex nihilo*. Chamberlen and Briscoe were surely very calculating in adding large numbers of lucrative offices to their respective designs – as a way of ensuring that MPs, rather than grow resentful, would be able to share in the largesse. But even if such gratuities were bestowed upon some of the wealthiest, and by contemporary lights most deserving, elements of society, such a door once opened would be hard to close again. As one critic maintained of Briscoe's project, doling out money that hadn't been earned by hard labour 'is a levelling notion that must end in confusion and discourage all industry'.[23] There is delicious irony in such a pronouncement, addressed as it was to a parliament full of inherited wealth. But it is testament to the instinctive worries that Chamberlen's and Briscoe's schemes must have provoked among MPs.

The Lincoln's-Inn Bank of Asgill and Barbon

A third land-bank project of this period was led by John Asgill and Nicholas Barbon. It became known to contemporaries as the Lincoln's-Inn Bank, after the location of one of its offices in London. Asgill was a young lawyer, only recently called to the bar, a former business associate of Briscoe and a trustee for a small bank recently reorganized by Paterson (the so-called London Orphans' Fund). Barbon was considerably older, an MP for Bramber (a borough small enough that its support could be bought by the highest bidder) and a heavily-indebted London builder and property developer.[24] His only known prior connection to banking projects was having been named to the Commons committee to which the Briscoe-Brockman bill was referred in March 1695.

The design of Asgill and Barbon was far more conservative, safe from the kinds of objections that had been brought against those of Chamberlen and Briscoe.[25] They proposed a bank that would lend to gentry at low interest rates: 3.5 or 4 percent per annum depending on the frequency of payments. Landowners could borrow up to three-quarters of the normal sale value of their estates. All loans were to be perpetual; borrowers need only cover their interest obligations – though they would have the option of repaying their principal at any time, in whole or in part. Borrowers would receive their loans in the form of transferable paper 'bills' issued by the bank and made transferable by design. Landowners could then offer their bills in turn to creditors, tax collectors, etc. To give others an incentive to accept payment in this medium, the bills were to carry interest at 2 percent per annum, payable to bearer semi-annually at the bank. By various markings, each individual bill was to be tied directly to the estate for which it had originally been issued. So bill holders would have the stream of rental revenues from a particular property as security for payment of the 2 percent interest owed them by the bank – and ultimately the sale proceeds of that property as security for the value of the bill itself should the bank fail. Really, then, the proposed land bank was to be just an intermediary, indirectly borrowing from bill holders at 2 percent interest and re-lending to landowners at 3.5 or 4.0 percent interest. To make people more willing to accept and hold the bills, Asgill and Barbon further proposed that they be made payable on demand at the bank. To this end they invited investors to subscribe toward a £100 thousand specie reserve. All profits from the bank's operations would be distributed among the members of this group in proportion to their contribution to the specie reserve.

Few could have objected to the distributive consequences of a design of this kind. Landowners had the prospect of borrowing more cheaply only because the bank promised to furnish a service that might make creditors willing to lend more cheaply – namely the opportunity to hold an interest-earning asset convertible into specie upon demand. Rentiers might have been unhappy,[26] but would have garnered little public sympathy. Even if the operation were to go bankrupt, bill holders should eventually have been able to recover their principal in full; for landowners were the ultimate borrowers and the sale value of their estates was final security for the bills. The distribution of wealth would certainly have been altered. But no one was waving a magic wand to absolve landowners of their debts. Nor would creditors have been denied the right to recover the full value of their bills in specie if so desired.

The Lincoln's-Inn Bank project nevertheless had a key weakness; in its existing form investors had little incentive to contribute to the specie reserve. Asgill and Barbon blithely promised shareholders returns of 30 to 40 percent per annum on their investment.[27] But this would have been possible only if the bank had acquired all £2 to £3 million of existing mortgage lending in England while maintaining a specie reserve of only £100 thousand. The actual rate of return for specie investors was sure to be much lower. With a specie reserve in the more realistic range of say 20 percent of the bills outstanding and ignoring all administrative costs, the maximum attainable rate of return was only 7.5 percent. The actual dividend rate was sure to have been well below 5 percent.[28] At the time, much better returns were available to anyone with a large store of specie. Those lending into the Exchequer typically received 6 percent interest and an immediate 2 percent discount on the principal value of their loan; since Exchequer loans were often repaid in a half year or less, this translated into rates of return of 10 percent or better. The original investors in the Bank of England were earning dividends of 8 percent per annum on stock only 60 percent paid in – a 13.3 percent rate of return (though because of rising stock prices this rate was not available to anyone buying into the corporation in 1695). And still better results were available to anyone prepared to buy distant tallies at a discount and hold them to maturity (though such investments were considerably less liquid).

So Asgill and Barbon could not have been counting on their design, at least in the form originally advertised, to draw specie into their land bank. They must have had other, bigger game in mind. Given the subsequent course of events, their plan was surely for the Lincoln's-Inn Bank to be awarded the next big war loan. On an undertaking of this kind they could have replicated the tactics of the Bank of England: raising a loan in part from stock subscribers but as much as possible by issuing bills bearing interest at 3 percent. Given the relatively high interest rates being paid on government loans, the bank could then have furnished shareholders a much better rate of return – comparable to that being earned by the Bank of England. This would of course have made Lincoln's-Inn into a money bank of the usual kind, not a land bank; on any bills being issued in support of the war there would be the security only of specie pledged by stockholders. But by setting up initially as a land bank, and promising to carry on with that line of lending no matter what other opportunities might come along, the Lincoln's-Inn group could establish their bona fides with the landowning class. It didn't hurt to remind contemporaries, as Asgill and Barbon often did in their promotional literature, that the Bank of England had never delivered on its promise to lend on land.[29] In any new competition for a long-term government loan, the Lincoln's Inn Bank could therefore position itself as something other than the usual monied oppressor of landowners.

Certainly some in London were aware by mid-1695 that a new war loan was on the way. That summer, Paul Foley (speaker of the House of Commons) and Robert Harley (Foley's nephew and fellow Herefordshire MP) had worked with the court on a comprehensive plan for raising money during the coming session.[30] Already in June Foley had proposed a design expected to generate £7 million.[31] Harley later bragged that in a speech at the opening of the 1695–96 session of parliament he had 'chalked out the lines for the whole proceedings' that year.[32] Since the session later featured an act for a loan of £2.6 million, he must have known such an undertaking was on the way. This would explain why Foley's and Harley's younger brothers, Philip and Edward respectively, put themselves forward in July as trustees for the Lincoln's-Inn Bank and why Edward wrote his father immediately after being elected: 'I trust God will please to give his blessing to it so as that it may prove of service to the whole nation'.[33]

Since their design didn't require legal-tender status for the bank's bills, Asgill and Barbon did not need to wait upon a parliamentary statute. They set to work to put their project into operation as soon as possible. In late May 1695 they issued a broadside describing the design[34] and opened two offices – one at Lincoln's-Inn to receive specie subscriptions and another in the Strand to exchange specie for bills.[35] A series of ads in the London *Post-Boy* invited specie subscriptions and reported totals received to date. By 13 July the initial £100 thousand target had been reached; so a subscribers' meeting was called to elect twenty-one trustees. In August a broadside was printed to advertise the concept to potential borrowers.[36] A formal constitution appeared a few days later, listing several dignitaries among the trustees.[37] That month the bank also began publishing a *Monthly Account* in which it was announced that the specie reserve target had been raised first to £250 thousand and then to £350 thousand. The first bills were issued in October.

All of this would have helped smooth the way for their bank being the source of any new war loan in the coming session of parliament. For with the organization already in operation and its bills having a known currency even before the session had begun, there could be no doubts of the kind that had plagued Paterson's projects. And Asgill and Barbon would already have had an opportunity to prove to MPs that they were honouring their promise to lend to landowners.

Duelling projects

The rise of this new project was a grave threat to Briscoe and Chamberlen. It was most unlikely that parliament would choose to authorize more than one new bank during the coming session. And their new competitor would have a big leg up by being already in operation, with an established credit. So both men decided to alter their plans, following the lead of the Lincoln's-Inn group and trying to set their banks into operation straight away. Briscoe was apologetic about this. He claimed he would have preferred to wait upon parliament's approval and direction. But 'some gentlemen who pretended they could not understand my scheme while the bill was depending before the House of Commons', i.e. Asgill and Barbon, had gone ahead with a design stolen from him. So he needed to act now to protect his intellectual property.[38] He had one more reason for going ahead now: because most people 'will not believe anything possible until they see it effected'.[39]

The original design of both projects required that their currencies be made legal tender by parliament before they could begin operating. So to go into operation straight away meant extensive changes. The two projectors responded in the same way: by working a specie reserve into their designs. This would require diverting a portion of the potential spoils from landowners to monied men. For not otherwise would the latter agree to invest some part of their specie holdings. The central problem for Briscoe and Chamberlen was how to balance off these competing interests and keep both groups happy.

Briscoe was first off the mark. In June he invited landowners to subscribe to a new undertaking that he named 'The National Land Bank'. Claiming to be worried about further plagiarism, he revealed almost nothing at this point. He promised only that subscribers would be able to borrow from the bank at interest of 3 percent and that if subscriptions for £100 thousand (annual value) were received, he would call a meeting to provide further details. A call for £1 million in money subscriptions went out in August; investors were promised 3 percent interest on their specie contribution and a share of any remaining profits. The initial target for land subscriptions having been reached, an investors' meeting was called for 10 September. Over the next few weeks, the committee chosen that day arranged for the election of 60 trustees and 36 directors, published a list of subscribers,[40] approved a constitution and a design for the bills, acquired office space, hired employees and set salaries. Seventeen of the trustees and eleven of the directors (including six of the top ten vote-getters) were members of the House of Commons. Speaker Foley was chosen one of the trustees; so was Mint Master Thomas Neale, who a few days later came first in the election for the first slate of directors.

Though Briscoe never published a clear description of his business plan for the National Land Bank, its core features seem to have been as follows.[41] The directors would issue bills equal in value to the bank's subscribed capital (specie contributions plus the sale value of land subscriptions). The bills would be redeemable for specie upon demand and pay interest to bearer at about 3 percent per annum. Investors were to be a mix of monied men and landowners; the former would contribute specie (for circulating the bills) and the latter would pledge their estates (as further security for interest and principal on the bills). The directors decided early on to aim for subscriptions of £1 million in money and £4 million (sale value) in land. Specie subscribers would be paid 3 percent interest on their cash contributions plus a proportionate share of any remaining profits.[42] Land subscribers would get only a share of the profits, plus an option to borrow from the bank at cost (3 percent). For purposes of calculating dividend shares, landed estates would be valued at three-quarters of their purchase price. So a monied man contributing £1.5 thousand in specie would get the same profit share as a landowner subscribing an estate of £100 per annum (£2 thousand sale value). Since the bank could profit only by lending at an interest rate higher than it was offering to specie investors and bill holders, the ultimate goal must have been to snag a large war loan (though no one ever declared this in writing).

This version of Briscoe's land-bank project would have been less contentious than his previous iteration. No longer were landowners being asked for a merely fictional 'settlement' of their estates. Their contribution was now to be a very real one: providing collateral security for all bills in circulation. Had the bank failed, land subscribers would have been on the hook for the principal value of any bills still outstanding. Consequently, any dividends they received would have been a return on a tangible investment – albeit one that didn't require any up-front cash from them.

Briscoe boasted that his institution alone deserved the title of a land bank. For unlike the Lincoln's-Inn Bank, the National Land Bank would involve landowners in its governance (trustees and directors were to be elected only from among the subscribers) and provide them with a share of the profits.[43] Indeed, landowners would have done reasonably well out of the project. They could have anticipated a healthy annual dividend without having to supply any money. And they were taking on a level of risk that under normal circumstances would have been quite low. With a 20 percent specie reserve, an annual income deriving from a public tax and with a parliamentary guarantee, plus a healthy rate of interest on its bills, a run on the bank was unlikely. The principal weakness in Briscoe's design arose rather in connection with the money subscribers. Even if the bank had received the same interest rate of 7 percent eventually granted on that session's war loan, specie investors could not have done as well as the original investors in the Bank of England.[44] And since the bank's first proposal to the Treasury was for a war loan at 5 percent, money subscribers would have been chary unless they had reason to think the bank was going to profit by other means.[45]

Chamberlen waited longer; not until August did he begin trying to put the Office of Land Credit into practice. A 'constitution' was being drafted and bills would begin to be issued as soon as an annual rent charge of £50 thousand had been subscribed (all subscriptions to be void if that target were not met). Starting in late September, Chamberlen ran a series of eight advertisements in a London commercial weekly inviting landowners to subscribe their estates.[46] In late November he announced that the subscription target had been reached and an inaugural meeting would soon be called. In a printed constitution published not long afterward, Chamberlen claimed that subscriptions had reached £100 thousand per annum and could be raised to £200 thousand if needed.[47]

In most respects the new design differed little from previous offerings.[48] The Office would still issue zero-interest 'bills of credit' on security of land subscriptions and still for 100 times the annual rental income subscribed. Most of these bills would be made over to the subscribers in one way or another, with 20 percent being held back to cover the costs of administration. In the current iteration, subscribers would get 60 percent of the bills for themselves and a further 20 percent would be invested on their behalf in a suitable joint-stock company. Finally, subscribers would still have to gradually pay back the bills they were given up front: 100 payments equal to the subscribed annual rental, paid any time in the next 150 years and always in the Office's own bills. The main difference was that now the bills were also to be redeemable for specie upon demand. To furnish the necessary reserve, landowners would themselves have to ante up hard cash for ten times the annual value of the rents subscribed. These specie contributions were to be paid into the Office in instalments over the first four years; the bills of credit would be paid out to subscribers in similar instalments over the same period. In return for their specie contributions, subscribers would be credited with the equivalent value in additional shares in the joint-stock corporation.

This version of the project, had it worked as planned, would still have released all subscribing landowners from debt.[49] But now they faced a substantial new hurdle – raising £1 thousand in specie at a time when their estates were heavily taxed and might already be fully mortgaged. And without a legal-tender clause, the undertaking had become far riskier for subscribers. Given that bills were to be redeemable upon demand, it would now be possible for a run by bill holders to bankrupt the Office. Since Chamberlen did not plan to pay interest on its bills, the Office would have been more susceptible to a run than its competitors. And if a run bankrupted the Office, subscribers' estates would have to be sold off to cover bill holders' losses.

During that summer and carrying right on into the 1695–96 parliamentary session, the three opposing camps issued a spate of broadsides and pamphlets attacking one another and arguing the superiority of their own approach. A Briscoe supporter asserted that the Chamberlen and Asgill-Briscoe groups had been taken over by 'cunning sparks … who have called one another in print impudent k[naves], libellers, stock jobbers'.[50] But Chamberlen had labelled Briscoe too a stockjobber, harping on his earlier involvement in a joint-stock corporation.[51] And an anonymous writer for Asgill and Barbon (Chamberlen thought it was Barbon himself)[52] accused Briscoe of having set up the National Land Bank only from spite, hoping thereby to weaken the Lincoln's-Inn Bank by drawing away the support of some part of the landowning class.[53]

The squabbling hampered all three projects. The banks of Briscoe and Asgill-Barbon needed a war loan in order to prove profitable. Unsure which of the two was destined to win that looming battle, specie subscribers would have been reluctant to make any firm commitments. The prospect of parliament raising the coin during the coming session would have given them additional pause. In any case, all three projects showed signs of being unable to turn specie subscriptions (which after all were just written expressions of interest) into actual cash contributions. The Lincoln's-Inn group had initially offered a 6 percent discount to those specie subscribers who made their first payment before 23 October.[54] This must not have sufficed, for some time later they raised their offer to 10 percent per annum.[55] In early November the directors noted that 'several subscribers of money to the National Land Bank have neglected to pay their money'. For their encouragement the bank offered to pay interest on the full amount of their subscription from the date of their first 10 percent instalment payment.[56] But the strategy doesn't seem to have worked, for in December the directors were offering to extend the payment deadline to early January, as long as money subscribers paid both their first and second instalments at that time.[57] Nor was Chamberlen having much success raising money in the fall. For, as we shall see in Chapter 9, by December he was offering extremely high rates of return to anyone prepared to invest specie in his operation.

Summary

During the Nine Years' War, numerous entrepreneurs were eager to establish a banking project of some kind. Given widespread perceptions that the Bank of England was trying to monopolize the nation's cash, parliament was certainly open to the idea of establishing a new bank. But to obtain parliament's favour, that institution would need to find a way of conferring benefits upon landowners. Two rather fantastic projects claimed to be able to restore landowners to their rightful place in society; one promised to liberate them from mortgage debt and the other to transform them into lenders in their own right. For either goal to be attained, however, parliament would have to confer legal-tender status on the relevant new currency. A third project was much more modest; landed men would benefit only by being able to borrow more cheaply. Needing no legal-tender clause, its promoters proceeded to put their bank into operation. The hope was that its bills would have attained a ready currency before the new parliamentary session, making it the most likely candidate for supplying a large and lucrative new war loan. The two earlier projects were forced to remodel themselves to incorporate a specie reserve, so that they too could prove themselves viable in advance of the parliamentary session. Unfortunately, their designs were flawed, making them unlikely to succeed. Yet their very existence was enough to create doubt in the minds of investors, causing them to withhold cash contributions until a clear winner had emerged. Monetary uncertainty arising from the deteriorating state of the silver coin would have aggravated the situation. So everything was still up for grabs as the nation headed into a new parliamentary session in November 1695. As we shall see, this played into the hands of certain whig members of the Treasury, who further exacerbated the uncertainty in the hope of keeping *any* of the projects from succeeding.

Notes

1. See *CJ*, 19 Jan. 1695; and l'Hermitage Reports, 25 Jan. / 4 Feb. 1695 and 29 Jan. / 8 Feb. 1695.

2. At least two proposals for large new Bank loans that session may be found among Montagu's papers. See 'Proposal for a Fund of Interest 1695' (2.5 million) and 'For Their Majesties Service for ye Yeare 1695' (1.5 million) in Montagu Papers, fols. 63 and 81–82.

3. Horsefield, *British Monetary Experiments*, pp. 103ff.

4. We can follow their history by the series of broadsides he printed for circulation in London, roughly one per parliamentary session: *An Humble Proposal to the Honourable the House of Commons* (1690); *Dr. Hugh Chamberlen's Proposal to Make England Rich and Happy* (November 1690); (with Dalby Thomas) *A Proposal for Encouraging of Persons to Subscribe Towards a Common Stock* (1691); 'The Proposal for the Fishery Stock Formerly Presented to the Members of Parliament' (1692), printed in *The Tunnage Bank Compared with Dr. Chamberlen's Land Fund of Credit* (1694); *Dr. Chamberlen's Petition and Proposals for a Land-Bank to Increase Trade* (1693); 'An Easie Method to Enrich the People by Raising So Many Millions of Money as the Parliament Please' (1694), printed in *Some Useful Reflections Upon a Pamphlet Called A Brief Account of the Intended Bank of England* (1694); *A Proposal by Dr. Hugh Chamberlain in Essex Street for a Bank of Secure Credit to Be Founded Upon Land* (1695); *Positions Supported by Their Reasons, Explaining the Office of Land-Credit* (1696, a pamphlet rather than a broadside); and *An Abstract and Brief Illustration of the Proposal of the Office of Land-Credit* (1697).

5. See Chamberlen, *Dr. Chamberlen's Petition*, p. 1; and Chamberlen, *Short Abstract*, p. 1.

6. *CJ*, 5 Feb. 1694.

7. Chamberlen's projects were never defined any more precisely than this. Surely there would have been some additional strictures had the project ever been put into practice. For by this general formula, landowners would have been entitled in principle to pay no rents whatsoever for the first 50 years of any loan contract with the Office.

8. Chamberlen, *Dr. Hugh Chamberlen's Proposal*.

9. Horsefield, *British Monetary Experiments*, p. 180; Tindall, *Some Remarks*, p. 1.

10. Chamberlen, *Rod for the Fool's-Back*, p. 3.

11. An ad for the third edition appeared in the *Post-Man* on 5 March 1696.

12. *CJ*, 29 Mar. 1695. A copy of the bill has survived (BL, Harley MS 1250, fols. 109–14) as well as a summary (Codrington MSS), fols. 44–9, along with a list of possible objections and answers prepared in advance by Brockman (BL, Add. MS 42593, fols. 52–54).

13. *CJ*, 4 Apr. 1695.

14. Chamberlen, *Proposal by Dr. Hugh Chamberlain*, p. 1.

15. Briscoe, *Discourse*, 2nd ed., p. 66.

16. Briscoe, *Discourse*, 2nd ed., p. 66.

17. See for instance Briscoe, *Discourse*, p. 55.

18. Paterson, *Brief Account*, p. 3.

19. Paterson, *Brief Account*, p. 5.

20. Brockman used the term 'chimera' (BL, Add. MS 42593, fol. 54), just as Lowndes had earlier dismissed Paterson's bills as 'fictitious cash' (Montagu Papers, fol. 77v).

21. Chamberlen tried to make this a virtue of his proposed currency. High-denomination brass tickets, unlike milled money, were sure to remain in circulation domestically. Parliament could stop fiddling with laws against melting coin and exporting bullion (*Some Useful Reflections*, p. 22).

22 Briscoe's bills would surely have become convertible into specie after a few years. For interest payments on a large war loan would have furnished his bank with a highly dependable source of regular cash infusions. But this would have been no help to the Treasury when the bank's loan first came into the Exchequer – the time when it most needed convertibility.

23 Briscoe, *Proposals for Supplying the Government with Money*, p. 20. Though this passage is from a work published under Briscoe's name, it was written by a critic. For details see Horsefield, *British Monetary Experiments*, pp. 183–84. Note that for contemporaries the term 'levelling' had much the same connotation as 'communism' does today.

24 Horsefield, *British Monetary Experiments*, pp. 196–97.

25 The following description draws from three publications by Asgill and Barbon: *Proposal for a Subscription*; *Account of the Land-Bank*; and *Settlement of the Land-Bank*.

26 See for instance *Reasons Offered Against the Intended Project, Commonly Called The National Land-Bank*, in which the author argued against any project to lower the rate of interest because it would rob income-trust heirs of a corresponding part of their properties.

27 Asgill and Barbon, *Account of the Land-Bank*, p. 2.

28 Asgill and Barbon promised that a third of all interest income would be invested in some interest-bearing asset, to provide collateral security for the Bank's bills. Mortgage lending was bound to be very expensive to administer, since it required a large legal staff to inspect title. There were also to be 20 full-time 'trustees' at salaries yet to be decided. Finally, Asgill and Barbon were to be credited with £5 thousand in free stock between them.

29 See for instance Asgill and Barbon, *Settlement of the Land-Bank*, p. 1; and Asgill and Barbon, *Proposal for a subscription*, p. 1.

30 Horwitz, *Parliament*, pp. 155–6.

31 Henry Guy to Portland, 5 June 1695, University of Nottingham, MS Pw A 506 (henceforth I will refer to MS Pw A 501–15 collectively as 'Guy Letters to Portland'), fol. 2r.

32 Letter to Methuen, 30 June 1696 (in RCHM, *Manuscripts of the Duke of Portland*, p. 577).

33 Letter of Edward Harley to Sir Edward Harley, 1 Aug. 1696 (BL, Add. MS 70018, f. 17).

34 Asgill and Barbon, *Proposal for a Subscription*.

35 Asgill and Barbon, *Account of the Land-Bank*, p. 2.

36 Asgill and Barbon, *Account of the Land-Bank*.

37 Asgill and Barbon, *Settlement of the Land-Bank*.

38 Briscoe, *To the Lords*.

39 Briscoe, *Freehold Estates*.

40 National Land Bank, *List of the Names*.

41 The available record is so thin and ambiguous that previous commentators, myself included, failed to grasp the essentials (see for instance Horsefield, *British Monetary Experiments*, pp. 186–88; and Kleer, 'Fictitious Cash', pp. 89–90). I stitched the following account together from a manuscript copy of the bank's minutes (Senate House Library, MS 61 [hereafter 'National Land Bank Minutes']) and a scattering of Briscoe's broadsides and pamphlets: *Advertisement*; *To the Lords*; *Following Proposals*; *Freehold Estates*; and *Proposals for Raising Money*.

42 The directors later decided that landowners could avail themselves of this offer only after December 1696–freeing up the specie reserve to support for-profit lending.

43 Briscoe, *Mr. Briscoe's Reply*.

44 The new war loan was for £2.5 million. For a loan of this size a specie reserve of £1 million would have been overkill; suppose the Bank had gone ahead with a 20 percent specie reserve and kept the same 1:4 ratio between money and land

subscriptions. Gross revenues would have been £100 thousand per annum (the difference between an interest rate of 3 percent on the bills and the loan interest rate of 7 percent). Specie investors would have been awarded £15 thousand off the top (3 percent interest on their £500 thousand specie contribution) plus 43 percent of net revenues (since their £500 thousand contribution was deemed equal to £666.7 thousand in land subscriptions). If costs had consumed say half a percentage point of gross interest income, the end result would be annual payouts of £46.2 thousand and £41.3 thousand for money and land subscribers respectively. For specie subscribers this would have translated into an annual rate of return of 9.3 percent. A rate-of-return calculation would not be very meaningful for landowners, since they were investing no actual capital (just shouldering some risk should the bank fail). For this investment anyone subscribing an estate with an annual rental value of £100 could expect to receive a dividend of £31.2 per annum. If Briscoe had succeeded in getting them excused from paying the land tax, the same individuals would have pocketed a further £20 gain.

45 It is possible they were optimistic. For in Nov. 1695 the directors decided to accept running-cash deposits at 2.3 percent – money that the bank could have invested in tallies bearing much higher interest rates. And they might have hoped to follow the example of the Bank of England and get people to deposit their specie in return for notes that paid no interest at all.

46 Houghton, *Collection.*

47 Chamberlen, *Constitution of the Office.*

48 I have assembled the following account from the following few works by Chamberlen: *Brief Narrative; Proposal by Dr. Hugh Chamberlain; Several Articles.*

49 Consider again the case of someone subscribing an estate with an annual rental value of £150 or a sale value of £3 thousand. For pledging 2/3rds of his rental income to the Office and contributing a further £1 thousand in specie up front, a landowner would receive back £6 thousand in bills and £3 thousand in shares in a joint-stock corporation. With the £6 thousand in bills, assuming others were willing to accept them in payment, he could pay off his mortgage and the principal and interest on any loan he might have taken out to finance his specie contribution, and still have perhaps £2.5 thousand left over for himself. He could have reasonable hope that dividends from the joint-stock corporation would cover his annual payments to the Office, freeing up the whole of his rental income for his own uses.

50 Tindall, *Some Remarks*, p. 3.

51 Chamberlen, *Rod for the Fool's-Back*, p. 3.

52 Chamberlen, *Answer to a Libel.*

53 Asgill and Barbon, *Freeholder's Answer.*

54 *Monthly Account*, September.

55 *Monthly Account*, November.

56 National Land Bank Minutes, 16 Nov.

57 National Land Bank Minutes, 14 Dec.

Bibliography

Manuscript sources

British Library
   Add. MS. 17677 OO-QQ ('l'Hermitage Reports')
   Add. MS 42593
   Add. MS 70018
   Harley MS 1250

Codrington Library, All Souls College, Oxford University
    MS 152(5) ('Codrington MSS')
National Library of Scotland, Edinburgh
    Adv. MS 31.1.7 ('Montagu Papers')
Senate House Library, University of London
    MS 61 ('National Land Bank Minutes')
University of Nottingham
    MS Pw A 501–15 ('Guy Letters to Portland')

Printed primary sources

[Asgill, John, and Nicholas Barbon]. *An Account of the Land-Bank: Shewing the Design and Manner of the Settlement, the Profits to the Subscribers, the Advantage to the Borrowers, the Conveniency to the Lenders, That It Will Be the Support of the Nobility and Gentry of England, and a Publick Good to the Whole Nation.* London: T. Milbourn, 1695.

[Asgill, John, and Nicholas Barbon]. *The Freeholder's Answer to Mr. John Briscoe's Proposals for a National Bank: Shewing the Reasons Why They Will Rather Borrow Money of the Land-Bank Already Establish'd, Than Subscribe to His Proposals.* [London: s.n., 1695].

[Asgill, John, and Nicholas Barbon]. *A Proposal for a Subscription to Raise One Hundred Thousand Pounds for Circulating the Credit of a Land-Bank.* [London: s.n., 1695].

[Asgill, John, and Nicholas Barbon]. *The Settlement of the Land-Bank, Established Anno Dom. 1695: With an Abstract Thereof Annexed.* [London: s.n., 1695].

Briscoe, John. *Advertisement: I Have Been Desired...* [London: s.n., 1695].

B[riscoe], J[ohn]. *A Discourse on the Late Funds of the Million-Act, Lottery-Act and Bank of England: Shewing That They Are Injurious to the Nobility and Gentry and Ruinous to the Trade of the Nation: Together with Proposals for the Supplying Their Majesties With Money On Easy Terms, Exempting the Nobility, Gentry &c. From Taxes, Enlarging Their Yearly Estates and Enriching All the Subjects in the Kingdom.* London: [s.n.], 1694.

B[riscoe], J[ohn]. *A Discourse on the Late Funds.* 2nd edition. London: [s.n.], 1694.

Briscoe, John. *A Discourse on the Late Funds.* 3rd edition. London: printed by J. D. for Andrew Bell, 1696.

[Briscoe, John]. *The Following Proposals for, and Accounts of, a National Land-Bank Having Been Printed at London ...* Edinburgh: Joseph Blake, 1695.

Briscoe, John. *The Freehold Estates of England, or, England Itself the Best Fund or Security.* London: John Darby, 1695.

[Briscoe, John]. *Mr. Briscoe's Reply to a Pamphlet Intituled, The Freeholder's Answer to Mr. John Briscoe's Proposals for a National Bank.* [London: s.n., 1695].

Briscoe, John. *Proposals for Raising Money for the National Land-Bank.* London: John Darby, 1695.

Briscoe, John. *Proposals for Supplying the Government with Money On Easie Terms, Excusing the Nobility and Gentry from Taxes, Enlarging Their Yearly Estates, and Enriching All the Subjects in the Kingdom ... With a Suplement to His Explanatory Dialogue Thereupon.* London: [s.n.], 1694[/5].

Briscoe, John. *To the Lords Spiritual and Temporal and Commons in Parliament Assembled.* [London: s.n., 1695].

Chamberlen, Hugh. *The Constitution of the Office of Land-Credit Declared in a Deed by Hugh Chamberlen Senior, M.D. and Others, Joynt Undertakers and Managers Thereof: Inrolled in Chancery, Anno Dom. 1696.* London: T. Sowle, 1696.

[Chamberlen, Hugh]. *Dr. Chamberlen's Petition, and Proposals for a Land Bank to Increase Trade: Humbly Offered to the Honourable House of Commons, December 1693, and then by Them Referred to a Committee: With Some Remarks on the Practicableness and Usefulness Thereof.* [London: s.n., 1694].

[Chamberlen, Hugh]. *Dr. Hugh Chamberlen's Proposal to Make England Rich and Happy.* London: [s.n.], 1690.

Chamberlen, Hugh. *An Humble Proposal to the Honourable the House of Commons.* [London: s.n., 1690].

[Chamberlen, Hugh]. *Positions Supported by Their Reasons, Explaining the Office of Land-Credit.* London: T. Sowle, 1696.

[Chamberlen, Hugh]. *A Proposal by Dr. Hugh Chamberlain in Essex Street for a Bank of Secure Credit to Be Founded Upon Land.* London: T. Sowle, 1695.

[Chamberlen, Hugh]. *A Rod for the Fool's-Back, Or, Dr. Chamberlin and His Proposal Vindicated, From the Foul Aspersions of a Dirty Scurrilous Scribler, Who Pretends to Answer the Paper of the Comparison, Between the Doctor's Proposal, and Mr. Briscoe's.* London: John Whitlock, 1694.

Chamberlen, Hugh. *The Several Articles or Parts of the Proposal Upon Land-Credit, Rationally Explained.* London: T. Sowle, 1695.

[Chamberlen, Hugh]. *A Short Abstract of Dr. H. Chamberlen's Proposal to the Honourable House of Commons, the Last Sessions: And Also of Mr. John Briscoe's Present Printed Proposal Compared Together.* [London: s.n., 1694].

[Chamberlen, Hugh]. *Some Useful Reflections Upon a Pamphlet Called A Brief Account of the Intended Bank of England.* ([London: s.n., 1694]).

Chamberlen, Hugh. *The Tunnage Bank Compared with Dr. Chamberlen's Land Fund of Credit.* London: T. Sowle, 1694.

Chamberlen, Hugh, and Dalby Thomas. *A Proposal for Encouraging of Persons to Subscribe Towards a Common Stock of ---- for the Erecting and Managing of a Trade by a General Fishery.* [London: s.n., 1691].

Great Britain. Parliament. House of Commons. *Journals of the House of Commons.* London: House of Commons, 1803. Accessed online at http://www.british-history.ac.uk/commons-jrnl/.

Great Britain. Royal Commission on Historical Manuscripts. *The Manuscripts of His Grace the Duke of Portland: Preserved at Welbeck Abbey.* Volume III. Historical Manuscripts Commission, Vol. 29. Fourteenth Report, Appendix, Part II. London: HMSO, 1894.

[National Land Bank]. *A List of the Names of the Subscribers of Land and Money Towards a Fund for the National Land-Bank.* [London: s.n., 1695].

[Paterson, William]. *A Brief Account of the Intended Bank of England.* [London: s.n., 1694].

Reasons Offered Against the Intended Project, Commonly Called the National Land-Bank: Shewing the Same to Be Very Inconsistent with the Public Good and Benefit of the Nation. [London: s.n., 1695].

Tindall, William. *Some Remarks Upon the Bank and Other Pretended Banks, With Reasons Humbly Offered to the Consideration of the Present Parliament for Establishing a Real Land-Fund, or a Money and Land Bank; Under a Regular Managery, With Unquestionable Controuls and Checks Upon Them.* London: E. Whitlock, 1695[/6].

Contemporary periodicals

Collection for the Improvement of Husbandry and Trade. Ed. John Houghton. London. ('Houghton, *Collection*').
Monthly Account of the Land-Bank. Ed. John Asgill and Nicholas Barbon.
Post-Man. London.

Secondary sources

Horsefield, John Keith. *British Monetary Experiments, 1650–1710*. Cambridge: Harvard University Press, 1960.
Horwitz, Henry. *Parliament, Policy and Politics in the Reign of William III*. Newark: University of Delaware Press, 1977.
Kleer, Richard. '"Fictitious Cash": English Public Finance and Paper Money, 1689–97'. In *Money, Power and Print: Interdisciplinary Studies on the British Financial Revolution*, edited by Christopher Fauske and C. Ivar McGrath, 70–114. Newark: University of Delaware Press, 2008.

Part II

The political and policy narrative

7 The administrative debate on the state of the currency, September–November 1695

Here begins a narrative, three chapters long, of the course of debates, within the administration and in parliament, on monetary matters between September 1695 and April 1696. My concern at this point is just to get the details on the record as simply as possible. Parts of the story are interesting in their own right. But for the most part they are scaffolding for Chapter 11, in which I review the narrative to identify the political forces that were at work behind the scenes. There is also a chapter, part way through, on the various banking projects that were afoot at the same time – since it provides some context needed to follow the final part of the narrative.

In this chapter I summarize the course of the debate within the administration in the months leading up to the new parliamentary session that began in late November. There was the potential for all of the main policy issues to have been resolved by administrative fiat before the new session had even started. But as we shall see, for political reasons the administration eventually decided to leave all the hard decisions to parliament.

By summer's end it seems most in the administration had accepted that a recoinage was now in the cards. The Treasury attempted to take control of the internal policy debate by submitting to the lords justices in late September a complete and detailed proposal for how a recoinage might be managed in practice. This took the form of a long manuscript by Treasury Secretary William Lowndes, published two months later under the title *A Report Containing an Essay for the Amendment of the Silver Coins.*

The first three-quarters of the report was given over to the vexed question whether and how to raise the coin. Lowndes argued at length against altering the weight or fineness and in favour of raising the denomination by one quarter: for instance, the crown piece from 60d. to 75d. This would be equivalent to a Mint price of 77.5d. per ounce of sterling silver. Lowndes advised the change in part to help finance the losses from clipping but more so to protect any new, full-weight coin from being melted for export (the market price of silver bullion then stood at 77d. an ounce), attract bullion to the Mint and reduce the negative impact on the nation's tale of money once clipped coin was demonetized. In the final quarter of the report he tendered a plan for how concretely to go about a recoinage. 'Country mints' were to be established in nine other cities besides London. To each mint, including the one at London, would be annexed a 'change office' to which all hammered money could be brought for processing. Any coin weighing above 18 pennyweight per crown *pro rata* (93 percent of the Mint standard) would be specially marked and returned to the holder to circulate thereafter at the new higher rate of 75d. per crown *pro rata*. The rest would be taken in for recoining after tale and weight had been duly recorded. In return holders would be issued a 'bill' for an amount equal to the weight of the clipped coin times some special redemption rate. The exact rate chosen would depend on how much of the losses from clipping parliament was prepared to cover. For purposes of illustration Lowndes used a figure of 8s. per ounce – which he claimed would divide the losses evenly between individuals and the public.[1] This special redemption rate would be available only for a limited time (Lowndes proposed six months), after which all clipped money would be demonetized and accepted at the mints only at its (new) normal value by weight. Change-office bills were to be transferable and pay interest at 5 percent per annum. The bills of any given change office were to be repaid from the new coin being manufactured at its respective mint – in the same sequence in which the bills were originally issued. Since recoining would generate enough new money to repay only some portion of the bills, parliament would cover the rest by borrowing full-weight specie and/or bullion from the general public. Any bullion and heavy coin loaned to the Exchequer would be credited at the new, higher rate of 75d. per crown. Lenders were to be issued tallies bearing interest at 7 percent and repayable from some new tax that parliament would have to design and enact. Note that it was deliberate on Lowndes' part to propose a redemption price based on weight rather than face value. This would prevent clippers from doing further damage to the coin while a recoinage was under way. 'Clipping is perfectly obviated, for no man will clip off silver to sell at six shillings five pence an ounce by the market price when he may carry it to the king's change and there receive eight shillings per ounce for it'.[2]

Lowndes' main goal, as he declared in the opening paragraph of the *Report*, was to ensure that there would be 'sufficient coins to pay the king's taxes and revenues and to carry on the public commerce'[3] while a recoinage was underway. It is important to understand exactly how he hoped to achieve that outcome. He estimated England's total supply of silver coin to be £5.6 million by tale. The bulk of this, some £4 million, was clipped and so would disappear from circulation during a recoinage. In the interim the nation would have three other kinds of money upon which to draw. One was the bills given out by the change office. Another was guineas, though Lowndes was curiously silent about their importance to the overall money supply.[4] The third, and the one on which he laid a great deal of stress, was the estimated £1.6 million in good, full-weight silver coin still residing in the country. This specie would 'go a great way towards supplying the commerce and other occasions whilst the new money is making'.[5] But at the moment most of this money was locked away in private stores. The Commons committee resolutions of March 1695 had led many to believe the silver coin might soon be raised. If that happened, they would make a much better return from their heavy coin by simply holding onto it for now than by lending it out or using it in trade. So the key was somehow to make people stop hoarding their heavy silver coins. Lowndes believed 'it is not likely they will soon be brought to light without raising their value'.[6] So here was another good reason for raising the coin; the very act would convince people they had nothing further to gain by keeping their heavy money in store.

The lords justices may not have been convinced that a successful recoinage would require awarding a handsome prize to those hoarding heavy coin. For upon receiving Lowndes' report in late September, they decided to invite additional input. They asked for the views of Locke, Charles Davenant, Sir Christopher Wren, Dr. John Wallis, Sir Isaac Newton, Sir Gilbert Heathcote, Sir Josiah Child and John Asgill.[7] In early October four more names were added to the list: Charles Chamberlain, Sir John Houblon, Sir Joseph Herne and Abraham Hill.[8]

This was hardly a disinterested group. Heathcote was a Bank director, had loaned extensively to the government on his own account, and was a leading importer of naval supplies. Child was a long-time leader of the East India Company, which engaged in extensive exports of silver bullion. Asgill was invited presumably in view of his bank's anticipated role in a new war loan. Houblon, besides being an admiralty lord and mayor of London, was governor of the Bank of England and a leading importer from the Mediterranean. And Herne, also a leading member of the East India Company, was one of two partners in the syndicate that had long remitted Treasury funds for the English armies on the continent. Several others had patronage connections to one of the treasury lords and/or lords justices: Newton to Montagu, Locke to Somers, Davenant to Godolphin and Hill to Archbishop Tenison. Since appointments to several high-paying government offices were then very much in prospect, these latter individuals would have had a strong incentive to say what they thought their patrons wanted to hear.[9] Only Chamberlain (of whom little is known other than that he had been one of the commissioners for taking subscriptions to the Bank of England), Wallis (an Oxford mathematician who had served as a cryptographer for Nottingham in the early 90s) and Wren had no obvious stake in the outcome.

Perhaps surprisingly, only one of the advisors – Newton – favoured raising the coin. No one else believed this was necessary to protect the coin from melting. On their view, melting would continue apace whether the coin was raised or not. For bullion exports had nothing to do with the alleged high price of silver bullion (which reflected only the clipped state of the coin) and were driven instead by England's large trade deficit. They added that raising the coin would have many unhappy side effects; prices would soon rise in the same proportion, transferring wealth away from those on fixed incomes (like annuitants and landowners with long-term rental agreements) and raising the cost of financing England's army overseas. Child and Locke maintained quite explicitly that those who favoured raising the coin knew all this themselves but hoped to profit privately from the impact on their own holdings of heavy coin.

More importantly for our purposes, several of the submissions challenged Lowndes' reasoning that the only way to ensure the flow of tax revenues during a recoinage was to hand out a substantial premium to the holders of heavy coin. I set aside the cases of those (Wallis and Wren) who seemed unaware of the Treasury's problem or who thought it was already beyond hope (Heathcote). Two advisors believed it would be possible to muddle through without a recoinage or indeed a currency reform of any kind. Child thought the public was less troubled by clipped money than before and that together with Bank bills and guineas, the nation had enough currency to get by for now. Davenant maintained that the poor state of the coin had made people more willing to accept Exchequer tallies as money and so that the administration should concentrate instead on projects to improve the state of public credit. More intriguingly, Hill, Houblon and Locke showed there were other ways to recover a usable store of specie besides capitulating to expectations for the coin to be raised. Houblon proposed that parliament pass an act prohibiting the use of silver plate and affording a modest premium to those who brought it to the Mint for coining. By this means £2.5 million in new silver coin might easily be raised. This together with the £2.5 million in guineas already in the kingdom should be more than sufficient. Hill was more innovative still. He suggested that for a time the Mint be reserved only to the king's use. He proposed that the king then recoin all the clipped silver, as it arrived in the Exchequer on tax payments and loans, into new money 1/12th lighter than the current standard. After a healthy amount of this new money was in circulation, the various denominations of silver coin (crowns, halfcrowns, shillings, etc.) could be declared impassable one at a time, holding off on the next type until its predecessor had been recoined and returned to circulation. The resulting losses from clipping could be made to fall upon either the current holders or the crown. Either way, as long as the Mint was reserved only to the king's use, so that all gains from lightening the money could accrue only to him, hoarded heavy money must eventually come out of store. For those holding it could no longer hope to profit by waiting a little longer; and once it was made impassable they would have no other option but to bring it in for recoining. Locke proposed a similar but still simpler solution: by a surprise legislative decree, demonetize all clipped coin overnight, permitting it to circulate henceforth only at its value by weight (at the existing Mint standard). This would instantly foil all clippers, since the coin upon which they operated would lose exactly as much value as might be gained from clipping it. Clipped silver money, now returned to a known, dependable value, would immediately become available for commerce and tax payments (though it was more likely to be voluntarily handed in at the Mint to be manufactured into new, milled money). More importantly, heavy silver money would naturally return to circulation – since all hope of the coin being raised would now be at an end. This would impose all losses on those currently holding clipped coin. But no one had a right to compensation, since they had accepted it voluntarily and could have prosecuted those who proffered it. Even Newton acknowledged the distributive problem posed by any proposal to raise the coin. If the public was to bear the cost of recoining all the lighter money, it seemed only fair that it should also be allowed to realize the profit from raising the heavy coin. But he confessed he had not yet figured out a way to make this happen.[10]

One other aspect of the advisory literature deserves notice. Several of the designs for a recoinage featured two new wrinkles that would eventually make their way into Commons bills: retiring clipped money from circulation one denomination at a time and making sure that the process for redeeming it was channelled through the Exchequer. Neither of these ideas had been present in Lowndes' *Report*. Both seem to have come originally from Abraham Hill; at least his was the earliest (explicitly-dated) submission in which they were mentioned. But they must have appealed to the Treasury. For they appeared again in Newton's submission and were features of the first recoinage bill that Montagu submitted to the Commons. The first proposal was consistent with Lowndes' goal of keeping as much specie as possible in circulation while a recoinage was underway. The second was also sure to be advantageous to the Treasury. It would encourage receipt of taxes and loans at the Exchequer, since only by submitting their money there would holders of clipped coin put themselves in line to have their losses made good to them.

William arrived back in England on 10 October[11] and quickly took control of the administrative debate.[12] At a cabinet meeting on 16 October, he ordered the council to meet with the treasury lords (while he toured the country in preparation for the upcoming Commons elections) and explore all possible means of resolving the nation's monetary problems. But he made it clear that the Mint standard was not to be altered unless absolutely necessary. Expert advice continued to come in during the month of October.[13] But by month's end, in keeping with the king's instructions, the group had resolved to ask Lowndes to come up with a new recoinage plan, one that would retain the existing monetary standard.

Lowndes' new plan, which the lords justices eventually approved and forwarded for William's consideration, was a blend of Locke's recommendations and Lowndes' own earlier design.[14] On the one hand, clipped money would be demonetized overnight and circulate henceforth only at its value by weight. But those holding clipped money were to be promised full compensation for their losses. Specifically, each market town was to have a public office to which people might bring their clipped coin for processing. They were to be issued a receipt for any difference between tale and value by weight. These receipts, transferable and interest-bearing, could presumably be presented for reimbursement at some later date, after the necessary taxes had been appointed and the corresponding revenues raised. Once registered in this way at a public office, clipped money would be cut in two (so it could not be presented for compensation over and over again) and returned to its owner. Thereafter it could continue in circulation, though now only at its value by weight.

In this design we can see the Treasury's continuing concern for keeping up the tale of the specie; the proposed receipts could compensate for the sudden loss of half the face value of the clipped money. It is probably for the same reason that Lowndes objected against his own revised plan that it would cause the market price of guineas very quickly to fall back to normal. He noted too that it would remove any incentive for people to bring their clipped money to the Mint for recoining. This may have reflected a worry that clipped coin cut in half and forced to circulate by weight would hardly prove an effective currency.[15] But the council decided nevertheless to present the new plan to William upon his return to London.

In the end the administration decided instead, for political rather than technical reasons, to leave the whole matter to parliament. The lords justices presented Lowndes' new plan to William on 10 November. Clearly there was disagreement within the group about whether to implement it. Godolphin and the Duke of Devonshire advised against proceeding, upon this or any other plan, without already having parliament's approval in hand; otherwise the administration would have no political cover should public unrest break out.[16] Somers and Secretary of State William Trumbull argued the opposite position. Deferring to parliament would mean sacrificing a great part of the coming session to that debate. Furthermore, the key element of surprise would be lost. Parliament would have to announce a compensation scheme and a date when it would take effect. The moment that happened, all silver coin would be clipped right down to whatever weight parliament declared as the minimum eligible for compensation. No decision was made that day. William must have sent the matter back for a joint decision by the council and Treasury. For those two groups met again on 12 November, this time without him. It was at this session that Davenant's long paper was read. He stressed the political dangers of pursuing a recoinage while a war was under way. The problem of compensation would create great disputes in the Commons on account of a contest between the monied and landed interests. And it might cause 'difficulties, tumults and disorders' to break out among the people, from suspicions – however groundless – that government was favouring some by ensuring they got new coin back from the Mint sooner than others.[17] Devonshire and the Duke of Shrewsbury added that parliament might take it ill were they presented with an administrative solution as a *fait accompli*, especially one that compelled them to find the means with which to finance compensation. Godolphin noted they must be unanimous in so weighty a matter, for none would want to stand out as having advised a solution that might later prove a disaster. Everyone else accepted this point. The next day Somers brought to council the outline of a royal proclamation for demonetizing clipped money. But now even he thought it best to wait until parliament met. The group must have resolved upon this course of action, for after this date the matter of the coinage disappeared from council minutes.

Notes

1 Lowndes assumed that clipped silver money was on average half its normal weight. So taken in by weight at the usual mint price of 5s. 2d. per ounce, the loss on an average crown piece (which weighed 0.968 ounces) would have been 30d. That same clipped crown coin taken in by a change office at the rate of 8s. per ounce would have netted the holder a bill for 46.5d., entailing a loss of only 13.5d. (since the face value was 60d.). So in fact a rate of 8s. would have assigned 55 percent of the loss to the state and 45 percent to the holder.
2 Lowndes, *Report*, p. 135.
3 Lowndes, *Report*, p. 3.
4 He noted only that their current market price was too high and that a recoinage would lower them to a more appropriate price of 25s., putting an end to the current gold-silver arbitrage trade and the resulting downward pressure on the exchange rate (*Report*, pp. 111–13).
5 Lowndes, *Report*, pp. 85–6.
6 Lowndes, *Report*, p. 114.
7 Lords Justices Minutes, 27 Sep.
8 The submissions of all but Asgill, Chamberlain and Herne have survived. Most are printed in Takemoto, 'Historical Documents', from a manuscript collection held at the Senate House Library (MS 62). Davenant's contribution, 'Memorial Concerning the Coine of England in Which Are Handled These 4 Questions', has been printed in Davenant, *Two Manuscripts*. Several drafts of Hill's submission, 'Reflections on the Coin Now Currant', are preserved in the British Library (Harley MS 1223, fols. 176–180; Sloane MS 2902, fols. 17–42 in passim). See also Hill's manuscript, 'Additional Reflections on the Coin Now Currant 1695' (BL, Harley MS 1223, fols. 181–82 (though, dated 26 Nov. 1695, it could not have influenced the lords justices' decision earlier that month).
9 Immediately after his second submission to the lords justices, Locke asked Somers to put his name forward to Secretary of State Shrewsbury for the office of mint master, even though Somers had informed Locke that 'Mr. Newton has been recommended as proper for that place' (letter of 4 Nov. 1695, in Coxe, *Correspondence*, p. 400). The appointment eventually went to Newton and it was Montagu who wrote to tell him this (Scott, *Correspondence of Newton*, p. 195). It was already common knowledge that a trade council of some kind was in the works. Davenant, Locke, Newton and Wren all explicitly proposed a body of this kind, hoping perhaps to strengthen their case for being appointed to that body. Locke and Hill were eventually named to the council that was created in 1696.
10 Takemoto, 'Historical Documents', p. 136:67.
11 Luttrell, *Brief Historical Relation*, p. 3:536.
12 The following brief account draws from RCHM, *Manuscripts of Buccleuch*, pp. 242, 253, 255; and Cabinet Minutes.
13 By this point council had received the submissions at least of Heathcote (4 Oct.), Hill (11 Oct.) and possibly Houblon. Wallis' contribution and Locke's first submission were ready by 23 Oct. It is unclear when Newton's memorial arrived. But it may have been around this same time or shortly thereafter. For the queries to which Locke responded in his second submission – read to a joint session of council and treasury lords on 31 Oct. – seemed directed to propositions set forth on the first page of Newton's report.

14 Kelly, working from the same evidence, came to a different conclusion. He believed that in Lowndes' new plan 'Locke's principles were fully accepted' (Intro. to *Locke on Money*, p. 30). I attribute this difference of opinion to the fact that Trumbull's minutes of the key council meeting of 4 Nov. are brief, rather cryptic and very hard to interpret.

15 Somers later reported the same two objections to Locke in a letter of 15 Nov. 1695 (in de Beer, *Correspondence*, pp. 5:461–2). Treasury officials later criticized Locke's call for making clipped coin go by weight, objecting that it would force everyone to carry around a set of scales with them just to make their everyday purchases (see letter of Pawling to Locke, 7 Jan. 1696, in de Beer, *Correspondence*, p. 507).

16 Burnet later wrote that cabinet was worried the proclamation might cause all money to stop circulating, resulting in a commercial crisis, and that people would refuse to believe the promise of future compensation and riot against being made to bear the losses from clipping themselves (Burnet, *History*, p. 4:265).

17 Davenant, *Two Manuscripts*, pp. 30–33.

Bibliography

Manuscript sources

British Library
   Add. MS 72566–67 ('Cabinet Minutes')
   Harley MS 1223
   Sloane MS 2902
National Archives
   SP 44/274 ('Lords Justices Minutes')
Senate House Library, University of London
   MS 62

Printed primary sources

Burnet, Gilbert. *History of His Own Time: With Notes by the Earls of Dartmouth and Hardwicke, Speaker Onslow, and Dean Swift: To Which Are Added Other Annotations.* Vol. 4. Ed. Martin Joseph Routh. Oxford: University Press, 1833.

Coxe, William (ed.). *Private and Original Correspondence of Charles Talbot, Duke of Shrewsbury, with King William, the Leaders of the Whig Party, and Other Distinguished Statesmen.* London: Longman, Hurst, Rees, Orme & Brown, 1821.

Davenant, Charles. *Two Manuscripts by Charles Davenant.* Edited by Abbott Payson Usher. Baltimore: Johns Hopkins University Press, 1942.

De Beer, E. S. (ed.). *The Correspondence of John Locke.* Vol. 5. Oxford: Clarendon Press, 1979.

Great Britain. Royal Commission on Historical Manuscripts. *Report on the Manuscripts of the Duke of Buccleuch and Queensberry, K.G., K.T., Preserved at Montagu House, Whitehall.* Vol. 2: *The Shrewsbury Papers.* Ed. R. E. G. Kirk. London: HMSO, 1903.

Lowndes, William. *A Report Containing an Essay for the Amendment of the Silver Coins.* London: printed by Charles Bill and the executrix of Thomas Newcomb, deceas'd, printers to the kings most excellent majesty, 1695.

Luttrell, Narcissus. *A Brief Historical Relation of State Affairs from September 1678 to April 1714.* 6 vols. Oxford: Oxford University Press, 1857.

Scott, J. F. (ed.). *The Correspondence of Isaac Newton.* Vol. 4: *1694–1709.* Cambridge: University Press, 1967.

Takemoto, Hiroshi. 'Historical Documents Relating to the Reformation of the English Coinage (Circa 1695): Fourteen Articles by Locke, Newton and Others'. *Osaka Keidai Ronshu* (Proceedings of the Osaka University of Economics) 134–36 (March-July 1980): 213–34; 181–203; 53–88.

Secondary sources

Kelly, Patrick Hyde. Introduction to *Locke on Money,* by John Locke, 1–121. Oxford: Clarendon Press, 1991.

8 The act for remedying the ill state of the coin, November 1695–January 1696

In this chapter I offer a short summary of the process by which a recoinage design was settled upon and embodied in the 'Act for remedying the ill state of the coin of the kingdom' (7 & 8 Will. 3, c. 1) that came into effect on 21 January 1696. I also do the same for the two other coinage-related bills passed this session: one for funding the losses from clipping (7 & 8 Will. 3, c. 18) and another for encouraging people to lend full-weight coin and plate to the state to help offset the sudden drop in the money supply that would occur while the clipped coin was being repaired (7 & 8 Will. 3, c. 19).

The new session of parliament began on 22 November 1695. The subject of the coin first came up in the Commons on 29 November, during the session's first discussion, in a committee of the whole house, on the state of the nation. Clarke attempted on this day to get the House to request a royal proclamation for simply demonetizing all clipped money and leaving it in circulation, though henceforth to go only at its value by weight. But by 4 December the committee had voted instead to have all the clipped money called in and recoined.[1] Though the details had yet to be worked out at that point, this was tantamount to a decision to compensate holders for their clipping-related losses – meaning that the Commons would have to find the necessary funds.

The Lords first debated the state of the coin on 4 December.[2] Rochester and Monmouth advised a royal proclamation that would demonetize all clipped money as soon as possible. A series of ministers (Torrington, Pembroke, Shrewsbury and Godolphin) countered that this might lead a stop of trade and so to public unrest. They pressed instead for leaving clipped coin in circulation for a further time and building up an alternative supply of coin that could facilitate trade while the clipped money was being recoined. Monmouth's motion nevertheless won the day. The Lords resolved to invite the Commons to join with them in petitioning William for a proclamation to demonetize clipped coin immediately.[3] Rochester proposed such an address to the Commons the next day. It is worth noting, perhaps, that Rochester and Monmouth were both opposition politicians at this time (one tory and the other whig). So their motion for making the coin go by weight was probably tantamount to making all losses fall upon those currently holding the coin. Though they would have argued this policy on principled grounds, their real motivation may have been a hope that imposing losses on members of the general public would lead to widespread political unrest and so the demise of some current ministers.

On 6 December the Commons began debating how it should respond to the Lords' request. In the end they just quietly ignored it. Instead, on 10 December the House approved the recommendation from its own committee of the whole to proceed with a recoinage. Specifically it was resolved that clipped money be recoined into specie of the same weight and fineness as existing milled coin, that all clipping-related losses be covered by the public (though only for genuine, not also counterfeit, coin), that clipped money be retired gradually (first crowns and half-crowns, then all smaller denominations, and for each denomination in two stages: first for all uses but tax payments and Exchequer loans and then for any purposes whatsoever), and finally that compensation be afforded for a limited time simply by receiving all clipped coin at full face value in payment of taxes and upon Exchequer loans. Note that of the small-denomination coins the Commons proposed to retire only those that had been clipped 'within the ring'. This amounted to a call to keep all clipped, small-denomination coins in circulation. For money clipped within the ring would have been slightly below half of its standard Mint weight and contemporaries agreed that on average clipped money had lost half its normal weight.[4] The aim no doubt was to restrain public unrest. Since such money was used principally by the poorer sort, keeping most of it in circulation would help sustain everyday commerce during a recoinage (hopefully while offering limited scope for clippers to do further harm). The same concern drove the decision to recall the rest of the coin only in stages; the hope was that some part of the previous tranches would have been recoined and returned to circulation before the next one was retired. The decision to offer full value for clipped money paid in upon taxes and Exchequer loans meant in effect that all losses from clipping would be absorbed in the first instance by the crown. The Commons committed to find the funding with which in turn to compensate the crown.

On 12 December the Commons instructed a committee, consisting of the Chancellor of the Exchequer and about twenty other MPs, to prepare a draft address to the king for a royal proclamation that would set the deadlines for retiring the various denominations of clipped money.[5] The address was ready two days later, approved by the full House that same day and then presented to William. The Lords chimed in on 16 December with their own address, asking William to set a date after which clipped money should become impassable. On 17 December, the king replied to both Houses that he would issue a proclamation as soon as possible. The Treasury and lords justices met that same day to decide the timelines that would be written into the proclamation.[6] Their recommendations are set out in Table 8.1. In the actual proclamation, dated 19 December and published in the *London Gazette* for 19–23 December, all but the stage-one deadlines for crowns/half-crowns and shillings were shortened by another 10 or 11 days.

Table 8.1 Dates originally proclaimed for retiring the several types of clipped money

Coin type(s)	Stage 1	Stage 2
Crown and half crowns	1 Jan. 1696	London & area: 13 Feb. 1696
		Rest of England: 2 Mar. 1696
Shillings	13 Feb. 1696	13 Mar. 1696
All others	13 Mar. 1696	13 Apr. 1696

Source: *London Gazette*, 19–23 December 1695.

On 17 December Montagu presented the Commons with a recoinage bill. No copy has survived. But judging from the various amendments on record, for the most part it just replicated William's proclamation (giving it parliamentary force) and spelled out the practical means by which clipped money was to be taken in. It seems the idea was to establish public offices in major cities and towns at which clipped silver could be tried for authenticity before being accepted in tax payments. The bill was debated daily between 20 and 24 December. Judging from the committee minutes, nothing of substance was altered at this stage; only three relatively minor changes were made.[7] Only one of them needs mentioning (since it will come up again later). A clause was added for establishing 'country mints'. These were to be a few additional sites, four or five major cities outside London, to which members of the public could bring clipped money to be tried for authenticity and then recoined.[8] At no point was there any apparent opposition to the bill. Bonnet noted that whenever it came up for discussion, a lot of members left the chamber. He thought this was because, as MPs themselves avowed, 'this is a matter of which they understand nothing'.[9] I consider this a key characteristic of the whole recoinage debate, one to which I shall return in subsequent analysis.

The recoinage bill passed the Commons the next sitting day (due to the Christmas break, 27 December). No doubt the idea was for the Lords to approve it right away so that the statute might be in effect before the first key demonetization deadline (namely for 1 January) had arrived. Instead the upper house moved to address the king to push back the deadlines in his proclamation[10] and then over the next few days proceeded to make several very significant changes to the bill.[11] First, they proposed that public compensation for clipping-related losses be made generally-available rather than limited only to clipped coin being submitted for tax payments or Exchequer loans. The public offices to be appointed for trying clipped money for tax payments could easily be extended to meet this purpose too. Second, pursuing a suggestion from the Duke of Leeds, they wanted any clipped coin that wasn't being paid in for taxes to remain in circulation at its value by weight. Specifically, the plan was to implement Lowndes' earlier idea of recording the tale and weight, cutting the clipped money in half and handing it back to the owner together with an interest-bearing bill for any difference between the values by tale and by weight. Third, the Lords elected to remove the wording about country mints; all clipped money would have to come to the London Mint for recoining. Finally, they added clauses for making it legal to export English coin and temporarily halting imports or new coining of gold guineas. The Lords were done with the bill by 3 January and returned it to the Commons that same day.

The Lords' proposed changes were occasioned in part by a sudden stop of trade that seems to have broken out in late December. There were early warning signs already at mid-month. One contemporary wrote, three days after the Commons voted to retired clipped money in stages and a fortnight before the first demonetization deadline had arrived, that 'half-crowns are already refused and great confusion will in all likelihood follow'.[12] Another observer thought that half-crowns stopped being current when the royal proclamation was released and claimed that people began refusing clipped money of any kind as soon as the Lords started debating the Commons' coinage bill.[13] Bonnet confirmed this diagnosis a few days later:

> For though it is only the crowns and half-crowns that have been cried down, no one wants to part with his merchandise for any other species either. For everyone knows that these coins will soon be in the same state [as the crowns and half-crowns], and upon which, if there won't be loss, there is at least risk, on account of the large number of counterfeit pieces (or ones suspected of being so), with which the holders will be stuck.[14]

The Lords' motions to push back the deadlines for discontinuing the currency of clipped money and extend compensation to all coin (not just that paid into the Exchequer) were justified as ways of easing the stop of trade. For such measures would have helped assure members of the general public that it was still safe to accept clipped coin in payment.

The Commons also began paying close attention to the problem of the stop in trade. On 31 December the House resolved to go next day into a committee of the whole to debate how to prevent the recoinage from having such an effect.[15] On the appointed day, Sir John Lowther (first lord of the Treasury earlier in William's regime, when the tories had been in power) confessed that he had changed his mind and now thought that clipped coin should be allowed to remain in circulation by weight. He proposed the same plan that tory-leader Leeds had put forward in the Lords two days earlier: to let people, at the same public offices to be appointed for trying the coin for tax payments, register a claim for compensation and then have their clipped money back at its value by weight.[16] Some MPs argued for carrying on with the present recoinage bill and addressing any shortcomings in it by means of a second, later bill. Others wanted to start afresh and either lower the weight or raise the denomination.[17] The next day the Commons received a petition from several London tax collectors complaining that the local land-tax receiver was refusing to accept the clipped money in which they were tendering payment. MPs responded by petitioning the king to issue another royal proclamation, this time ordering tax receivers to take clipped money (the previous proclamation had said only that after 1 January clipped money could be used for nothing else but tax payments). A new proclamation to this effect was issued on 4 January.[18] The Commons would probably have gone on debating the subject and proposing additional measures. But with the return of the recoinage bill from the Lords on 3 January, they were forced to turn their attention for a time to this more pressing matter.

It is impossible to know whether the measures already taken had their intended effects. The contemporary press usually gave little or no coverage to economic issues. We are forced to rely upon passing references in personal correspondence or in the diplomatic dispatches. Judging by those standards, the crisis probably abated in fairly short order. For after the first week of January or so, there are no further references to a stop of trade.

Now began a week-long contest between the two Houses over the Lords' proposed amendments to the Commons' recoinage bill. On 4 and 6 January (5 January being a Sunday), the Commons went through the amendments one by one. They accepted a few, but only relatively minor ones. The significant changes – to make compensation available to everyone (not just those paying taxes), to let clipped money remain in circulation by weight, to kill the country mints, to end the coining and importation of guineas for a time and to legalize coin exports – were all rejected. On 7 January the bill thus marked up was sent back to the Lords for their reconsideration. Two days later the Lords responded that they were prepared to abandon all their earlier changes except that calling for the country mints to be scuttled, upon which they insisted. At a joint conference of the two Houses on 11 January, the Lords argued against country mints on the grounds that it would be too dangerous to involve so many additional people in making new coin; this would offer potential counterfeiters too much opportunity to learn the secret for edging milled coins. The Commons seems to have decided a day earlier that if the Lords proved inflexible on the country mints, they would use their right, established by long practice on the part of both Houses, simply to abandon a bill in dispute and substitute a new one.[19] For on the next sitting day (13 January) Montagu brought in a new recoinage bill designed to replace the first one.

As soon as the Commons had returned the first recoinage bill to the Lords, it resumed the debate begun a week earlier on how best to prevent a further stop of trade while the recoinage was under way. On 8 January, in a committee of the whole house on the state of the coin, two very remarkable resolutions were reached: to extend public compensation even to counterfeit clipped coin and to compel tax collectors also to accept this sort of money.

Upon learning of this decision, Locke was astounded.[20] And an acquaintance wrote that 'the goldsmiths laugh in their sleeves', for this now licensed them quietly to manufacture imitation clipped coin with a very high alloy content and turn it in upon Exchequer loans as though it were perfectly good money.[21] But a plausible justification was offered in the House: that uncertainty about which coins were genuine and which counterfeit had given tax collectors all the handle they needed, despite William's latest proclamation, to go on refusing clipped money and that only by attacking this problem at the root could the currency of clipped coin be restored.

That same day the committee approved a few other coinage-related resolutions. Three of them seem of a piece and together amounted to a proposal for a completely different way of retiring clipped money from circulation. The three resolutions in question were to: a) offer a premium of 5 percent to those supplying the government with milled or broad money; b) offer a bounty of 3d. per ounce (equivalent to about 5 percent) to anyone bringing silver plate to the Mint for coining; and c) appoint commissioners in every county to exchange the heavy money thus drawn out of hoard, and/or milled coin newly-minted from silver plate, for any clipped money that would be brought to them (presumably redeeming the latter at full face value). In sum, the goal was to provide another mechanism, entirely outside that for tax collection already appointed, by which people might get compensation for their clipped money – one that would immediately bring hoarded heavy coin into circulation. A final resolution seemed consistent rather with the policy direction already being taken of affording compensation only when clipped money was used to pay taxes. This was a proposal namely for letting people pay the whole year's worth of the coming land tax at once, instead of in quarterly instalments as usual. All of these resolutions were approved by the full House the next day and an additional bill was ordered to be brought in by which they might be implemented.

The replacement recoinage bill that Montagu presented to the House on 13 January differed from its predecessor in five main ways. First, gone was all the language about establishing public offices to try clipped money for authenticity. This was because, second, the new bill incorporated two of the resolutions approved by the House of 9 January: namely to extend compensation even to counterfeit clipped money and compel receivers to take that sort of coin too. Third, the timelines for retiring clipped money from circulation and receiving compensation were significantly relaxed. People could use clipped money for paying taxes until 4 May and for making Exchequer loans until 24 June. And they could use *all* their clipped money for this purpose; no longer were the several denominations to be discontinued in sequence. Fourth, the Exchequer was immediately to begin melting down and recoining all the clipped money already in its possession. Finally, unclipped hammered money could remain in circulation as long as its owners punched a hole through the middle; after 10 February, any hammered money not marked in this way, and any punched money that showed signs of having been clipped, would become impassable. For the purposes of this clause, 'unclipped' was defined as any money retaining at least half of the lettering around the outside edge; money clipped to this extent would have been about three-quarters the weight of newly-minted coins. All the above changes seem closely connected to worries about a stop of trade. They appear designed both to restore currency to clipped money for a few months longer and to make as large as possible a supply of coin available while the bulk of the clipped money was being reminted.

The bill made its way through parliament in very short order. A Commons committee of the whole house finished with it in a single day (15 January), doing little more than specifying dates for the blanks customarily provided in new bills. A day later the full House approved the committee amendments, adding two more of its own (one of them for sixpence coins to continue in circulation as long as they had not been clipped within the inner ring). The bill passed the Commons a day after that. In the Lords it passed through the committee stage in a single day and without amendment. This was despite the fact that the new version still contained the wording about country mints that had earlier been in contention between the two houses. The Lords noted this fact but declined to make an issue of it. The bill was approved by the full House on the 20th and received royal assent the next day.

This still left the whole question of how to fund the losses that the crown would incur by taking tax payments and Exchequer loans in clipped money received at face value. The Commons had been steadily working away on this piece of the puzzle while the recoinage bills were under discussion. Already on 17 December the House had resolved: a) to provide the crown with £1.2 million for this purpose;[22] and b) to begin considering how to raise the necessary funds. On 19 December a committee of the whole house resolved to tax dwelling houses (except those of low-income families), with rates tripled and quintupled for moderately- and very-large houses respectively (as measured by the number of windows). The tax was to be paid by inhabitants rather than owners. On 30 December the committee further decided to raise the necessary funds over a period of seven years. These recommendations were approved by the full house on the final day of the year. A matching bill received first and second reading on 9 and 10 January respectively. A committee of the whole house made some progress on the bill three days later. But thereafter it simply dropped off the map for a time. Not until 7 March did the committee resume discussions. I will pick up the bill's story at the appropriate point in Chapter 10.

Finally, what of the remaining four of the additional recoinage-related resolutions the Commons had approved on 10 January? One of them, for letting people pay the whole of the coming year's land tax up front, was ordered on 17 January to be implemented by the committee already working on the bill for that tax. It was eventually included as §67 of the resulting statute, which received royal assent in mid-February. Another, for appointing county commissioners to receive clipped and pay out milled money, disappeared without a trace. The other two, to offer premia on milled and full-weight hammered money and upon plate, were worked into a bill first presented to the Commons on 20 January. The story of that bill too is better told in Chapter 10, since it got caught up in the later Commons debate on the high price of guineas.

Notes

1　BL, Harley MS 1274 (hereafter 'Commons Committee Minutes'), fol. 3r.
2　RCHM, *Hastings Manuscripts*, pp. 4:310–12.
3　*LJ*, p. 604.
4　Judging by images of small-denomination silver coins from the reigns of James I and Charles II (available at http://www.coins-of-the-uk.co.uk/pics/), the distance from centre to the inside edge of the inner ring accounted for about 70 percent of the normal radius. So using the standard formula for calculating surface area (and thus weight), a small-denomination coin clipped to the inner ring would have been reduced to 49 percent of its normal Mint weight: $\pi(0.7r)^2/\pi r^2$. As Lowndes himself noted, by this time the only hammered money still in circulation was from these older reigns (*Report*, pp. 102–6). Anything more recent was milled (and so unclipped) money, most of which Lowndes thought had already been melted for export.
5　*CJ*, 12 Dec.
6　*CTB*, Minutes, 17 Dec.
7　Commons Committee Minutes.
8　The other two modifications were to extend compensation to *all* hammered coins in circulation (not just those that could be certified as having been made at the London Mint) and to raise the benchmark for keeping clipped shillings and sixpence in circulation to about three quarters of the standard Mint weight. (I take this to be the meaning of an amendment that only 'such pieces as have both rings or the greatest part [i.e. at least half] of the letters appearing thereon' would be allowed to remain in circulation.)
9　Bonnet Reports, 27 Dec. 1695/6 Jan. 1696.
10　I can find no record of such an address having been made nor of the deadlines being postponed.
11　The following account builds from the Lords Journals, the summary of committee minutes and calendar of associated papers provided in item 978 of Great Britain, House of Lords, *Manuscripts of the House of Lords, 1695–97*; and l'Hermitage Reports, 31 Dec. 1965 / 10 Jan. 1696.
12　Letter of Harvey to Mercier, 13 Dec. 1695, in RCHM, *Downshire Manuscripts*, p. 598.
13　Letter of Walker to Hatton, 31 Dec. 1695 (BL, MS 29566, fol. 128r).
14　Bonnet Reports, 3/13 Jan. 1696.
15　*CJ*, 31 Dec. 1695.
16　Letter of Popple to Locke, 2 Jan. 1696, in de Beer, *Correspondence*, p. 498.
17　L'Hermitage Reports, 3/13 Jan. 1696.
18　*London Gazette*, 2–6 Jan. 1696.
19　I take this to be the meaning of an instruction on 10 Jan. 1696 that a committee already appointed to draft a follow-up recoinage bill have leave to prepare 'one more bill' relating to the coin.
20　Letter to Clarke, 13 Jan. 1696, in de Beer, *Correspondence*, p. 518.
21　Letter of Wheelock to Brounower, 9 Jan. 1696; in de Beer, *Correspondence*, p. 510.
22　L'Hermitage puts the corresponding committee motion on 13 Dec. 1695 (l'Hermitage Reports, 13/23 Dec. 1695).

Bibliography

Manuscript sources

British Library
  Add. MS. 17677 OO-QQ ('l'Hermitage Reports')
  Add. MS 29566
  Harley MS 1274 ('Commons Committee Minutes')
Geheimes Staatsarchiv, Preußischer Kulturbesitz, Berlin
  I. HA Geheimer Rat, Rep. 11, Nr. 1792–1811 ('Bonnet Reports')

Printed primary sources

De Beer, E. S. (ed.). *The Correspondence of John Locke*. Vol. 5. Oxford: Clarendon Press, 1979.

Great Britain. *Statutes of the Realm*. Edited Alexander Luders and John Raithby. London: G. Eyre and A. Strahan, 1810–22. Accessed online at http://www.british-history.ac.uk/statutes-realm/.

Great Britain. Parliament. House of Commons. *Journals of the House of Commons*. London: House of Commons, 1803. Accessed online at http://www.british-history.ac.uk/commons-jrnl/.

Great Britain. Parliament. House of Lords. *Journals of the House of Lords*. Vol. 15: *1691–96*. London: HMSO, 1767–1830. Accessed online at http://www.british-history.ac.uk/lords-jrnl/vol15/.

Great Britain. Parliament. House of Lords. *The Manuscripts of the House of Lords, 1695–1697*. House of Lords Manuscripts, Volume 2 (new series). London: HMSO, 1903.

Great Britain. Public Record Office. *Calendar of Treasury Books*. Volume X: *January 1693 to March 1696*. Edited by William Shaw. London: HMSO, 1931. Accessed online at http://www.british-history.ac.uk/cal-treasury-books/vol10.

Great Britain. Royal Commission on Historical Manuscripts. *Report on the Manuscripts of the Late Reginald Rawdon Hastings, Esq., of the Manor House, Ashby de la Zouch*. Volume II. Edited by Francis Bickley. London: HMSO, 1930.

Great Britain. Royal Commission on Historical Manuscripts. *Report on the Manuscripts of the Marquess of Downshire Preserved at Easthampstead Park, Berks*. Vol. 1: *Papers of Sir William Trumbull*. London: HMSO, 1924.

Lowndes, William. *A Report Containing an Essay for the Amendment of the Silver Coins*. London: printed by Charles Bill and the executrix of Thomas Newcomb, deceas'd, printers to the kings most excellent majesty, 1695.

Contemporary periodicals

London Gazette.

9 Banking projects and public finance, early 1696

Introduction

The next part of the parliamentary story – a contest over whether or not to lower the value of the guinea by statute – unfolded hand-in-hand with yet a third main issue of public finance during this session: how exactly to raise the large, new loan that would round out the revenues needed for the coming year's military campaign. Since I propose in the next chapter to weave those two narrative strands together, I need in this one to provide some background and context for the war loan. Specifically, I continue the story, begun in Chapter 6, of the contest between several different groups of bank projectors to be awarded the anticipated new loan. I also need to add two new players to the story: a new land-bank project formed from a union of the Briscoe and Asgill-Barbon groups and a new bank proposed to be erected within the Exchequer itself.

The story needs one small piece of context. Though the Commons didn't officially decide the matter until February 1696, many expected from early on in the session that the new war loan would be funded by means of an existing tax on salt.[1] This tax (actually a pair of levies: a duty on imported, and an excise on domestically-manufactured, salt) was first enacted in March 1694. At the time it was granted only for a three-year period (5&6 W. & M., c. 7). Judging from the pamphlet literature, it seems that parliamentarians were thinking about making this tax perpetual as a way of funding a new perpetual war loan just like the one around which the Bank of England had been built.

The story also grows more complicated insofar as there were now two further prospects for lending to the crown. Specifically, some projectors hoped to build a banking operation on the strength of a new stock of specie that might be provided to them by the government itself – without need of a drive for private subscriptions such as the various land-bank projectors had already begun. The specie source in question could be either clipped silver coin or guineas. The proposals turned on the fact that holders of both kinds of coin were about to experience large losses: from clipped silver when it stopped going at face value and from guineas when their market price fell back to normal. The core idea was to offer to lend government the money it would need to compensate private citizens for these losses. The loan, however, would take the unusual form of absorbing the losses rather than of contributing actual specie. Handled appropriately, this would present an opportunity to establish new paper currencies and acquire control of large parts of the clipped silver (once recoined) or guineas to use as a specie reserve.

We can already see the basic principle at work in the previous parliamentary session, in some of the projects submitted to the Commons committee for preventing clipping. Of the twenty-one submissions received that winter, a third contained banking-related proposals. They all had the same two core ideas. One was for everyone to give their clipped money to the crown at face value and get back two kinds of notes. The first ordered that they be paid back the same weight in new, milled coin as soon as the Mint could supply it. The second would entitle them to eventual government compensation, with interest, for the resulting loss in face value (the difference in tale between the original clipped and the new milled coin). The latter note would be repaid only very gradually, on whatever schedule the government decided it could afford. And of course it would also be transferable, payable to bearer. The second core idea was to funnel the entire process through a bank, existing or new. In effect, the loss of face value would be treated as a loan made by the holders of clipped money to the government. And the bank would serve as a loan intermediary, collecting the specie, paying it into the Mint, issuing the two kinds of notes and repaying both kinds as circumstances permitted. Since some of the notes were sure to be held rather than immediately cashed, whatever bank handled the process would quickly become the functional equivalent of the Bank of England. Two projectors (Stampe and Gathorne) called for the government itself to serve as the bank in question, by issuing tallies and Mint 'notes' respectively. Another projector (da Cosera) implicitly proposed the creation of a new bank, by recommending that five or more 'eminent merchants' be appointed as 'commissioners' to receive the clipped coin and issue out 'bills', lend the silver needed to restore the nation's coin to its full weight, and then oversee 'discharge' of the bills. Neale recommended giving the job to the Bank of England, Dalby Thomas to an 'office' (presumably the Office of Land Credit being flogged by his associate Chamberlen), and Briscoe to some unnamed agency – surely the same land bank he would be proposing to the Commons later in the 1694–95 session.

The idea of a recoinage bank returned during the 1695–96 session, accompanied this time by proposals for what we might call a guineas bank. The projects in question were brought to the Commons' attention in three main bunches: ahead of the session, immediately after the House had settled on a specific plan for the recoinage and during the debate later in the session on what to do about the high price of guineas. In this chapter I show how several new entrants to the banking scene, as well as each of the already-established banking contenders, responded to these two new lending possibilities. I also explore how the various players positioned themselves in regard to the session's biggest public-finance prize: the pending large, new war loan.

The newcomers

The new session saw two new banking projectors step forward: Daniel Beeckman and Thomas Whately. Neither attempted to take control of the war loan. Perhaps they had already conceded that territory to the Lincoln's-Inn group. Or more likely they preferred the lending possibilities presented by the losses on clipped coin and guineas, since such projects would eliminate the need for a specie-subscription drive of the usual sort. Beeckman, because he wrote before parliament had even begun meeting and so before the guineas question had come to the fore, directed his thoughts only to the issue of clipping. Because Whately wrote later in the session, after the Commons had already decided on a recoinage plan, he should have focused only on guineas. But his project also contained a proposal for financing the losses from clipping – an idea he was repeatedly told had come too late.

Beeckman set out a banking project that promised a low-cost, gradual solution to the clipping problem, without need of a recoinage.[2] He proposed establishing a whole series of banks across England, one in every town with a post office or market. The banks' main business would be to transmit funds between centres via the equivalent of inland bills of exchange made payable in these 'petty chambers'. The king's taxes would be paid into the nearest chambers, providing the latter with start-up cash reserves. Taxes could then be remitted to the Exchequer via paper orders made payable in one of four corresponding regional 'grand chambers' in London. The operation would finance itself with a small 1.25 percent charge on all money orders. With such a banking system in place, a one-shot recoinage would be unnecessary. Instead the various petty chambers could gradually send portions of the clipped coin in their reserves up to the London Mint to be melted and made whole. He asserted that a small tax of £40 thousand per year would suffice to cover the resulting losses.

Whately too proposed setting up a new nation-wide network of banks, one per market town. But these banks were to focus exclusively on lending to the crown. The earliest version of his project called for the general public to lend all its clipped silver to the crown.[3] A later permutation would have the public lending all their guineas.[4] Both versions called for the crown to absorb all the losses resulting from monetary reform. Everyone was to bring their clipped coin (first version) or guineas (second version) to the nearest bank. The clipped money would be taken in at face value and the guineas at 30s. apiece. In return holders would be given 'bills' issued by their local bank: a third with a very early repayment date (after a few months – once new milled coin began issuing from the Mint) and the other two thirds to remain in circulation until the local bank decided to call for their repayment. The banks would turn their clipped coin and guineas over to the Exchequer as loans (the clipped coin first having to be melted and recoined, the guineas immediately thereafter reduced to their former market value). The Exchequer would pay each local bank back a certain proportion of its loan in new milled money, once the Mint had made sufficient quantities ready. But the rest of the local banks' entitlements would be treated as an ongoing loan on which the Exchequer would periodically pay interest and, if a given local bank chose, some portion of the principal. The local banks, or 'loan offices', would look after distributing interest income and principal to local bill holders. There would be no need for a specie reserve because the bills could not be redeemed for specie upon demand; they simply conferred the right to collect a corresponding share of whatever interest and/or principal was periodically paid out from the Exchequer to the local bank. The bills would be made transferable and legal tender anywhere within 10 miles of the issuing bank (including for tax payments). So these were not so much banks as an early version of present-day money-market funds – though with shares much more easily transferable. In a companion piece, Whately tried to persuade his readers that his proposed lending offices, rather than being a hindrance to the anticipated new parliamentary land bank, would have strengthened it.[5] He saw the two organizations working in partnership. Had the parliamentary bank accepted the loan offices' bills as money, the currency of the latter would have been greatly strengthened. And the bank would have found the bills useful assets to hold, as they would have paid much better returns than mortgage loans offered at the rates then being proposed by the bank's projectors.

Chamberlen's Office of Land Credit

During the new parliamentary session Chamberlen was still trying to build a specie reserve for his Office. Starting in late December, he began running a series of eighteen weekly advertisements in a London merchant newspaper, in which 'monied-men' were invited to subscribe their specie to the bank.[6] He offered to repay them in four annual instalments at an interest rate of 15 percent. In a broadside published around this time, Chamberlen repeated this offer and further proposed a 20 percent premium on any funds contributed toward his joint stock of trade.[7]

I haven't found any published offer from the Chamberlen camp for his Office to administer the intended new war loan. He did fault Briscoe and Asgill-Barbon for their efforts to secure that loan. He maintained that in taking on such a project they would be failing to make good on their previous promises to look after the borrowing needs of landed men.[8] By implication, the Office would focus on mortgage lending. On the other hand, he did profess himself willing to take over the Bank of England's £1.2 million loan (presumably at a much lower rate of interest) and to fund all the losses from clipping.[9] In fact he published a detailed plan for how the latter task might be handled. His 'Proposal for Making Good the Light and Clipt Money' called for the Office to issue bills equal in value to the tale of all the clipped money being brought into the Exchequer.[10] The bills would be made payable in three months and the new-milled coin, as it issued from the Mint, would be returned to the Office for this purpose. But Chamberlen no doubt expected some healthy portion of the bills to remain in circulation, enabling the Office to finance the 50 percent loss in tale without calling in any further specie supplies of its own. Referring to parliament's estimate that this loss would come to £1.2 million, he offered the government a choice between paying off this loan over 15 or 30 years, at £120 thousand or £60 thousand per annum respectively. This implied interest rates of 5.56 and 2.85 percent respectively.

Nor have I spotted a proposal from the Chamberlen camp to finance the anticipated loss on guineas. But an offer to this effect, floated in Blackwell's *Essay Towards Carrying on the Present War*, sounds very much like a Chamberlen project. Blackwell proposed that some unnamed entity give out zero-interest 'bills of credit' in exchange for clipped money received at full face value and guineas taken in at 30s. Specie holders would get their guineas back immediately, though with a hole punched in them and reduced to 20s. in value. And they would recover the equivalent weight of their clipped silver as soon as it could be recoined. The bills issued to cover their losses would remain in circulation indefinitely; at least Blackwell gave no thought to how they might be retired. He advised only that they be made legal tender. In keeping with the Chamberlen approach, he also recommended that still more bills be issued to finance investment in a new royal fishery.

Chamberlen must have been perceived as a credible threat by his land-bank competitors. For in December two anonymous authors took the trouble of criticizing the Office in print. One, a Briscoe supporter, carefully analyzed the structure of Chamberlen's Office and sought to expose its weaknesses.[11] The other produced a witty satire that made the Doctor look a fool and painted his Office as a hopeless affair.[12] Chamberlen published two rather lengthy replies to the latter piece in which he tried to turn the tables on his competitors.[13] Briscoe and Asgill, he claimed, had both worked for him earlier and now, having betrayed him, were turning against each other. Their designs would 'cheat the world'. The only way for them to be made profitable was by 'issuing out a vast credit, more than they have a fund to answer'.[14]

The National Land Bank

The National Land Bank clearly hoped to be awarded the session's new war loan. Meeting a week before parliament began sitting, the directors decided to ask the king that it be conferred upon them. Tired of being taxed to finance loans that profited only monied men, and confident that they would fare better by lending to the crown themselves, their band of freeholders was 'able and ready to supply your majesty's emergent occasions with considerable sums of money and at a more easy interest than ever your majesty has been hitherto supplied'.[15] It is probably around this time that Briscoe approached the Treasury with a proposal for the coming parliamentary session.[16] The National

Land Bank was prepared to furnish a large loan, either of £2 million in perpetuity at 5 percent or of £1.2 million with blended payments of principal and interest for 25 years (implying an interest rate around 6.7 percent). His only condition was that receivers be directed to accept the bank's bills in payment of taxes, just as they now did, he claimed, with the bills of the Bank of England. He was quick to point out in this connection that the bills of his bank too would be convertible into specie upon demand.

Perhaps as insurance, the National Land Bank also offered to become the bank of the recoinage. Three short works were published to that end around this time.

In one broadside, Briscoe proposed that for the next six months, taxes be made payable only in hammered coin.[17] The Exchequer would transfer this money to the Mint for recoining, but take bills from the National Land Bank for its value by tale and pay those bills out to the various military paymasters. The bank, using subscriptions already collected, would undertake to make the bills payable, any time after their three-month due date, in specie upon demand. The Treasury would assist the bank in this connection by turning over all the new milled coin manufactured by the Mint from the hammered money paid in upon taxes. Since the tale of that new coin would come on average to only half the value of the bills issued by the bank, the difference would be treated as a loan made by the bank to the Treasury. Briscoe proposed that the loan amount be set at £1.6 million (a little above parliament's estimate of the losses from clipping). The Treasury would gradually pay this sum back to the bank, with interest, by way of a £100 thousand annuity (payable no doubt in specie) to run for the next forty years (implying an interest rate of about 5.5 percent).

In a second broadside, Neale similarly proposed that all the new coin, as it came from the Mint, be given to the National Land Bank (of which recall he was a trustee and director) and they be credited with a loan for the difference between tale and weight. But he estimated the loss from clipping at only £1 million and proposed a slightly lower interest rate of 5 percent.[18]

Finally, the anonymous author of a short pamphlet argued for setting up a network of agents across the country to take in all the clipped and counterfeit coin on the nation's behalf and lend that money to the Exchequer.[19] The writer requested a meeting with a parliamentary committee to discuss the terms upon which they might be compensated for this loan. Undoubtedly the organization would have proposed something similar to what Briscoe and Neale had already offered.

Had any of these initiatives been pursued, the National Land Bank would have ended up with a massive new specie reserve and a large number of its bills and/or notes in circulation – instantly establishing itself as a formidable competitor to the Bank of England. Parliament never implemented the suggestion. But the National Land Bank tried for a similar outcome on its own initiative, by declaring that anyone bringing in clipped money be given bank notes for the corresponding value in tale.[20] The bank could then have loaned this money in turn into the Exchequer at face value, lining itself up for repayment in new milled coin a few months down the road.

I haven't found any published proposals from the National Land Bank for turning the pending loss on guineas into a new public loan. This is probably because, sometime late in January, Briscoe decided to join forces with Asgill and Barbon. As we shall see, the new partners focused on the session's main war loan and had their own reasons for wanting to keep guineas high.

Proposals from inside the Treasury

Montagu's group was also at work behind the scenes, trying to keep a new parliamentary bank from getting off the ground. They must have decided that there was little or no prospect for getting the Commons to borrow instead from the Bank of England. In the eyes of many country MPs, that institution, dominated by monied men, was the problem rather than the solution. So instead they sought to supply parliament with attractive alternatives to a land-bank project. The strategy seems to have been to set out multiple proposals and hope that one of them took.

One pamphlet from this period seems to have had such a purpose. It called for the establishment of a truly public land bank, as opposed to the private undertakings that were already afoot.[21] Its twenty or thirty directors were to be appointed by parliament. Bank branches would be established in London and six other English cities. The banks collectively would be authorized to issue £4 million in bills. This money could be invested as the directors saw fit – presumably for the most part upon mortgages. The bills would not have legal-tender status; the idea rather was that they could be cashed on demand. To generate the necessary specie reserve, parliament would levy a permanent land-tax surcharge of a half shilling per pound – money that would be paid into the nearest office. This would generate an annual revenue flow of £200 thousand, which by current standards was a 'property' worth 20 times that amount or £4 million – hence the assigned issue ceiling for these banks. Profits would be distributed back to landowners in proportion to their contribution to the local land tax. Indeed, the writer promised, after a time profits would become large enough to outweigh the land tax required annually of landowners. So at some point money would flow only outward from the banks to landowners.

For our purposes the most important features of this pamphlet were contained in the accompanying analysis of public finance for the coming session. With a banking system of the kind proposed, our anonymous author argued, there would be no need to use the salt tax to fund a new parliamentary land bank. That revenue source could be used instead as the basis for a conventional long-term loan, which the Bank of England should be asked to supply. Indeed, the author warned, it was dangerous to be hasty in setting up new banks that had the same remit as the Bank: lending to the crown. The proposed new public land bank wouldn't be a concern in that way; it would be confined to lending upon land in the countryside, leaving the business of money loans to the Bank of England where it properly belonged. Indeed, there doesn't 'at present seem any occasion or haste for setting up new [private money] banks'.

Similarly, another work of this period reads like an attempt to cut the ground out from under the project of a parliamentary land bank.[22] The core idea was to establish a 'mint office' in the Exchequer from which £2 million in new 'bills' would be issued. The bills were to carry interest at a farthing (¼d.) a day per £100 (equivalent to 0.4 percent per annum) and were to be made legal tender and acceptable in payment of taxes. These bills would be offered out in exchange for clipped crowns and half-crowns (which were to be declared impassable after a certain date) taken in at face value. This specie would be melted down and, after recoining, given over to the Exchequer, which would use the money in turn to pay navy and army wages. The bills would remain in circulation until the nation could afford to repay the principal. So far this was just another recoinage bank. But the really important design features were contained in the fine print. First, only proper sterling coin was to be taken in, not counterfeit money. To ensure this outcome, 'a sufficient number of skilful persons' would need to be appointed as 'commissioners' with the task of trying the clipped coin to distinguish genuine from counterfeit. The author later explained that these were to be 'at least twenty goldsmiths of known reputation'. Second, the new mint office in the Exchequer was to be staffed with 'a sufficient number of officers of known reputation, [such] as comptroller, treasurer, accountant and their clerks'. These officers were to have their places and salaries 'for life'.[23] The pamphlet never explained who these individuals might be, but it is a safe bet that they too were to be drawn from among the goldsmiths' ranks. The piece reads therefore as the scaffolding for a quiet bribe from the Treasury. Had a measure of this kind passed parliament, goldsmiths would have been expected to withhold their specie stores from the prospective National Land Bank if they hoped to obtain lifelong sinecures in the new mint office. Those MPs who were themselves goldsmiths, or allied with them, might also be influenced in the House to argue against, rather than for, a parliamentary land bank.

The most interesting entry from this period, surely also from Montagu's group, was the broadside *Mint and Exchequer United*. It too called for the losses from clipped money to be financed by a bank. But this was to be an entirely new bank situated within the Exchequer. Much more aggressive than the 'mint office' of the previous proposal, this organization would finance not only the losses from clipping but a further £2.8 million of the year's military campaign. Specifically, it would issue a total of £4 million in new 'bills': interest-bearing, assignable and payable to bearer. The bills would be payable in specie on demand. The necessary reserve would be furnished in part by a parliamentary tax designed to quickly raise £1 million in coin (naturally the salt tax was proposed for this purpose). The rest of the reserve would be supplied by assigning to the Exchequer all the new milled money returning from the Mint. The new bills would be offered in exchange for any clipped money or plate brought to the Mint for coining. They would also be issued out to those military offices 'where money in specie is not necessary'. To encourage the bills' circulation, they would be accepted in payment of taxes – a privilege that the anonymous author proposed also be extended to the notes of the Bank of England and of the so-called 'Million Bank' (with which Mint master Neale was associated).[24] Bills could even be sent out to receivers-general in the counties, there to be exchanged directly for clipped coin. In short, this proposal was designed to deprive the anticipated new parliamentary land bank not only of the large war loan it hoped to se-cure, but also of the tax fund currently earmarked for paying the interest on that loan and of the goldsmiths most likely to be its founding subscribers. The project would have appealed to MPs on account of its public nature and the very economical interest rate of 3d. per diem per £100, or about 4.6 percent. An almost identical proposal was set out in another pamphlet published around this same time.[25] The author called for the creation of a new 'national bank' that would issue £4 million in 'bills', in denominations between £5 and £50 and paying interest at 2.5 percent, to be used for the war and also given in exchange for clipped money.

The Lincoln's-Inn Bank and the Land Bank United

There are no proposals on record from the Asgill-Barbon group for routing clipped silver or guineas through their bank's coffers. This is probably be-cause they already had the inside track on the session's biggest piece of public lending and so did not need to plead their case with the Commons. The only really significant move from this group came in early February, when Asgill and Barbon joined forces with Briscoe to form what was for a time styled the Land Bank United.[26] Asgill and Barbon had proposed as early as July 1695 that Briscoe come in with them.[27] Briscoe declined the offer at the time, maintaining that his was the better design and if anything they should join with him.[28] Chamberlen boasted that the merger of early 1696 was motivated by a fear that his Office 'would swallow them both up'.[29] But more likely it was a response to problems that became apparent to the two sets of projectors in January. First, it seems neither organization was faring well in the drive for specie subscriptions. For a manuscript version of their new joint 'scheme' declared that acquiring a 'fund of money' to circulate bank bills 'has been hitherto attempted in vain'.[30] More importantly, they felt threatened by the proposal recently issuing from the Treasury for a new public bank: the Mint and Exchequer United. The very name chosen for their partnership hints as much. This concern is also very clearly indicated in a broadside published by Briscoe around this time.[31] There he sought to persuade MPs that it would be better to award the session's war loan to the Land Bank United than to the Mint and Exchequer United. It would be better for the landed man to lend money on his own credit than 'for the Exchequer to have his money and the credit too'. He alleged that the proposed Exchequer bank was really a partnership with the Bank of England, formed to 'prevent the establishment of the Land-Bank'. Sensing the danger, the two groups decided they could no longer afford the luxury of squabbling among themselves.

Since the two component land-bank projects had differed very significantly, the new partnership required that they agree upon a hybrid design. The central problem, both now and as the project made its way through parliament, was how to involve landed men – specifically how to assign them some part of the profits while still leaving enough to motivate monied men to contribute their specie. A range of proposals was floated, some more generous to landowners than others. Most of them assumed a perpetual loan of £2 million on which the government would pay interest of 7 percent per annum and committed the bank for the next seven years to lend a further £500 thousand per annum on mortgages at 3.5 percent interest. One version called for the bank to gather £2 million in money subscriptions and £140 thousand per annum (rental value) in land subscriptions, the latter as collateral security. A quarter of the profits would go to landowners and the rest to money subscribers. Land subscribers would also be entitled to borrow three-quarters of the subscribed (sale) value of their estates at 3.5 percent.[32] Another version was identical in most respects except that land subscribers would later (in about six months, once legal title to their lands had been ascertained) replace a quarter of the money subscribers – who would be refunded their money with interest.[33] A version proposed by Neale in late February was still less generous to landed men.[34] The bank would collect £2 million in money subscriptions and a further £1 million in land subscriptions (£100 in rental value being deemed the equivalent of £500 in stock). Every year, land subscribers would have to pay the bank, in cash, a fifth of the rental value of their estates. (To balance things out, Neale also called for specie investors to be charged interest at 4 percent per annum on any part of their subscriptions not actually paid in.)

The problem with all these plans is that they threatened to depress rates of return for money subscribers to levels insufficient to attract their interest. Asgill later wrote that, like the Bank of England, his bank had originally hoped to call in only 60 percent of the value of the money subscriptions.[35] On that assumption, the gross return available for money subscribers on the original loan would have been 11.7 percent at best (£7 in interest for every £100 of stock purchased at £60 per share). But if, say, a quarter of overall returns were to flow to land subscribers, the 8.75 percent left over for money subscribers was less than what they could have earned on a standard short-term Exchequer loan (if it came with the usual 2 percent premium). Earnings could have been improved only by borrowing extensively at low rates of interest (like the Bank of England, principally through bills) and re-lending at much better rates (on tallies, etc.). But here the bank's prospects were hampered by the requirement that it lend extensively on mortgages at the same rate it was charging for its bills: 3.5 percent. So it isn't too surprising that the bill for a parliamentary land bank, introduced later in the session, was eventually stripped of any language relating to investor participation by landowners: clauses which, as one contemporary put it, 'gave us [MPs] so much trouble'.[36]

The Bank of England

Even in the early days of the new parliamentary session, the Bank of England was jousting with the two leading land-bank projects. Asgill later charged that after the Lincoln's-Inn bank had published its 'settlement', the Bank of England 'made a violent opposition'.[37] Specifically, it refused to accept any of the notes issued by their bank. This was a considerable blow, he charged, because the Bank had great market power; any currencies that it refused to accept 'are left destitute and necessitated', 'a dead weight in the hands of the owners'. The Bank also offered to match the proposal of the National Land Bank for lending the state what it would need to cover the losses from clipped silver.[38] And in late December it worked to defeat an attempt by the Lincoln's-Inn bank to acquire parliamentary standing through a legislative back door.[39]

In late January, just as the Briscoe and Asgill-Barbon groups were uniting, the Bank began a very aggressive campaign to ward off the prospect of a second parliamentary bank. The directors ordered a committee to explore methods, including a petition to the Commons, for preventing 'the setting up a new bank by act of parliament'.[40] One result was an offer from the Bank to finance the new loan at a rate lower than the land-bank group was offering.[41] Bank officials also visited the Treasury in person to argue that it would be 'unreasonable' and a 'prejudice to his majesty's service' to establish another bank.[42] Their reasoning was spelled out in a pamphlet published around this time.[43] The original subscribers had clearly been assuming that the Bank would be the only institution of its kind. For only so could the Bank be assured of a market for its bills. Without bills, which enabled the Bank to borrow low and lend high, shareholders would have been earning a rate of return on their specie contributions no higher than the 8 percent the government had agreed to pay on the war loan. The subscribers would never have agreed to invest under such circumstances, since they could easily have earned a better rate by using their specie instead to discount tallies. Furthermore, the directors maintained, the king's finances would suffer if the Bank's credit was undermined. For the Bank had been the sole cause of the recent reductions in the market rate of interest and in the discounts on Exchequer tallies. The Bank may also have been behind the pamphlet, *Reasons Against a Land Bank*, which offered similar arguments but also stooped to misrepresentation and innuendo: in this case, trying to persuade England's gentry that the land-bank project was a sinister design to seize their estates and subject them to forced sale.

Finally, the Bank of England worked behind the scenes to try to drive large quantities of guineas into its coffers and improve its access to the flow of public specie. On 9 March 1696 the directors read a proposal, written presumably by one of their members, for the Bank to absorb the public's losses from guineas and treat this loss as a new loan to the government. Specifically, the Bank would agree to take in guineas from the general public at whatever price parliament decided was appropriate (probably 30s.), giving depositors notes that entitled them to withdraw the same amount in tale, but in guineas rated now at 21s. 6d. The Bank was counting no doubt upon a large quantity of the new notes remaining in circulation, so that far from having to pay out more guineas than they took in, they might retain some of the influx and thus bolster their specie reserves. Furthermore, the proposal called for the government to treat the resulting losses as a perpetual loan, on which it would pay the Bank interest at 5 percent per annum. Since interest payments from the Exchequer, as always, would be in specie, this would have furnished the Bank with new inflows of coin on a regular basis. In a bid to strengthen its specie position still further, the Bank also asked that parliament agree to raise the current £1.2 million limit on its bill issues. Two directors were ordered that day to deliver the proposal to an (unnamed) MP. But nothing ever came of it.

Notes

1 Commons Committee Minutes.
2 Beeckman, *To the Honourable the Commons*.
3 Whately, *Advantageous Method*.
4 Whately, *Now Is the Time*.
5 Whately, *Interest of the Land-Bank*.
6 Houghton, *Collection*.
7 Chamberlen, *Office of Land-Credit*.
8 Chamberlen, *Answer*, p. 22.
9 Chamberlen, *Some Remarks*.
10 Contained in Chamberlen, *Collection*.
11 Atwood, *Safe and Easy method*, pp. 3–4.
12 *Bank dialogue*.
13 Chamberlen, *Answer to a libel;* and Chamberlen, *Some Remarks*.
14 Chamberlen, *Some Remarks*, p. 3.
15 National Land Bank Minutes, 19 Nov. 1695.
16 Briscoe, 'Proposals Humbly Offer'd to the Right Honble the Lords Comrs of the Treasury', Montagu Papers, fol. 114.
17 Briscoe, *To the Honourable the Knights*.
18 Neale, *About Mending the Coyn*.
19 *Humble Proposal for National Banks*.
20 National Land Bank Minutes, 28 Dec. 1695.
21 *Proposal for Erecting a General Bank*.
22 R., *Proposal for Supplying His Majesty*.
23 R. *Proposal for Supplying His Majesty*, pp. 2, 7, 5.
24 This bank dealt in the tickets of an earlier £1 million lottery, which were a kind of annuity and which the bank offered to discount for those needing ready money.
25 Hodges, *Groans of the Poor*, pp. 11–13. This pamphlet is usually attributed to Sir William Hodges, leader of the Cadiz merchant firm Hodges & Haynes. But it was almost certainly written rather by another William Hodges: the author of several earlier pamphlets proposing relief for sailors' wage arrears.

26 In *Reasons humbly offered*, Briscoe dated their agreement to 3 February 1696.
27 C., *Letter from a Citizen*.
28 Briscoe, *Mr. Briscoe's Reply*, p. 2.
29 Chamberlen, *Answer to a Libel*, p. 21.
30 'Scheme for a Nationall Land Bank', in Montagu Papers, fol. 104.
31 Briscoe, *Reasons Humbly Offered*.
32 Asgill, Barbon and Briscoe, 'Scheme for a Nationall Land Bank'.
33 Asgill, Barbon and Briscoe, *Proposals Made to the Honourable House of Commons*.
34 Neale, *National Land-Bank*. The arguments of this pamphlet were echoed in *Only Way of Subscribing Land*. Let us assume gross returns of 7 percent per annum throughout and, for simplicity, ignore all investment costs. Then under the first plan described above, landowners would have received £35 thousand (one quarter of £140 thousand) per annum for pledging £140 thousand in rental estates as security. On Neale's plan, they would have had to pledge £200 thousand in rental estates and received back only £30 thousand per annum (a third of the annual interest of £210 thousand less their annual cash contributions of £40 thousand).
35 Asgill, *Remarks on the Proceedings*, p. 22.
36 *Second Discourse*.
37 Asgill, *Argument*, p. 2.
38 *Some Short Proposals* contained an offer almost identical to Briscoe's, except that it called for the project to be handled by the Bank of England, rather than the National Land Bank, and at a slightly lower interest rate of 5 percent. The Bank may have been behind a similar *Proposall to Make Good the Coyn*. This pamphlet, probably written by Thomas Haynes, suggested that the losses from clipping be financed by in part by issuing Bank of England bills and in part by a new £1 million lottery loan (also to be provided by the Bank) that would be used to purchase plate for rapid coining.
39 The anonymous author of the wonderfully comic pamphlet, *Tryal and Condemnation*, claims that the Lincoln's-Inn bank submitted a clause for inclusion in a bill 'for enlarging the times to come and purchase certain annuities' (later enacted as 7 & 8 Will. 3, c. 5). This probably occurred at a committee of the whole house on 28 Dec. Nominally the aim of the clause was to give the Lincoln's-Inn bank right of first refusal on some new long-term government loans. But apparently the clause was worded in a way that would have conferred corporate status upon the trustees. Bank of England supporters discovered the 'stratagem' and managed to have the clause withdrawn.
40 Bank Minutes, 29 Jan. 1696.
41 Bank Minutes, 7 Feb.
42 Bank Minutes, 5 Feb.; *CTB*, Minutes, 5 Feb.
43 *Reasons for Encouraging the Bank of England*.

Bibliography

Manuscript sources

Bank of England Archive
   G4/1-2 ('Bank Minutes')
British Library
   Harley MS 1274 ('Commons Committee Minutes')
National Library of Scotland, Edinburgh
   Adv. MS 31.1.7 ('Montagu Papers')

Senate House Library, University of London
MS 61 ('National Land Bank Minutes')

Printed primary sources

[Asgill, John]. *An Argument, Proving, That the Reason Given by the Directors of the Bank of England, Against Settling Any Other Bank, Viz. Because They Are Already Settled, Is the Highest Reason for It.* [London: s.n., 1695].

[Asgill, John]. *Remarks On the Proceedings of the Commissioners for Putting in Execution the Act Past Last Sessions for Establishing of a Land-Bank.* London: printed and sold by the booksellers of London and Westminster, 1696.

[Asgill, John; Nicholas Barbon; and John Briscoe]. *Proposals Made to the Honourable House of Commons by the Land Bank United for Raising Two Millions, or More.* [London: s.n., 1696].

[Atwood, William]. *A Safe and Easy Method for Supplying the Want of Coin, and Raising as Many Millions as the Occasions of the Publick May Require.* [London]: printed for Roger Clavel, 1695.

A Bank Dialogue Between Dr. H. C. and a Country Gentleman. [London: s.n., 1695].

Beeckman, Daniel. *To the Honourable the Commons of England Assembled in Parliament.* [London: s.n., 1695].

Blackwell, John. *An Essay Towards Carrying On the Present War Against France and Other Publick Occasions: As Also for Paying Off All Debts Contracted in the Same, or Otherwise: And New-Coyning of All Our Moneys, Without Charge ...* London: author, 1695.

[Briscoe, John]. *Mr. Briscoe's Reply to a Pamphlet Intituled, The Freeholder's Answer to Mr. John Briscoe's Proposals for a National Bank.* [London: s.n., 1695].

Briscoe, John. *Reasons Humbly Offered for the Establishment of the National Land-Bank.* [London: s.n., 1696].

Briscoe, John. *To the Honourable the Knights, Citizens, and Burgesses in Parliament Assembled.* [London: s.n., 1695].

C., D. *A Letter from a Citizen of London to His Friend in the Country, Concerning the Land Bank, Established by a Deed of Settlement Enroll'd in Chancery; and the Land Bank Proposed to be Established by Mr. Briscoe.* London: [s.n., 1695].

[Chamberlen, Hugh]. *An Answer to a Libel Entituled, A Dialogue Between Dr. H. C. and a Country-Gentleman.* London: T. Sowle, 1696.

Chamberlen, Hugh. *A Collection of Some Papers Writ Upon Several Occasions Concerning Clipt and Counterfeit Money, and Trade, So Far as It Relates to the Exportation of Bullion.* London: Benjamin Tooke, 1696.

[Chamberlen, Hugh]. *The Office of Land-Credit, Encouragement to Mony'd Men.* [London: s.n., 1696].

[Chamberlen, Hugh]. *Some Remarks Upon a Late Nameless and Scurrilous Libel Entituled, A Bank-Dialogue Between Dr. H. C. and a Country-Gentleman.* London: T. Sowle, 1696.

Great Britain. *Statutes of the Realm.* Edited Alexander Luders and John Raithby. London: G. Eyre and A. Strahan, 1810–22. Accessed online at http://www.british-history.ac.uk/statutes-realm/.

Great Britain. Public Record Office. *Calendar of Treasury Books.* Volume X: *January 1693 to March 1696.* Edited by William Shaw. London: HMSO, 1931. Accessed online at http://www.british-history.ac.uk/cal-treasury-books/vol10.

H[aynes], T[homas]. *A Proposall to Make Good the Coyn of this Kingdom, Without Diminishing the Species Thereof.* [London: s.n., 1696].

Hodges, William. *The Groans of the Poor, the Misery of Traders, and the Calamity of the Publick: For the Spoiling of our Money, for the Want of our Money, and for the Loss That Will Befal the King and the Nation, If There Be Not as Much Money Coined in the Room of It, to Pay Our Taxes, Drive Our Trades, Pay Our Rents, and the Poor to Buy Bread; And an Humble Proposal to Raise Four Millions of Money for His Majesty's and the Nation's Use.* London: [s.n.], 1696.

An Humble Proposal for National Banks, Whereby the Land Will Be Freed from Taxes, the King More Plentifully Supplied Than Ever, and the Nation Receive Many Other Great Advantages. [London: s.n.], 1696.

The Mint and Exchequer United: Being a Method to Furnish His Majesty with Two, Three, or Four Millions Immediately, at the Present Charge But of One Million or Less, and Supply the Want of Coin Till New Money Can Be Had. [London: s.n., 1695].

Neale, Thomas. *About Mending the Coyn.* London: F. Collins, 1695.

Neale, Thomas. *The National Land-Bank, Together with Money: So Composed as Not Only to Be Easie Understood, and Easily Practiced, But More Capable Also of Supplying the Government With Any Sum of Money in Proportion to What Fund Shall Be Settled.* [London: s.n.], 1695[/6].

A Proposal for Erecting a General Bank, Which May Be Fitly Called The Land Bank of England. London: E. Whitlock, 1695.

R., L. *A Proposal for Supplying His Majesty with Twelve Hundred Thousand Pounds, by Mending the Coin, and Yet Preserve the Ancient Standard of This Kingdom.* London: John Whitlock, 1695.

Reasons Against a Land Bank: Contained in a Dialogue Between a Yeoman, a Merchant, and a Land-Banker. [London: s.n., 1696].

Reasons for Encouraging the Bank of England: I. In Respect of Justice and Common Right, II. Of Its Usefulness and the Publick Good. [London: s.n., 1696].

A Second Discourse About Banks: Between a Brigadier, a Lawyer, a Merchant and a Goldsmith. [London: s.n., 1696].

Some Short Proposals Humbly Offer'd to the Consideration of Parliament for Regulating of the Coin. London: R. Baldwin, [1695].

The Tryal and Condemnation of the Trustees of the Land-Bank at Exeter Exchange for Murdering the Bank of England at Grocers-Hall. [London: s.n., 1696].

Whately, Thomas. *An Advantageous Method of Extricating the Nation Out of its Present Difficulties.* London: printed by T. Milbourn for the author, 1696.

Whately, Thomas. *The Interest of the Land-Bank to Promote the Country Loan-Banks.* London: author, 1695/6.

W[hately], T[homas]. *Now Is the Time: Or, the Proposal of the Loan-Bank Seasonable.* London: printed by T. M. for the author, 1695/6.

Contemporary periodicals

Collection for the Improvement of Husbandry and Trade. Ed. John Houghton. London. ('Houghton, *Collection*').

10 Guineas and the National Land Bank, February–April 1696

In this chapter I offer short overviews of parliamentary debates and legislative proceedings on the high price of guineas and the possibility of a second large, perpetual war loan. The first problem was addressed by special-purpose clauses added to two bills that were already underway for other reasons but served as timely vehicles: one for continuing certain existing duties on wine and vinegar (7 & 8 Will. 3, c. 13) and the other for encouraging people to bring plate to the Mint for coining (7 & 8 Will. 3, c. 19). The second set of debates resulted in the salt-tax act that authorized the creation of both the National Land Bank and 'Exchequer bills' (7 & 8 Will. 3, c. 31). I consider the two together because, as we shall see in the next chapter, they were intimately related.

The Commons opts for a National Land Bank

On 3 February 1696 the Commons began discussions on the final large piece of the year's war supply. In a committee of the whole house on supply, it was resolved to make perpetual the existing salt tax, as a fund to pay interest of 7 percent per annum on a perpetual loan of £1.7 million.[1] The committee resolution was approved by the full House the next day. L'Hermitage reported that the salt tax was regarded as one of the best funds available. By this he meant that its revenues were dependable in both amount and timing. Perhaps too it was less politically contentious than others, such as the tax on shipping tonnage by which interest on the Bank of England's £1.2 million loan was funded. He added that the salt tax was the revenue source upon security of which the land-bank group proposed to lend – 'provided it is agreed to establish it by an act of parliament like the royal bank'.[2] The connection between the two must have been general knowledge. For that week the market price of Bank of England stock declined very sharply.[3]

On 10 February the Commons, in a committee of the whole on ways and means, debated where it would borrow the perpetual loan that was to be funded by the salt tax.[4] Three options were considered. The first two were that the money should come from the Bank of England or an Exchequer bank respectively. The first idea never came to a formal vote and didn't even feature in the committee minutes; it was mentioned only by Luttrell. The House divided on a motion to pursue the second possibility; the question was lost by a vote of 112 to 196. Then, without a further division, the House resolved that the loan be supplied by 'a national land bank to be settled by new subscriptions' and that no one owning stock in the Bank of England could subscribe to the new bank. The contest was thus between court and country: the one wanting the loan to be managed by the Bank of England or the Treasury and the other hoping to see it vested in a bank in which, at least in principle, landowning parliamentarians were to have a large say. [5] The motion to prohibit subscriptions by members of the Bank of England was likewise intended to keep the monied men associated with that institution from seizing control of the new bank through the back door. Luttrell noted that shares in the Bank of England fell still further this day, from £93 to £87. At a special shareholders' meeting two days later, the Bank resolved to ask the Commons that, if it was intent upon creating a second bank, the public loans at least be divided evenly between them: £1.6 million apiece.[6] It's not clear if the request was ever made; at least it never appeared in the formal parliamentary record.

The committee finished its meeting of 10 February by asking that the Treasury provide the House with accounts of the revenues from existing duties on salt, tonnage and coal. The report, presented four days later, shows that all three taxes had generated significantly less than the Commons initially anticipated.[7] When the committee on ways and means next met, on 20 February, this led to two new motions. One was to discontinue the duties on tonnage and coal after 17 May 1696. The other was to add a further £845 thousand to the £1.7 million the House had already agreed to borrow and use this money to replace the revenues lost by cancelling the coal (£565 thousand) and tonnage (£140 thousand) taxes and to supplement the salt tax fund for a year (£140 thousand). No one would have been surprised by the decision to cancel the coal tax. It had only another year to run anyway, had already fallen far behind and was extremely unpopular (in January the Commons had been presented with numerous petitions against it). But it was most unusual for the Commons to terminate the tonnage tax. It still had another two years to run and was no further behind than the salt tax. There had been no mention of it earlier in the session, except for an order from the House to the committee a few days earlier to consider funding some of its shortfall.[8] And, most important of all, this was the tax that parliament had earmarked to fund the first four years of interest on the Bank of England's original £1.2 million loan. To add insult to injury, the committee proposed that the next year's worth of the Bank's interest be paid from the loan being raised by its challenger and made no provision for replacement funding beyond that year. It seems very likely that these blows were intentional. Certainly the Bank would soon be complaining of them. But they also had the effect of tying the Bank's short-term fortunes to the success of the nascent national land bank and of making the Bank of England's access to the flow of public specie far less certain. The tactic was very effective, for in the end the Bank of England was deprived of its normal £100 thousand per annum specie influx for the next two years. In October 1696, and only after putting considerable pressure on the Treasury, the Bank was given £100 thousand in tallies on the salt tax and promised quick payment in cash.[9] But no actual cash was forthcoming that year.[10] Only in May 1698 did the Treasury finally order payment to the Bank in specie, and even that funding had to be specially carved out of the year's new land tax.[11]

The ways-and-means committee had finished its work on the land-bank bill by 20 February 1696 and was scheduled to report to the full House on 24 February. But on the appointed day William called the two houses together to announce that he had uncovered a Jacobite plot to assassinate him. The Commons turned its attention for a time to declaring its support for William and providing him with the powers needed to identify, track down and execute the conspirators. One of its measures was to approve a so-called 'Association': a document, one that all MPs were invited to sign, declaring William the rightful king of England. Since the tories were firmly committed to the principle of hereditary rule, many of them found the declaration very distasteful and either refused to sign it or did so only with a considerable delay. The whig junto stigmatized all non-signatories as closet Jacobites, seeking thereby to weaken the tories' standing in the Commons. Only on 6 March did the House finally get around to receiving the committee report on the land-bank bill. The several resolutions were approved with only one minor amendment and without a division. The House ordered a small committee, with a very country flavour,[12] to prepare and bring in a suitable bill.

A draft of the land-bank bill was presented to the Commons on 14 March, given first and second reading on 16 and 18 March, and referred to a committee of the whole that was scheduled to begin meeting on 23 March. On the appointed day the committee began by receiving a petition from, and hearing arguments by counsel for, the Bank of England.[13] The Bank complained that it was utterly inappropriate to terminate the tonnage duty. That tax was supposed to continue until 1698, so removing it now would lessen the Bank's credit. No borrower would unilaterally withdraw the security for a private loan; parliament should certainly not do so either. At the very least the bill should be amended to give the Bank first claim upon any revenue coming in from the loan. But it seems the Bank's concerns were completely ignored. For once counsel was dismissed, the committee simply proceeded to work its way through the draft bill in a very routine way, filling in the blanks for dates and amounts and adding innocuous bits of wording here and there. In the three meetings held before the end of the month, there was no apparent controversy nor even a single division on the bill.

The debate over the high price of guineas

I now retrace my steps a little to tell the story of a debate that was unfolding in the Commons during the same weeks that the question of a national land bank was under consideration.

On 21 January the Commons gave second reading to the bill 'to encourage the bringing in of milled, broad or unclipped monies to be exchanged by commissioners in the several parts of this realm, with the common people, for their clipped monies; and for the encouraging of persons to bring plate into the Mint to be coined'.[14] This bill, you will recall, resulted from the motions passed on 9 January in response to the stop of trade. The House resolved to send the bill to a committee of the whole and then divided over a motion to instruct the committee also to consider the price of guineas. By this last phrase the House meant deciding whether to set an official price on guineas and, if so, at what specific level. So the question was whether to let the committee for the bill handle this issue or debate it rather in some other setting. The motion was lost 87 to 110. It's very hard to know what was at stake in this division. The names of the tellers for (Bickerstaffe and Moore) and against (Blount and Moyle) give us a little information. The latter two were both court supporters and ardent, even radical, whigs. The former were both tories and, at the time, opponents of the court (though Bickerstaffe had supported the court earlier in William's reign, when it was largely a tory administration). This suggests that opposition politicians were hoping to start dealing with the guineas question right away while at least some members of the court wanted to postpone the discussion.

Though the committee was ordered to meet on 24 January, the *Commons Journals* make no further mention of it until 4 February. That day the House issued two new instructions that were clearly suggestive of a desire by some to raise the coin. First, the committee was empowered to receive a clause 'to prevent the melting down and exportation of coin'. Second, it was ordered to 'consider of a further encouragement [i.e. beyond the 5 percent already recommended on 9 January] for bringing in plate to be coined and broad money to be exchanged for clipped money'.

The committee sat on 6 and 8 February.[15] On the first day it agreed to double, from 3d. to 6d. (i.e. from 5 to 10 percent), the bonus on plate brought to the Mint for coining. On the second day the committee began by considering a petition that had been received in the House earlier that day, from a group of London merchants, complaining of the effects of guineas going at 30s. Though forced to receive guineas at this price, the merchants claimed they were unable to get the same high price when using the same guineas to pay their taxes or bills of exchange. They claimed that large quantities of guineas were still being imported from Holland in an arbitrage trade by which some were earning profits of at least 25 percent per cycle. Implicitly the merchants wanted the House somehow to bring the price of guineas down. After the committee discussed this petition, a clause for setting an official price on guineas was read twice and then withdrawn. Finally, the committee read, but made no decision, on a clause for preventing the export of coin. Though the bill was ordered into committee again on 12 February, it was another whole month before the next meeting actually took place. We have absolutely no record of discussions internal to the committee and so no sense of what the issues might have been or of the positions being taken by the several camps.

Fortunately a great deal of light is shed by an extensive and very intense debate on the guineas question, in another setting, just a few days later. On 9 February the House decided to meet in a special committee of the whole 'to consider of the high price of guineas'. The meeting was scheduled for 13 February and the officers of the Mint were ordered to supply that day a report on the number of guineas that had been coined since spring 1694. On the morning of the appointed day the House received four further petitions about guineas, all from London merchants and/or tradesmen. Three favoured reducing the price gradually and one was for returning the price to normal in a single, large step. The latter petition argued that guineas were still selling for 22s. in Holland, and so that the only way to stop the current, harmful arbitrage trade was to lower the English price of guineas to that level right away. That afternoon the House went as ordered into a committee of the whole. The committee began by considering the Mint's report. The results must have stunned MPs. First, the number of guineas coined in the past eleven months was very large: 721 thousand. More importantly, some of the 140 individuals on the list really stood out. The Mint had manufactured an almost unbelievable 140 thousand guineas for one man alone, above 40 thousand each for another four and more than 10 thousand each for a further eleven. This information would have reinforced the belief that certain unscrupulous individuals were profiting from an arbitrage trade, importing gold and guineas and exporting silver bullion derived from clippings or melted coin. That the sixteen men in question were almost all goldsmiths would only have confirmed widespread suspicions.[16] This must have greatly strengthened the case for a bill first presented the day before and passed two weeks later, directing the Mint to stop coining gold until the new year (7&8 Will. 3, c. 13).

Then the committee proceeded to discuss whether an official price should be set on guineas and, if so, at what level. This was the most remarkable debate of the session to date, lasting until 10 that night – almost unheard of. Fortunately, we have a partial record.[17] It offers a most surprising view: almost the very opposite of the story usually told about the recoinage. Montagu, Smith and Littleton – all members of the whig junto – proposed raising silver coin by 20 percent and letting guineas fall to whatever level was needed to bring the gold:silver ratio in England into line with that prevailing abroad. (Though they didn't cite a specific figure, this would have been about 25s.) Members of two fairly distinct sets of MPs opposed raising the coin and offered instead a range of alternative strategies. One group may fairly be classed as critics of the court party. It included such country stalwarts as Foley, Sir Christopher Musgrave and John Howe, but now also Seymour, Heneage Finch (Nottingham's son) and Sir Richard Temple (tory MPs who had supported the court when Nottingham and Leeds were in power, but who were now in opposition). Curiously, the latter group was joined on this occasion by two MPs who usually supported the crown's priorities: Thomas Lord Coningsby and Lowther. Speakers from the two groups proposed either leaving guineas to find their own level (Howe, Seymour, Coningsby, Lowther and Temple), setting a (high) ceiling above which they would not be permitted to rise (Musgrave) or setting a relatively high price and then gradually reducing it over time (Foley). Their respective lines of reasoning aren't that important, since they probably don't speak to their real motivations. But Montagu's group maintained that the price of gold had to be brought into line with that of silver to prevent the current arbitrage trade, while the others focused on the losses and unrest that would result from reducing the price of guineas – especially all at once to their normal market value. Of those who spoke after Montagu, only the first responded to Montagu's proposal for raising silver coin. Musgrave, sounding on this occasion rather like Locke, argued that this would be a kind of state-sanctioned clipping (making money go for more than the value of the metal contained in it) and would be to repeal the decision made earlier in the session to keep silver at the current Mint standard. Note that those who opposed a high price for guineas didn't necessarily favour Montagu's approach. Clarke believed that there had been wide support for the idea of reducing guineas all at once to 22s., but that Montagu and other revenue officials had prevented this outcome, wanting to leave the door open for raising the coin at some later date.[18] In any case, at the end of a long day, the committee resolved to fix no definite price upon guineas and merely to set a ceiling of 28s.

It took a few weeks for a slightly modified version of this resolution to be implemented. On 15 February the committee resolution was reported to the full House, which divided over the question whether to support it. The vote, 164 to 129, seems again to have divided along country-court lines.[19] The House then ordered that its decision be written up as a formal clause and added to a supply bill already underway at the time. Of the committee meeting, two days later, at which the supply bill in question was debated we know nothing except that a date of 25 March was set for the guineas ceiling to take effect.[20] It seems the court had not yet surrendered and was hoping at least to lower the ceiling before the supply bill was sent up to the Lords. Abbott wrote Hill that some were very keen to keep guineas high but that others '(who I think are in the right) are struggling to bring them down'. He feared that unless parliament reduced guineas further, all the new milled money would be hoarded and the exchange rate remain low (from expectations that a high rate of guineas would necessitate raising the silver coin), making it impossible to finance the army in Flanders via bills of exchange.[21] On 28 February, when the bill came back from committee, the House debated lowering the ceiling further to 26s. The question for retaining the existing ceiling was lost 140 to 194. Again the vote seems to have fallen out along country-court lines.[22] On 2 March the Commons passed the bill as amended. When it came up in the Lords a few days later, the guineas clause occasioned a long debate, lasting until 6 PM. In the end it was approved by a margin of 34 to 28. Bonnet noted this day that there were widespread expectations for a further act that session by which guineas would be lowered all the way to 22s.[23] The bill passed the Lords on 7 March and received royal assent that same day (7 & 8 Will. 3, c. 10). The new ceiling on guineas was still scheduled to come into effect on 25 March.

It seems the new legislation caused an immediate decline in the market price of guineas. We can't know for sure, since after the first week of February London price currents stopped reporting prices for guineas and precious metals for a while. But we get a hint from a series of lottery advertisements placed in London newspapers in February and March. In ads for the 'golden adventure for 6000 guineas', the '£10,000 adventure' and the '£61,000 adventure', undertakers declared the rates at which they were willing to accept guineas for ticket purchases. Up until early March the quoted price was always 30s. But by 12 March the figure had dropped to 25s.[24] This must have been in response to changing market conditions, since the new legislative ceiling on guineas did not come into force until 25 March.

The committee on the window-tax bill finally met again on 7 March, after a delay of almost two months. It is not as though major work was needed; this day the committee made only one minor amendment (arranging for the tax to be collected by land-tax commissioners) and then declared itself ready to report to the full House.[25] The bill seems to have been uncontroversial. The amendments were all accepted on 18 March without a division. It passed both the Commons (23 March) and the Lords (2 April) without a division. Normally William gave his royal assent to revenue bills the same day they were passed in parliament. In this case he waited for over a week (7 & 8 Will. 3, c. 18). The likely explanation for all these delays is that the Treasury knew there was no urgency in this case. The whole point of the act was to enable the Exchequer to borrow the specie needed to finance the difference between the tale and weight of the clipped money that it would be taking in upon taxes and loans before 24 June. Given the terms of the recoinage statute, any loans received before 24 June could be made in clipped money. So the loan clause for this act (§30) stipulated that Exchequer borrowing could not begin until that day. Otherwise the measure would simply have added to, rather than helped repair, the crown's losses from clipping.

On 10 March, after a delay of almost a month, the Commons finally returned to the bill on plate and heavy and milled coin. In this case, however, the matters under consideration were both urgent and controversial. In the next chapter I speculate on why the bill was delayed for so long and came back at this particular juncture. For the moment I will confine myself to a simple description of the further course of events.

It seems that on this day Montagu's group again tried, and failed, to obtain a measure for raising the silver coin. The committee read and then divided over 'a clause for the value of silver and gold'.[26] Bonnet reported that it was in fact a proposal to raise the price of silver coin and lower that of gold.[27] A motion to approve the said clause failed by a narrow margin of 82 to 85. From this day forward, accordingly, the *Commons Journals* dropped the first part of the bill's title and referred to it simply as 'the bill for encouraging of persons to bring plate into the Mint to be coined'. There is no record of the debate at committee. The minutes report only the tellers for and against: Thomas Bere and William Monson. This tells us little, since it seems both were court whigs.[28] But Freke and Clarke, writing to Locke that night, gave a lengthy report.[29] They began by complimenting Locke for having correctly detected, distant though he was from London, the same 'designs of a certain set of men as we that daily converse with them and receive fresh instances of their unwearied attempts to obtain their end'.[30] Freke and Clarke were referring specifically to an initiative coming from within the Treasury to keep guineas high and use their high price as justification for raising the silver coin. The market price of guineas had recently fallen back to normal (namely, 21s. 6d.). But in the past few days they had risen again to 24.5s. after Exchequer officials, claiming an order to this effect from Godolphin, started accepting them at 26s. Then at the Commons committee meeting on 10 March, 'a design was manifested to have raised the crown from 5s. to 6s.'. The 'designers' lost by only three votes, after a long debate in a thin committee. In the wake of that decision, everyone in the Treasury was denying that anyone there had ever ordered guineas to be received at 26s. Freke and Clarke attributed these efforts to raise the coin to 'the monkey': their code word for Montagu. They added that, according to Somers, in the wake of this failed attempt Montagu had promised to stop trying to raise the coin, realizing that 'his leader [William] was going to sink him' if he persisted. But they feared Montagu 'keeps his nature and will be a monkey still'.

On 19 March, when the committee finally reported back to the House, there were two more attempts to get the coin raised. The House began by considering the committee's first amendment: to remove the clauses for raising the silver coin and lowering gold. This led to a motion that the bill be sent back to committee for further discussion. The proposal failed without a division. But after the remaining amendments were approved, someone (we don't know who) offered a motion that probably had similar intent: to add a clause for 'settling the price of guineas'. Unlike the guineas clause already enacted, which had merely imposed a ceiling, this was a proposal for setting an official price upon guineas – a fixed rate at which they would be required by law to circulate. The House debated this clause the next day and divided on a motion to set the price at 25s. This figure was approved by the narrow margin of 167 to 163. But then the House divided again on the question whether to make the clause part of the bill. This time the motion failed, albeit by another close vote of 146 to 155.

It seems the politics of these two divisions were quite complex. Unfortunately we have no record of the debate. Judging just from the tellers, it looks like the proposal for setting guineas at 25s. was favoured by opponents of William's regime and resisted by the court party.[31] But one contemporary interchange reveals a more complex situation.[32] Richard Hill wrote from Antwerp to Blathwayt in London to ask whether there was any truth to the report that Blathwayt had voted for guineas at 25s. Hill could hardly believe such a thing, since in all his recent letters he had been telling Blathwayt how the lowness of the London-Antwerp exchange rate was making it impossible to obtain funding for the army in Flanders. Hill acknowledged the argument by which many MPs had justified voting for setting guineas at 25s.: that it would keep guineas from being exported to finance the army in Flanders. But if the goal was to keep guineas at home, Hill continued, then 'you must call us [here in Flanders] all home also'. For without a lower exchange rate or guinea exports, there would be no way to finance the army. Blathwayt confirmed the report.[33] He had voted for guineas at 25s., he said, because while this would not be good for the remittance operations of the Bank of England it was very much in the interest of 'the king and old England'. And 'let me tell you, the country gentleman had then Mr. Lowndes and other honest men in his company'. Unfortunately Blathwayt didn't explain his reasoning any further. Bonnet believed that those pushing for guineas at 25s. were intent upon diminishing William's popularity. The government would have lost a great deal of the purchasing power from the revenues granted by parliament that session had it been required to receive guineas at the Exchequer at 25s. and then used them to pay the forces abroad (where guineas were valued only at the equivalent of 21s. or 22s.). So the king would have been forced to issue a royal proclamation lowering guineas to 22s. The court's supporters in the Commons had been hoping to avoid such an outcome and wanted instead to make parliament the author of so unpopular a decision. Bonnet added that the second division that day was an unexpected victory for the court, attained by taking advantage of the departure of a few of the country party who thought the battle had already been won after the first motion passed. Locke thought that the motion for guineas at 25s. had been pushed by supporters of the National Land Bank (so that in the coming subscription they could 'put off their guineas at a high rate to the cost of the government') and by those in the Treasury who continued 'to compass their so long laboured design of raising the denomination of our coin'.[34] According to Luttrell, people still expected an official price to be set upon guineas at third reading of the bill.[35] L'Hermitage believed that some would press to reduce them to 22s. but that supporters of the land bank hoped to keep their price at 25 or 26s. – seeing in this a means of increasing subscriptions.[36]

The pamphlet literature of this period tells us a little more about the political forces likely to have been at work in the guineas debate. A few writers argued that failing to lower guineas to their normal rate would have a negative impact on the king's ability to finance the war overseas.[37] This suggests that at some level the debate may have been about the war; keeping guineas at a higher rate was a convenient way for politicians opposed to William's regime to do the war effort some harm. If the dispute was at base about support for the war, it is telling that most of the pamphlets favouring a lower price for guineas made no mention of this issue and instead emphasized the need to stop the current arbitrage trade in gold and silver.[38] This could mean that the war was a relatively unpopular cause, but that people didn't feel free to make their opposition public. Conversely, those arguing for guineas at 25s. may genuinely have believed this was essential for the regime's fiscal situation more broadly, whatever its impact on the war effort. In this connection consider two pamphlets published around this time: *An Essay for Lowering the Gold and Raising the Silver Coin* (usually attributed to John Blencowe) and *A Further Attempt Towards the Reformation of the Coin* (by R. Ford). Both argued for raising the coin and letting guineas fall to a level that would bring them into line with gold:silver ratios on the continent. And both argued that such a policy was needed to keep the money supply up, by getting heavy silver coin out of hoard and preventing the tale of guineas from falling quite so much as it otherwise would. Finally, both expressed the worry that without such changes the nation's finances would be in a very poor state. By the terms of the recoinage statute, Blencowe noted, all the good silver money coming out of the Mint would have to be used to repay existing long- and short-term Exchequer loans. In what currencies then were the year's taxes to be paid? This could only be by means of 'the old broad money, with the help of gold'.[39] Raising the coin would bring the former out of hoard; keeping guineas relatively high would prevent a further reduction in the tale of the nation's tale of coin. This may have been the kind of reasoning that led Blathwayt, Lowndes and other members of the court party to vote for guineas at 25s. Indeed it is the same position that Lowndes himself had advocated in the *Report*.

The conflict over the price of guineas resumed in the Commons a few days later, upon third reading of the plate bill. On 26 March the House divided three times over an initiative to lower the price of guineas – namely on the questions whether to: 1) add a clause for a new, lower ceiling (173–129); 2) make that ceiling 22s. (166–146); and 3) add the clause to the bill (183–135). The new 22s. ceiling was set to take effect on 10 April. Again we have no record of the debate. But judging from the tellers, the vote seems to have divided along whig-tory and not necessarily court-country lines – with the tories opposing a lower ceiling.[40] This was a considerable shift in attitude from a few days earlier, when a majority of the House had been willing to fix guineas at 25s. On Bonnet's telling, this was because in the interim several MPs had been told that William wanted parliament to fix guineas at as low a price as possible.[41] Presumably this information compelled MPs like Lowndes and Blathwayt to change their votes, even against their better judgment.

The guineas issue was contested one last time, on this occasion when the plate bill got to the committee stage in the House of Lords. The report in the *Journals*, as always, was entirely colorless: 'after some time' spent debating the bill, the Lords chose to pass it without amendment.[42] The only sign of conflict visible in the *Journals* was the fact that fifteen lords,

Rochester and Nottingham among their number, registered their dissent against the bill's passing. Fortunately the diplomatic reports are more informative.[43] After second reading on the 30th, the House had merely skirmished over the guineas clause. The only memorable event that day, Bonnet reported, was the wry observation that Nottingham, who a year ago had found fault with the government for letting the price of guineas climb (at the time it stood at 24s. or 25s.), now wanted to keep them high. The real battle came on the 31st, when Nottingham was joined by Leeds, Rochester and thirty other lords in opposing the clause. In this position they were supported, Bonnet claimed, by goldsmiths, merchants and more than fifty members of the Commons. Their reasoning was that guineas were still valued in Holland at the equivalent of 24s. – a claim for which they supplied evidence in the form of letters from abroad and testimony from a merchant specializing in bullion exports (Isaac Pereira). Consequently, if guineas were reduced to 22s. in England, they would all quickly be transported abroad, depriving the nation of a great deal of its money supply. The question for retaining the guineas clause was debated for five hours and carried 53 to 33. The act (7 & 8 Will. 3, c. 19) received royal assent on 10 April – the very day the new price ceiling was to come into effect. Price currents began quoting guineas at 22s. later that week. But one contemporary newspaper reports they had already been circulating at that rate by as early as the end of March.[44]

Two pamphlets of note were published hard on the heels of the Commons' decision to lower guineas to 22s.: Temple's *Some Short Remarks Upon Mr. Lock's Book* and Barbon's *Discourse Concerning Coining the New Money Lighter*.[45] They are significant because they suggest a change in strategy on the part of those politicians pushing the cause of the National Land Bank. Until now the country majority in the Commons had successfully resisted all of Montagu's efforts to raise the coin and settle a price upon guineas. But now that guineas had been lowered to 22s., suddenly here were two MPs, aligned with the land bank,[46] proposing that the coin be raised. Both maintained that England's silver money should be coined lighter, so that its denomination would exceed the market value of the bullion it contained. Temple proposed no specific figure. Barbon recommended reducing the weight of new coin by a sixth and raising the denomination of existing heavy silver coin to 6s. per crown *pro rata*.[47] This would attract silver to the Mint for coining and keep English coin from being melted for export. Both claimed that raising the coin would have no impact on domestic prices. Locke thought their arguments would convince no one, 'unless it be such as are of their minds for other reasons than their arguments'.[48] Note that neither Temple nor Barbon proposed setting a price upon guineas; they argued only that lowering guineas to 22s. had been a mistake because it reduced the money supply. In fact, Barbon maintained that fixing the price of guineas, whether at 22s. or 25s., would do nothing to preserve the nation's silver coin.[49]

The bill for the National Land Bank, April–May

The salt-tax bill, on which in March the House had been making steady progress without any apparent controversy, seems to have hit a major snag in early April. The committee met on 1 April to continue working its way through the text. But there was a conflict of some kind that day, since the committee divided over the inclusion of certain unspecified clauses. It is hard to know what was at issue. But a pamphlet published around this time gives a very good clue.[50] It dates to 1 April a split between the Briscoe and Asgill-Barbon camps. While the work in question is very satirical and funny, there is no reason to doubt its dating of the conflict. For the work was clearly designed to influence MPs' future voting on the bill by portraying Briscoe as having sold out to the Bank of England. Specifically it claims that he had ceded his 'freeholders', i.e. those MPs who had subscribed land to his bank, to Obadiah Sedgwick (MP and deputy-governor of the Bank) for the remainder of the session, with a view to getting the land-bank bill dismissed. Moreover it hints that the main reason for Briscoe's departure was a sense that in the design of the bill the main goal of his group, which was to have an actual land bank, had been subjugated to the priorities of the Lincoln's-Inn camp, which was interested only in a traditional money loan. This dispute was very likely at the root of the division in committee on 1 April. For the tellers for and against, Sir John Bolles and Harley, were then trustees of the Asgill-Barbon and Briscoe banks respectively (assuming that the *Journals* meant Edward rather than Robert Harley).

Over the next few weeks the prospects for a parliamentary land bank dimmed considerably, opening the door for Montagu's alternative Exchequer-bills scheme to be inserted into the bill. At its two next meetings, on 8 and 13 April, the committee worked on a side issue: how to raise a little more money, now that it was agreed the salt tax probably would not generate enough revenue by itself.[51] But things were not going well for the National Land Bank. L'Hermitage reported that there had been no great press of new subscribers and that 'a sort of dispute' had arisen between the directors of the two component banking projects.[52] This raised the prospect that the bank would fail to obtain parliamentary approval and that the loan would be raised instead through the Exchequer by way of perpetual annuities. People would much prefer this anyway, l'Hermitage added, over the alternative of having to join a new bank. At the committee meeting of 15 April, first reading was given to a clause for financing the loan instead by means of 'Exchequer bills'.[53] By this term the Commons had in mind the loan scheme proposed in *Mint and Exchequer United* in which the Exchequer itself would borrow directly from bill holders. Since nothing else was recorded in the minutes that day, it seems likely the discussion on Exchequer bills was a lengthy one. Luttrell wrote a day later: 'Tis believed at last the land bank will be turned into an Exchequer bank'.[54] At the next committee meeting, on 20 April, the Exchequer-bills clause was approved for inclusion. There was a division on this motion; but in the end opponents of the clause 'yielded' without forcing an actual vote. This was presumably the result of a compromise. For the committee immediately proceeded to add another clause. This one entitled the National Land Bank to redeem any existing Exchequer bills and take over the whole loan should it collect enough subscriptions to qualify for parliamentary standing. This implies that the battle had merely been deferred and would now come down to how well the bank's subscription drive fared once the act was passed. L'Hermitage nevertheless concluded that the Commons had resolved 'not to establish a land bank' and that the loan would come instead from the Exchequer, acting like a bank.[55] As usual, Bonnet was more careful; he thought the land bank was now 'the least important part of the bill' and that the loan would be furnished whether or not it succeeded. For 'the Exchequer itself will become a bank'.[56] L'Hermitage thought one of the main reasons the land bank had miscarried was the decision to reduce guineas to 22s. The bank's most ardent supporters had been people with guineas who hoped to pass them off, in their subscription payments, at 30s. apiece. But now that guineas were going at 22s., 'all the good reasons they offer [for establishing the bank] have vanished'. When the House debated the committee report on 21 and 22 April, the bill kept its basic form without any apparent contest; the only divisions at this point were over a couple of side issues. The House also added a clause stipulating that, if the revenues from this act should prove insufficient to pay interest on the Bank of England's £1.2 million loan, this money would be made good to them from the first revenues approved by parliament in the next session. The bill passed third reading on 24 April and was approved by the Lords without amendment three days later. William came that very day to give his assent and close the session.[57]

The design embodied in the act (7 & 8 Will. 3, c. 31) offered little in the way of a genuine land bank. Originally the Lincoln's-Inn project had been a land bank only in the sense that its directors were committed to lending some minimum amount on land mortgages. Briscoe's original design, by contrast, had promised to turn land owners into lenders and bank directors. Under the Land Bank United this aim was scaled back to the much more modest goal of allowing landowners to count land subscriptions as the equivalent of a specie contribution and claim some increasingly-modest share of the profits arising from a large war loan. In the least generous versions, landowners would also have had to contribute some specie of their own, although on a deferred basis. By the time of the act, the land component of the bank had been scaled back even further. There was still a commitment to lend up to £500 thousand per year on mortgages at the low rate of 3.5 percent per annum. But now all investors would have to contribute at least three-quarters of their subscription in hard cash – or at least make a commitment to deliver the same on demand. Landed estates or other streams of income could be used only as security for paying the final quarter of a given investor's subscription (see §75). Presumably for this purpose estates would have been capitalized at 15 to 20 times their annual rental values. In other words, for the final quarter payment of, say, a £6 thousand subscription, a landowner would have needed to mortgage title to an annual rental income of some £75 to £100. The projectors were implicitly assuming that, like with the Bank of England to date, the final quarter or better of an investor's subscription would never actually be called upon.

For the rest, the so-called National Land Bank would have been nothing but another money bank like the Bank of England. The details provided in the statute imply that the directors would have followed the Bank of England's lead and paid their loan into the Exchequer in the first instance in bills of the new bank. The specie needed by military paymasters would have been supplied to them a little later from the contributions of shareholders and bill holders (allowing for the possibility that some suppliers would agree to accept payment in bills and then choose to hold the same). The statute did not specify the rate of interest that would be offered on the bank's bills. Presumably it would been the same 3 percent being offered on bills of the Bank of England.[58] This had already been proven a rate of return sufficient to induce large numbers of private persons to hold such assets as short-term investments. If any decided to cash their bills when they came due, the bank would have needed to find new investors to hold them in turn. And surely the trustees would have hoped to do better still and, like the Bank of England, draw in additional loanable funds by offering zero-interest notes to anyone depositing specie. The bank's specie stocks would also, in theory, be regularly replenished with specie from the Exchequer, whether in payment of its annual £100 thousand interest charge or by way of principal and interest payments on those near-term tallies in which it chose to invest. Shareholders would profit by receiving interest at 7 percent per annum on a loan only part of which they had paid themselves (having in effect borrowed the rest from bill holders at 3 percent) and by the difference in interest rates between any additional assets (mostly tallies at 5 or 6 percent) and corresponding liabilities (bills at 3 percent and maybe notes at zero). The commitment to lend on mortgages at 3.5 percent would have been something of an albatross around the bank's neck. This might perhaps have been minimized by interpreting 'five hundred thousand pounds per annum' to mean a total of £500 thousand in any given year rather than an additional £500 thousand every successive year.

As with the Bank of England, certain conditions were imposed for the loan to go ahead as planned, and fallback procedures were put into place in case these conditions were not met. Government-appointed commissioners had until 1 August 1696 to collect subscriptions for at least half of the loan amount (§16). Should they fall short of this target, there would be no royal grant of incorporation – no National Land Bank. Instead those who had subscribed would be treated as private lenders to the crown, each annually receiving – individually and directly from the Exchequer – an appropriate share of the fund set aside for paying interest on the loan. The difference was crucial to subscribers' financial prospects. For without corporate status, the subscribers would not be able to issue bills and so borrow at low interest from bill holders. Instead they would have to contribute the full value of their shares themselves – reducing their rate of return to a straight 7 percent per annum and eliminating any possibility for further profits by using additional bills and notes to buy short-term assets like Exchequer tallies. Nor could subscribers have escaped their fate should they fail to attain corporate status. Upon subscribing they were required to pay commissioners, in cash, a quarter of the sum for which they had signed on; otherwise the subscription was not valid. This down payment would be forfeited if investors neglected to pay the remaining three-quarters of their subscription before 1 January 1697 (§17).

Of course, from the government's perspective, the fallback position of converting subscriptions into personal loans was most unsatisfactory. If the commissioners fell short of the target needed for incorporation, that would mean at least half the loan had not yet been received. And it was most unlikely that additional individual lenders would rush in to fill this void. For they would need to pay the whole of their loans in specie and would get in return an asset – a 7 percent perpetual annuity – that would be relatively hard to turn back into ready money should they suddenly need it: much harder anyway than shares in a joint-stock corporation like the proposed National Land Bank. At a time when liquidity was already in very short supply, few were likely to pursue such an investment strategy.

The prospect of so large a loan failing was a very grave risk for the government to be taking on during a time of war. This presumably aided Treasury officials very considerably in persuading the Commons to add a further backup plan to the bill: the several articles pertaining to Exchequer bills. These sections authorized the Exchequer to begin taking in loans right away, giving the lenders either tallies with interest at 7 percent or 'bills of credit' payable on demand with interest at 3d. per diem per £100 (equivalent to about 4.6 percent per annum). With the Exchequer bills concept, the Exchequer was in effect replicating the intended National Land Bank. The people likely to lend specie in exchange for Exchequer bills were the same individuals who would otherwise have ended up holding bills of the National Land Bank. And by cutting out the middle man the Exchequer could afford to give investors a better rate of interest: 4.6 instead of 3 percent. The statute stipulated that the Treasury could not issue more than £1.5 million in tallies or Exchequer bills before 1 August (§67) and that if the National Land Bank was incorporated it had the right to redeem any Exchequer tallies or bills already issued (§74). In effect this positioned the National Land Bank, once it was in operation, to replace any Exchequer bills already in circulation with its own bills and thereby take over the whole of the loan for itself.

Of course for the Exchequer-bills plan to succeed, someone somewhere would have to keep a large pool of specie at the ready, so that the bills could be cashed upon demand. A contemporary pamphlet, issued right after the relevant clauses were first proposed for inclusion in the bill, argued that this money could not come from the Exchequer itself.[59] For all the funds kept there had already been appropriated by parliament to specific purposes. The anonymous author of this piece asserted that the source 'must be the Bank of England'.[60] By this back door, then, the Bank of England would 'come to be possessed of the whole fund, to the total defeat of the Land Bank'. Technically this was incorrect. The statute was silent about the existence and source of any specie pool. But it did specify that principal and interest on Exchequer bills could be paid out of any money in the Exchequer that had previously been received from persons lending money under the terms of the act. So the proceeds from some Exchequer bill issues (or salt-tax tallies) could in principle be used to pay off other Exchequer bills. Whether the Exchequer-bills scheme could generate its own specie-reserve pool in this way remained to be seen. This depended on the extent to which members of the general public would be prepared to hold the new bills as interest-bearing assets rather than return them immediately for repayment in specie. For the statute explicitly specified that the bills were not to have legal-tender status; they must be accepted in payment either voluntarily or not at all. Note that the statute did at least implicitly supply a potential source of funding for an externally-financed specie pool. For it assumed, and set aside tax revenues sufficient for, interest payments at the rate of 7 percent. Yet if the Exchequer-bills scheme were implemented, interest would have been paid to lenders at the rate only of 4.6 percent per annum.

Notes

1 Commons Committee Minutes.
2 L'Hermitage Reports, 4/14 February 1696.
3 Quoted at £107 on 31 Jan., Bank shares had fallen to £93 by the next reporting date, 7 Feb. (Houghton, *Collection*). L'Hermitage stated it as a simple fact that the Commons decision had caused the decline.
4 Commons Committee Minutes; Luttrell, *Brief Historical Relation*, 11 Feb. 1696.
5 This is suggested too by the tellers on the division. For committees of the whole there were only two tellers, one per side. Sir Walter Yonge and Colonel John Perry belonged to the court and country parties respectively.
6 Letter of l'Hermitage to Pensionary Heinsius, 14/24 Feb. 1696, Nationaal Archief, Heinsius (3.01.19) 465.
7 The salt and tonnage duties had brought in £107 thousand and £125 thousand over the last 21 and 18 months respectively. The Commons had estimated that they would each generate £140 thousand annually. The duty on coal was £560 thousand in arrears.
8 *CJ*, 4 Feb. 1696.
9 Bank General Ledger 1, fol. 94.
10 *CTB*, Warrants, etc., 15 Nov. 1697.
11 *CTB*, Warrants, etc., 25 May 1698.
12 The first two members named were ex officio: the attorney- and solicitor-general. Of the other four, three consistently voted that session with the country party. John Conyers and Sir John Bolles were both tories and associates of Robert Harley. Bolles, who quickly refused the Association, had been elected both a trustee

and a director of Briscoe's National Land Bank in 1695. The third country member was reported only as 'Harley', so that we do not know whether Robert or Edward was meant. It could have been either, since Robert had worked with Foley over the summer to design the session's financial program and Edward was a director for the Lincoln's-Inn Bank. The final committee member, Joseph Tily, was something of an outlier. Though he too was a trustee and director for Briscoe's National Land Bank, he had subscribed to the Bank of England in 1694, voted with the court during the 1695–96 session, and that summer supported Montagu on the country mint at Exeter and the Exchequer bills scheme.

13 Commons Committee Minutes.

14 *CJ*, 21 Jan. 1696.

15 Commons Committee Minutes.

16 All but two (Grammar and Monger) are listed as goldsmiths in at least one of the following works: Price, *Handbook of London Bankers*; Heal, *London Goldsmiths*; and Prideaux, *Memorials of the Goldsmiths' Company*.

17 UK Parliamentary Archives, HC/LB/1/12, fols. 115–16.

18 Letter to Locke, 15 Feb. 1696, in de Beer, *Correspondence*, pp. 542–43. In their special code language, Clarke laid the blame on 'the monkey and some others of his brethren'.

19 The tellers for the motion, Henry Boyle and Francis Gwyn, consistently voted with the country party and, though tories, were on good terms with many whigs. John Elwill and an Onslow told against the motion. There were three Onslows in the House at this time. It cannot be Sir Richard Onslow, for the *Commons Journals* always referred to knights by their titles. Of Denzil and Foot Onslow, it was more likely the latter, since he was an excise commissioner while Denzil held no office. Elwill was a court whig, a receiver-general for Devon and Exeter, and an army contractor.

20 Luttrell, *Brief Historical Relation*, 18 Feb. 1696.

21 Abbott Letters, 21 Feb. 1696.

22 Once more Gwyn and Elwill told for the yeas and noes respectively. The other teller for the yeas, Sir Robert Davers, was a tory then in opposition. The remaining teller, Sir Henry Hobart, was a court whig, appointed in 1697 as a customs commissioner.

23 Bonnet Reports, 6/16 Mar. 1696.

24 See *Post-Boy* for 14 and 21 Mar. and the *Flying Post* for 12 and 19 Mar. 1696.

25 Commons Committee Minutes; *CJ*, 7 Mar. 1696.

26 Commons Committee Minutes.

27 Bonnet Reports, 10/20 Mar. 1696.

28 See their respective biographies in Hayton, *History of Parliament*.

29 Letter of 10 Mar. 1696, in de Beer, *Correspondence*, pp. 561–62.

30 They are referring to a letter that Locke wrote them on 6 March, excluded from the de Beer collection but reprinted in Davison and Keirn, 'John Locke', pp. 235–36. In that letter Locke maintained that there were two groups at work: those supporting the national land bank who wanted guineas to be as high as possible, and a second, unnamed group who hoped to raise the silver coin by 20 percent.

31 On the first question William Bromley and Sir Eliab Harvey were the tellers for and Sir Henry Hobart and Sir William Scawen the tellers against. Bromley and Harvey were both staunch tories who had refused the Association. Hobart was a whig who had fought alongside William in Ireland and voted consistently in favour of the court. Scawen was the one outlier, not known for being a strong supporter of the government. But as deputy-governor of the Bank of England he had his own reasons for voting against guineas at 25s. On the second question, the tellers for and against were Sir Marmaduke Wyvill and John Manley on the one

hand and Sir Walter Yonge and Roger Hoar on the other. Wyvill and Manley too had refused the association; the one was a high tory and the other even suspected of having worked with the Jacobites. Yonge and Hoar were both strong supporters of William's reign, whigs sharing the outlook of, and also friends with, Locke and Clarke.

32 Letter of Hill to Blathwayt, 2/12 Apr. 1696, BL Add. MS 9730.
33 Letter of Blathwayt to Hill, 10/20 Apr. 1696, BL Add. MS 56241 (henceforth 'Blathwayt Letters to Hill').
34 Letter to Clarke, 25 Mar. 1696, in de Beer, *Correspondence*, pp. 579–80.
35 Luttrell, *Brief Historical Relation,* 21 Mar. 1696.
36 L'Hermitage Reports, 24 Mar. / 3 Apr. 1696.
37 See for instance *Considerations About the Currancy of Guinea's*; *Letter to a Gentleman*; and *Reasons for Reducing of Guineas*.
38 See for instance Clement, *Dialogue*; *Considerations Most Humbly Proposed*; *Guineas at 21s. 6d.*; *Letter to an Eminent Member*; *Reasons for Reducing Guineas*; *Reasons for Reducing of Guineas*; *Some Observations Humbly Offered*; and *Some Remarks*.
39 Blencowe, *Essay*, pp. 22–23.
40 Those telling against a lower ceiling were, in order of the divisions: Francis Gwyn and Arthur Moore, Sir John Bolles and John Manley and Philip Bickerstaffe and Richard Fownes. All were tories who had refused to sign the Association, as well as supporters of a parliamentary trade council. Those telling for a lower price on guineas, again in order of the divisions, were: Coningsby and Sir Henry Hobart, Sir Godfrey Copley (the name of the second teller was not recorded) and Robert Molesworth and Salwey Winnington. All were whigs and prompt signatories to the Association, though Hobart had opposed a parliamentary trade council.
41 Bonnet Reports, 27 Mar. / 6 Apr. 1696.
42 *LJ*, 31 Mar. 1696.
43 Bonnet Reports and l'Hermitage Reports, 31 Mar. / 10 Apr. 1696.
44 *Post-Boy*, 31 Mar. 1696.
45 Temple's work was advertised in the *Post-Man* for 31 Mar. The earliest ad I could find for Barbon's pamphlet was in the 14 April edition of the *Post-Boy*. But in a letter of 8 April 1696 Locke mentioned it as being contemporaneous with Temple's publication.
46 Barbon was of course one of the land-bank projectors. Temple had been a leading member of the former tory administration and as such would have been supporting the land bank for political purposes.
47 Barbon, *Discourse*, pp. 90–91.
48 Letter to Freke and Clarke, 8 Apr. 1696, in de Beer, *Correspondence*, pp. 599–600.
49 Barbon, *Discourse*, p. 96.
50 *Mr. B--coe's Reply.*
51 Commons Committee Minutes.
52   L'Hermitage Reports, 10/20 Apr. 1696.
53 Commons Committee Minutes.
54 Luttrell, *Brief Historical Relation*, 16 Apr. 1696.
55 L'Hermitage Reports, 21 Apr. / 1 May 1696.
56 Bonnet Reports, 21 Apr. / 1 May 1696.
57 *CJ*, 24 Apr. 1696.
58 A short pamphlet published by land-bank supporters while the bill was still in committee explained that the rate would be no higher than 3.5 percent and would probably soon be reduced to 3 percent (*Computation Shewing*, p. 2).
59 *Substance of the Clause.*

60 Another pamphlet published around this time made the same claim. 'Nor is this
    Exchequer-bank any other than the Bank of England discounting Exchequer-bills,
    and so the Exchequer will be the Bank of England at Westminster and the Bank
    of England will be the Exchequer at Grocers Hall [the Bank's current abode]'
    (*Computation Shewing*, p. 3).

Bibliography

Manuscript sources

Bank of England Archive
    ADM7/1-2 ('Bank General Ledger 1' and 'Bank General Ledger 2')
British Library
    Add. MS 9730
    Add. MS. 17677 OO-QQ ('l'Hermitage Reports')
    Add. MS 56241 ('Blathwayt Letters to Hill')
    Harley MS 1274 ('Commons Committee Minutes')
Geheimes Staatsarchiv, Preußischer Kulturbesitz, Berlin
    I. HA Geheimer Rat, Rep. 11, Nr. 1792–1811 ('Bonnet Reports')
Nationaal Archief, The Hague
    Heinsius (3.01.19) 465
Parliamentary Archives, United Kingdom, London
    HC/LB/1/12
Shropshire Archives (Attingham Collection)
    X112/1/2/1 ('Abbott Letters')

Printed primary sources

Barbon, Nicholas. *A Discourse Concerning Coining the New Money Lighter: In An-
    swer to Mr. Lock's Considerations About Raising the Value of Money.* London:
    printed for Richard Chiswell, 1696.
[Blencowe, John]. *An Essay for Lowering the Gold and Raising the Silver Coin.*
    London: printed for Timothy Goodwin, 1696.
[Clement, Simon]. *A Dialogue Between a Countrey Gentleman and a Merchant Con-
    cerning the Falling of Guinea's: Wherein the Whole Argument Relating to Our
    Money Is Discuss'd.* London: printed by John Astwood for Samuel Crouch, 1696.
*A Computation Shewing That the Two Several Proposals Made to the Parliament for
    Raising Two Millions and a Half, Are Different, the One from the Other, as Much as
    Amounts to the Value of All the Lands in the Kingdom.* [London: s.n., 1696].
*Considerations About the Currancy of Guinea's, in Relation to the Silver-Coin of the
    Nation.* [London: s.n., 1696].
Considerations Most Humbly Proposed, in Relation to the Ill State of Our Money.
    [London: s.n., 1696].
De Beer, E. S. (ed.). *The Correspondence of John Locke.* Vol. 5. Oxford: Clarendon
    Press, 1979.
Ford, R. *A Further Attempt Towards the Reformation of the Coin: With Expedients
    for Preventing the Stop of Commerce During the Re-Coinage, and Supplying the
    Mint with a Sufficient Quantity of Bullion.* London: Thomas Cockerill, 1696.

Great Britain. *Statutes of the Realm.* Edited Alexander Luders and John Raithby. London: G. Eyre and A. Strahan, 1810–22. Accessed online at http://www.british-history.ac.uk/statutes-realm/.

Great Britain. Parliament. House of Commons. *Journals of the House of Commons.* London: House of Commons, 1803. Accessed online at http://www.british-history.ac.uk/commons-jrnl/.

Great Britain. Parliament. House of Lords. *Journals of the House of Lords.* Vol. 15: *1691–96.* London: HMSO, 1767–1830. Accessed online at http://www.british-history.ac.uk/lords-jrnl/vol15/.

Great Britain. Public Record Office. *Calendar of Treasury Books.* Volume XIII: *October 1697 to August 1698.* Edited by William Shaw. London: HMSO, 1931. Accessed online at http://www.british-history.ac.uk/cal-treasury-books/vol13.

Guineas at 21 s. 6d. Will Make Money Plenty: The People Will Bear It: Not Carry It to Holland, But Lend It to the King. [London: s.n., 1696].

A Letter to a Gentleman in the Country Concerning the Price of Guineas. [London: s.n.], 1696.

A Letter to an Eminent Member of Parliament About the Present Rate of Guineas, and the Influence They Will Have On Our Expected New Money. [London: s.n., 1696].

Luttrell, Narcissus. *A Brief Historical Relation of State Affairs from September 1678 to April 1714.* 6 vols. Oxford: Oxford University Press, 1857.

Mr. B — coe's Reply to the Almanack, Being Land and Money United: Or, B — coe & the B — k of E — nd Joined. [London: s.n., 1696].

Reasons for Reducing Guineas to 22s. a Peice. [London: s.n., 1696].

Reasons for Reducing of Guineas to Their True Value. [London: s.n., 1696].

Some Observations Humbly Offered to the Honourable House of Commons. [London: s.n., 1696].

Some Remarks on the Passing of Clip'd Six-Pences, and the High Rate of Guineas. [London: s.n., 1696].

The Substance of the Clause Offered to the Land-Bank-Bill: With Remarks Upon It. [London: s.n., 1696].

Temple, Richard. *Some Short Remarks Upon Mr. Lock's Book in Answer to Mr. Lounds and Several Other Books and Pamphlets Concerning Coin.* London: Richard Baldwin, 1696.

Contemporary periodicals

Collection for the Improvement of Husbandry and Trade. Ed. John Houghton. London. ('Houghton, *Collection*').

Flying Post. London.

Post-Boy. London.

Post-Man. London.

Secondary sources

Davison, Lee, and Tim Keirn. 'John Locke, Edward Clarke and the 1696 Guineas Legislation'. *Parliamentary History* 7, no. 2 (1988):228–40.

Hayton, David, Eveline Cruickshanks and Stuart Handley (eds.). *The History of Parliament: the House of Commons, 1690–1715*. 4 vols. Cambridge: Cambridge University Press for The History of Parliament Trust, 2002. Available online at http://www.historyofparliamentonline.org/volume/1690-1715.

Heal, Ambrose. *The London Goldsmiths, 1200–1800*. Cambridge: Cambridge University Press, 1935.

Price, F. G. Hilton. *A Handbook of London Bankers*. London: Leadenhall Press, 1890–91.

Prideaux, Walter Sherburne (comp.). *Memorials of the Goldsmiths' Company*. 2 vols. [London]: Eyre and Spottiwoode, 1896–97.

11 Connecting the dots

Monetary policies as means to political ends

Economic historians writing of the recoinage debate usually put front and centre the question of the Mint standard, making it out to be an analytical contest between court and country in which 'the Court party propounded undiluted Locke, while the Country party adopted as their Bible the *Report* of Lowndes'.[1] Relatively little attention has been paid to the later debates on guineas and the National Land Bank. When considered at all, the latter two have been treated as separate issues – the one a technical discussion about how best to stop arbitrage trading in gold and silver[2] and the other either another, separate court-country dispute[3] or a conflict emanating from competing whig and tory philosophies of economic development.[4]

In this chapter, by contrast, I draw upon the foregoing narrative of the three debates to argue that they were all very closely connected and divided politicians in ways that cut across court-country and whig-tory lines. I present them as the outworks of a complex, high-political battle being carried on behind the scenes. The core contest was between two camps that had formed within the administration by fall 1695.[5] One, led by the non-partisan politicians the Earl of Sunderland (William's most influential English advisor, though himself without office), Godolphin and Henry Guy (Treasury Secretary until spring 1695, when he had been chased from office by the junto-led bribery investigations), had decided to pursue an alliance with a group of country MPs managed by Foley and Harley. The latter would deliver, from the Commons, strong financial support for the war. In return they wanted the Commons to have a say in the crown's financial programme and in naval policy. During the 1695–96 session, the two foremost fruits of this alliance were to be a parliamentary land bank and a parliamentary trade council. I left the latter issue out of my narrative of the 1695–96 parliamentary session, since it had no direct connection with issues of money or public finance. But it would have been a significant political achievement for the country party. For it would have given the Commons decision-making power over some aspects of naval administration, including the right to order convoys for the protection of English trade fleets. As such it was another touchstone during the session, at least equal in importance to the prospective National Land Bank. It is telling that Davenant's recoinage submission to the lords justices argued the case for such a trade council and specifically advocated for the Commons being allowed to name the majority of its members. The other camp within the royal administration was led by junto-whig treasury lords Montagu and John Smith and MPs Thomas Wharton and Littleton. They had agreed, over the summer, to abandon their vindictive campaign of the previous session to prove the Duke of Leeds and other prominent leaders of the former tory administration guilty of corruption. But they still hoped to use their considerable influence within the Commons (which was based in large part on their talent for oratory) to persuade William to keep the former tory leaders on the sidelines and tilt his administration yet further in their direction. This would involve, among other things, securing Wharton's appointment as head of state in Ireland and moving Littleton into the Treasury position vacated in mid-1695 when Trumbull was made a secretary of state. This group pursued a financial programme that left no role for the National Land Bank and, like William and most other members of the court party, actively opposed a parliamentary trade council.

During William's reign, politicians could secure influence and power within the Commons only if they were capable of delivering (or also, as it turns out, obstructing) financial support for the war effort. For this was first on the king's list of priorities and so foremost in his thinking about which MPs should be invited to assist in managing the Commons (an offer usually accompanied by administrative appointments for them or their clients). And potential Commons leaders in turn had to design political programs capable of persuading a sufficient number of MPs to join them in getting the session's major pieces of financial legislation through the House. This led to a system of political barter that was well understood by insiders. So, for instance, Blathwayt wrote Richard Hill during an earlier session: 'our affairs [in the Commons] go on merrily with relation to [supply for] the land forces, for which the gentlemen [who were supporting army supply] will have the triennial bill, etc.'[6] The mere fact that Blathwayt was so brief means he expected Hill would have no trouble grasping his meaning: that a coalition of mainly whig MPs had agreed to support the court's requested level of army funding on condition the court worked with them to pass a bill requiring parliamentary elections every three years. This was the same sort of bargain that Sunderland and company had struck with Foley and Harley for the 1695–96 session; deliver a Commons majority for quick and generous support of the war effort and we will do our best to make sure that the Commons gets control of a major new source of public finance (thereby both cementing your political position in the House and giving you some say over whether the crown will receive any future war loans) and influence over the administration's handling of the navy (specifically to give a higher priority to protecting commercial shipping).

Montagu and associates understood that this new agreement posed a real threat to their power and influence within the administration. Their own rise to high office had come about in large part because of their ability to deliver a strong financial programme that had included a large war loan from the Bank of England. Should the National Land Bank prove a success, this would free William to demote the Montagu group (whom he disliked in any case for being very extreme, mercurial and ambitious) without harming his military finances. It would also clear the way for tory leaders like Nottingham and Leeds to return to the administration.[7] Yet because the bank would remain under parliamentary control, the country party would also have greater power.

So the central contest during the 1695–96 session of parliament was over the fortunes of the land bank and, ultimately, the distribution of political power within the nation. In this chapter I will argue that the latter struggle was evident in, and affected the shape of, debates within the administration and in parliament over the recoinage and the price of guineas.

The administrative debate

Lowndes' *Report* came as something of a shock to contemporaries. It was clearly an official Treasury statement, since it named the Treasury Secretary as the author, was printed by the king's own printer, and took the form of a recommendation to the treasury lords. And since the latter were always the crown's principal managers in the Commons and the report was distributed to all members of parliament, it amounted to a declaration that the Treasury aimed during the coming session to raise the silver coin. Many found this perfectly amazing. For such a policy threatened to further reduce the London-Antwerp exchange rate, which everyone knew was already doing great injury, even at its current level, to England's capacity to finance an army in Flanders. Indeed, the Bank's directors in Antwerp wrote London that the very appearance of the *Report* 'had frightened and astonished all persons on that side of the water' and caused the exchange rate to fall. The directors had been forced to send an emissary to The Hague to assure the Dutch government that 'this scheme was the notion only of one man and would not take effect'.[8]

It was a remarkable document too because it represented a sharp reversal of opinion on Lowndes' part. In a private memorandum written for the treasury lords earlier that year, Lowndes had strongly recommended *against* raising the coin.[9] The occasion was a request from the treasury lords for his evaluation of a recoinage scheme that had been submitted for their consideration.[10] The scheme was very similar to the one Lowndes would later recommend in his own *Report*.[11] Yet at this time Lowndes found lots to criticize about such an approach. Specifically, he worried that raising the coin would: a) diminish the crown's ability to finance the war (exchange rates would fall, making army remittances and naval stores more expensive); b) disrupt foreign trade (which would be disrupted by the change in exchange rates); c) reduce landlords' real income (long-term rents were fixed but commodity prices would probably rise); and d) make it hard for the government to obtain new loans (investors would fear being repaid with less coin, measured by weight, than they had originally loaned). Lowndes saw clipping-related losses as the central problem facing the Treasury in regard to a recoinage. Of the two main options available, raising the coin or appointing some new tax, he considered the latter the better way to go. If the treasury lords decided to go the other route, he wanted nothing to do with it and urged them to find someone else to work out the details.

How are we to explain the Treasury coming out in support of a policy which it knew would make it harder to fund the English army in Flanders, and the remarkable turnabout in Lowndes' own views? I believe that in September Lowndes came out in favour of raising the coin because the nation's monetary circumstances had changed a great deal since January, when he had last written on this question for the Treasury. Heavy silver coin had largely disappeared from circulation. Uncertainty about the future value of clipped coin had driven guineas to 30s. The exchange rate had already fallen to levels lower than they might go even if the Mint standard was actually changed. And in the spring a Commons finance committee had declared its support for raising the coin: a fact that Trevor had made public knowledge. If into this mix one were now to introduce a recoinage, thereby depriving the nation of the better part of the specie that remained in circulation, chaos might ensue. Lowndes sought remedial measures and believed the most promising prospect was to find some way of luring heavy silver coin out of hoard. Raising the coin promised to do this. Under the present circumstances, any negative impact on the army's situation from raising the coin would have to be viewed as the lesser of two evils; it was either that or risk having the year's entire financial program fail. It's not clear that all the treasury lords agreed with Lowndes' assessment or proposed plan of attack. The fact that Davenant, in his submission to the lords justices, advised against raising the coin suggests that Godolphin too thought this measure unnecessary or at least unwise. But a good number of treasury lords must have supported the idea. For there is no other way to explain the decision to print the *Report* and circulate it to all members of parliament just ahead of the new session. Montagu must have been among that group, given both his behaviour later in the session and the fact that Newton, his client, supported the strategy in his own submission to the lords justices. But Montagu took this position for reasons different than Lowndes'. As I argue later in the chapter, in Lowndes' proposal for raising the coin he saw a prospect for defeating the land-bank project upon which Godolphin, Foley and Harley were already engaged.

The recoinage bill

The parliamentary debate on the recoinage bill took an unexpected form. Judging from the pamphlet literature of 1695[12] and the coverage given in most secondary accounts, the parliamentary debate should have focused on the question whether to raise the coin. But in fact that issue figured hardly at all in the printed record. In the first Lords committee debate on the coinage, of which we have a good summary, the discussion centered entirely on whether to demonetize clipped coin right away.[13] No proposal to raise the coin ever made it to the floor of the Commons or featured even in the minutes of committees of the whole house or in Luttrell's daily record of political highlights. The closest it ever came to being the subject of an explicit vote was on 10 December, when the House approved a committee recommendation that 'all clipped money be recoined according to the es- tablished standard of the Mint, both as to weight and fineness'.[14] There was a division that day on a motion to remove the word 'both'. Bonnet reports that this amounted to a proposal to coin the new money with a higher alloy content.[15] But the question was lost by the very wide margin of 225 to 114. We have only the testimony of l'Hermitage that the issue of raising the coin figured once more in a Commons committee debate on 20 December.[16] But on that occasion there wasn't enough support even to bring the question to a division. Debate focused instead on issues almost completely ignored in the secondary literature – whether to: a) grant compensation only to taxpayers or more broadly; b) let clipped money stay in circulation by weight after be- ing registered for compensation; c) extend compensation also to counterfeit coin; and d) retain the proposal for establishing several country mints.

The debate went down these paths, to us unexpected, because it was al- ways more than just a technical discussion about how best to carry out a recoinage; at base it was an outpost of the larger struggle over the future shape of the administration. In a way the debate was both simultaneously. As Bonnet noted at the time (see p. 128), the matters at stake were very com- plex, well over the heads of most MPs. This enabled those politicians who were well-acquainted with financial issues to pursue objectives of which others might be entirely ignorant. A particular discussion might run along lines the average MP could grasp and about which many were surely quite sincere: for instance, whether a given measure would keep more money in circulation while the recoinage was under way. But the arguments by which that measure was defended or opposed could also function as mere handles for parliamentarians more in the know, men who were pushing for outcomes they favoured for other reasons altogether.

Raising the coin featured very little in the debates on the recoinage bill because this was not yet the appropriate time for that issue to come to the fore. Montagu wanted to put the question off until the House had formally decided whether to establish a national land bank. So the Commons vote of 10 December to alter neither the weight nor the fineness of the silver coin was not, as many scholars interpret it, a decision to retain the existing Mint standard. There had always been three ways of raising the coin: altering weight, fineness or denomination. The vote in question eliminated only two of them but left the third option still very much on the table – able to be brought into play later in the session. Bonnet was very conscious of this fact, noting quite explicitly that 'there is an issue on which the Commons has yet to rule' – namely whether to change the denomination of the money.[17] This is probably also why Locke's friends in London chose to have his book, *Further Considerations Concerning Raising the Value of Money*, published in late December, i.e. *after* the Commons had already passed the first recoinage bill – because they knew that the danger had by no means yet been averted.

The disagreement between Commons and Lords over how to compensate holders of clipped coin and whether to let the latter remain in circulation by weight may be traced to an early skirmish between Montagu and former tory leaders over the prospective fortunes of the land-bank project. It was Leeds who first proposed in the Lords that compensation be extended to all by means of specially-appointed public offices to which everyone could bring their clipped coin. And it was the tory and former treasury lord Lowther who broached the idea in the Commons a day or two later. Presumably Montagu opposed this measure. For though he was already perfectly familiar with the concept (it had featured in Lowndes' *Report*), it wasn't included in either of the two recoinage bills that he brought into the Commons that session. It is curious that Montagu should have excluded it. For such a measure would surely have helped increase the amount of currency in circulation while a recoinage was under way. But his opposition makes sense if we suppose that Montagu and associates hoped to divert specie away from the land-bank project. This is exactly what the recoinage bill in its original, and final, design promised to do. As soon as clipped coin was paid in for taxes – a use for which most of it was surely destined, since there was no other way to avoid the losses that must come from demonetization – it would be removed from circulation for several months and so unavailable for being subscribed to the bank. Nor would those interested in subscribing to the bank be able to use their holdings of clipped coin for that purpose; to avoid taking losses, they would have to invest that money instead in some other, short-term Exchequer loan. By contrast, if Leeds and Lowther had had their way, holders of clipped coin could both have obtained compensation and hung onto their money – freeing it up to be subscribed into the land bank at the appropriate time.

Montagu and associates may have had another reason for opposing any measure to make clipped coin go by weight. For as long as clipped money continued to circulate at face value, the market price of silver bullion was sure to remain high. And it was upon this fact that Montagu rested his later case for raising the coin. It allowed him to argue, a point on which many MPs were quite willing to be persuaded, that if new milled coin were kept to the existing standard, it would be melted as quickly as it came from the Mint. This realization may explain an apparent change of heart on Montagu's part. Writing to Locke on 5 December 1695, Freke complained of a shared acquaintance, almost certainly Montagu, who earlier that year had accepted their views on the advisability of making clipped coin go by weight but now thought it vital to let clipped coin remain in circulation at face value. This person, Freke remarked, was suddenly 'full of fears of I know not what dangers [that] may ensue if one could not with a clipped shilling pay a coach man'.[18] A month later Locke's friend Pawling reported a chance encounter with Montagu's older brother Christopher, then a commissioner for the stamp duty and also an MP. The older Montagu, knowing that Pawling favoured weighing, taunted him that the Commons 'had been considering of it and found it impracticable'. Another MP in the room, William Harris, chimed in 'that he satisfied many parliament men yesterday that money could not be weighed because there were not half scales enough to be had for the purpose and how could country people reckon grains, pennyweights, etc.'[19] Pawling, like Freke, was implying that the Treasury whigs were being disingenuous and had other reasons for their position than the ones they were stating. Locke and associates, as we shall see, thought it was their desire to profit privately from the recoinage. But Montagu and friends may have been thinking rather of the implications for the land bank's coming subscription drive.

The disagreement between Lords and Commons over the country mints, and within the Commons itself about whether to extend compensation also to counterfeit money, were probably also connected with the land-bank issue. In the first recoinage bill, the country mints were to be regional centers for trying coins to decide whether they were genuine or counterfeit. In principle the country mints became superfluous once the Commons decided to extend compensation to *all* hammered silver coin, even counterfeit. Yet they were retained in the second version of the bill, even though this was the one feature of the first bill that the Lords had insisted upon changing. And why was this, apparently such a minor feature of the bill, an issue over which the Lords were prepared to make a stand? I believe the explanation comes down to a small bit of corruption of the kind quite understood and accepted by contemporaries. By the statute there were to be at least four such operations, with the choice of location at the Treasury's discretion. For each mint multiple appointments would be required: local masters, wardens, etc. Montagu probably hoped to use the promise of these paid positions to buy support within the Commons for his coming fight against the land bank. Cooperative MPs would be rewarded, later in the year, with lucrative offices for them and/or their clients. This would explain too why the Lords fought hard to remove that clause; both Leeds and Godolphin wanted to see the land bank succeed and were trying to eliminate a potential obstacle. The remarkable decision by the Commons to extend public compensation even to counterfeit coin – which Locke and his friends could hardly believe – may have had a similar objective. Though at the time it was justified as a way of preventing the stop of trade, its real purpose may have been to weaken the case for retaining the clauses pertaining to change offices and country mints.

The plate bill and the guineas clauses

In a small pamphlet war that broke out during the monetary crisis of summer 1696, the earlier parliamentary debate on the high price of guineas came to be construed as a contest between court and country. Toward the end of the summer, an unnamed Jacobite supporter published an *Account of the Proceedings in the House of Commons in Relation to the Recoining the Clipp'd Money, and Falling the Price of Guineas*. The author maintained it was the court party that had pressed to recoin at the existing Mint standard and to lower guineas to 22s., and the country party that had tried to raise the silver coin and keep guineas high. The court had been thinking only of the English army in Flanders. Specifically, its goal had been to make gold and silver coin suitable for export to the continent, suppressing their value in England so they could be obtained more cheaply by the crown and used to maximum effect abroad. The country party was worried that such policies would deprive England of all its specie and generate the very loss of credit and stop of trade through which the nation was now suffering. The pamphlet proved very controversial, especially since it named the MPs alleged to have voted for and against guineas going at 22s. For this breach of parliamentary privilege, the House ordered the work burned by the common hangman and appointed an investigative committee to determine the identities of those involved in its production and distribution.[20] The committee concluded it had been written by Samuel Grascome, a non-juring Anglican clergyman. William issued a warrant for Grascome's arrest and offered a princely £500 reward for his apprehension.[21] The court also responded with an anonymous pamphlet of its own: *Reflections Upon a Scandalous Libel*. The author of this work sought to defend the decisions against raising the coin and for reducing guineas. But he entirely accepted the premise of the *Account*, that Montagu and the whole court party had pressed for these measures and the country party had opposed them.

Kelly was the first to notice that, in their private correspondence with Locke while the session was underway, Freke and Clarke offered a very different account of the guineas debate.[22] As we have seen, they maintained that Montagu and others in the Treasury were working behind the scenes that whole session to keep the market price of guineas relatively high with a view to getting the Commons to approve a measure for raising the silver coin by 20 percent. And indeed the minutes of a crucial Commons committee meeting in mid-February show Montagu arguing for exactly this outcome. In Locke's correspondence it is clear that the country party wanted to keep guineas high; but they were never identified as a group pressing for the coin to be raised.

I propose to explain both why Montagu and associates were proposing to raise the silver coin and keep guineas high and why, later, a writer for the court (presumably with Montagu's approval) nevertheless portrayed him as having pushed for the existing Mint standard and guineas at 22s. The short answer is that, near the end of the guineas debate, Montagu changed his position and it was later to his political advantage to position himself publicly as having supported all along the stance to which he came only at the end.

Locke and the College were shocked that the Treasury, under Montagu's leadership, was opposed to making clipped coin go by weight, wanted to raise the Mint standard and worked to keep guineas high. They were never sure about Montagu's motivations. Indeed, even Freke and Clarke on the scene in London confessed that as to 'the springs and tendencies of things [in parliament] we are strangers to the first [viz. the springs] and but guessers at the last [viz. the tendencies]'.[23] But reading between the lines of their correspondence that winter, they believed that many in the Treasury were hoping to use the recoinage to line their own pockets. Having access to the large flows of specie associated with taxes and Exchequer loans, public officials could cull out any heavy money and profit handsomely once the coin was raised. And in the meantime, monetary uncertainty offered them plenty of opportunity to gain at the expense of the state's creditors. Locke's friend Pawling described one such strategy.[24] He claimed that when anyone brought tallies for redemption, Exchequer officials began by offering payment in punched money that was obviously counterfeit. Then, when the tally holder offered to take payment instead in guineas at 30s., they claimed to have none – except that guineas would suddenly appear the moment a recipient agreed to take them at 30s. 6d. The Treasury men didn't seem to mind that their policies, in Locke's estimation, had also left the door open for goldsmiths to profit at public expense. The latter could lend clipped coin at full face to the Exchequer and, once repaid in milled coin, melt the latter down, turn it into simulated clipped money and start the process all over again.[25] Locke called it a 'perpetual circle of torment'. He and his associates, who constantly pushed for clipped silver to circulate only by weight because they believed this would instantly put an end to all such deceits, saw themselves as the sole defenders of monetary integrity and the public interest. Pawling teased that with all the corruption going on around them, it was time for Locke to flee the country: 'for you have attempted the ruin of their Diana and put a stop to that craft by which such k[naves] have got their gain'.[26] This was an allusion to a biblical story.[27] Allegedly two of Paul's disciples were almost killed by an angry mob at Ephesus, stirred up by silversmiths specializing in the production of shrines of the goddess Diana, after Paul had questioned her divinity.

But I think it more likely that Montagu regretted the peccadillos of public officials and saw them as the unavoidable cost of policies he was pursuing for other ends. Montagu understood that the success or failure of the National Land Bank would ultimately depend upon London goldsmiths and other tory monied men (many of them formerly goldsmiths themselves). For they were sitting on the better part of the nation's remaining store of guineas and heavy silver coin. With a policy of raising the silver coin by 20 percent and fixing guineas at 25s., Montagu was attempting to provide tory financiers with a means of making a handsome fortune that did not require their involvement in the National Land Bank. A bank of this kind might generate no more profit than a normal goldsmith-banking operation, especially since the version then on offer carried a large millstone around its neck: a commitment to lend at low cost to landowners. As such its existence mattered a whole lot more to the country politicians who hoped to use it to supply the crown with the loan it was seeking than it did to the financiers who might back it. But the land-bank project also represented an opportunity for a large set of the crown's would-be creditors to band together to demand concessions on the terms of their collective loan. Specifically, they could hope to cash in on the stores of specie that they had amassed in anticipation of the coin being raised. Montagu was therefore quietly offering tory financiers a trade-off. You may have a bank statute that will leave you free to negotiate with the government over the terms of your loan: no telling how that bargaining will shake out. Or you can have my support right now for a statute that will guarantee a 20 percent premium on any heavy silver coin in your possession and a reasonable rate for your guineas – a price you may well be unable to better even if you took the land-bank option because who knows where the market for guineas will eventually settle out? For this strategy to work it obviously had to be one or the other. Montagu would need to channel Commons proceedings so that those representing the goldsmiths' interests could get an act for a land bank or for raising the coin, but not both. Killing the land-bank project would do no harm to the crown's overall financial program, for Montagu could then hope to provide the necessary loan instead by means of a bank in the Exchequer.

Consider in this light the timing of the several efforts to get the Commons to approve resolutions for raising the coin and/or setting an official price on guineas. There had been three key moments in the Commons' handling of the new war loan. First, on 10 February the committee on ways and means resolved to borrow the money from a new national land bank rather than from the Bank of England or an Exchequer bank (a committee resolution of 10 February). Note that earlier on this same day the Treasury had brought in a list naming the goldsmiths on whose behalf the Mint had recently coined massive quantities of guineas. Second, on 6 March the House formally accepted the latter resolution (plus two new ones: to increase the size of the loan and to make the Bank of England's funding dependent upon the success of its competitor) and ordered that they be implemented in a draft bill. Finally, on 18 March the House approved the basic form of the bill and sent it forward to a committee of the whole for fine-tuning. The three main Treasury initiatives for raising the coin and/or setting an official price on guineas were undertaken, respectively, just after the land-bank project reached the foregoing three procedural milestones. The court party had the guineas question put off for a time when it was first raised in the House on 21 January. Instead the first serious debate on that issue occurred on 13 February: the very long session running well into the night and at which Montagu proposed raising the coin and setting guineas at 25s. The Treasury's second attempt to raise the silver coin came on 10 March: a move that clearly failed, resulting in the bill under discussion being stripped of the clauses for encouraging milled and heavy coin into the Mint (i.e. for raising the coin) and becoming henceforth a measure pertaining only to silver plate. Finally, on 19 March there was one last effort to get the clauses for milled and heavy coin back into the bill; and the Commons very narrowly defeated a measure to fix guineas at 25s.

On my reading, then, the Treasury whigs had thrice tried to split the goldsmith-banker camp off from the larger group supporting the creation of a national land bank. And three times they had failed. The goldsmiths chose to keep their support behind the land-bank group, seeing in this the more certain prospect for realizing a substantial gain on their specie holdings.[28] But the Jacobite plot to assassinate William presented the Treasury whigs with one last strategy: to get the Commons to agree to lower guineas all the way to 22s. This would have been understood by all concerned as a measure of support for the war and for the current administration. As such, it was an outcome that probably wouldn't have been attainable were it not for William's new popularity after the failed assassination attempt. This strategy was implemented on 26 March, at third reading of the plate bill. L'Hermitage maintained that this new development led the goldsmiths suddenly to lose all their enthusiasm for the land-bank project. It also led two land-bank supporters, Temple and Barbon, suddenly to publish pamphlets in which they publicly declared their support for raising the silver coin. Putting the pieces together, the Treasury had now thrown its support behind retaining the existing Mint standard and keeping guineas low, in the hopes of discouraging goldsmith-banker participation in the land-bank project. They had accepted that the land-bank project would be going ahead and were now doing their best to discourage subscriptions by the goldsmiths. This required that for the rest of the session and on into the summer, they position themselves as having been defenders of the currency's integrity all along. The Treasury whigs' new strategy forced the bank's remaining supporters, country politicians and bank projectors, to reposition themselves. Until now they had been opposed to raising the coin. For their best hopes lay in the current monetary situation, which made the value of guineas very uncertain and so would give goldsmiths and others a strong inducement to subscribe them into the land bank as a way of avoiding the losses they would suffer if the market price of guineas should fall. But now, late in the day and with the loss on guineas already having been suffered by all, they needed rather to raise expectations of the coin being raised and hopefully to restore uncertainty about the future value of guineas. For this would keep guineas and heavy silver coin in hoard and so strengthen the bank's hand in forthcoming negotiations with the Treasury over the terms of their loan. But others seem to have concluded the bank was now doomed to fail. In March the project lost ground and eventually ceded primacy to Montagu's Exchequer-bills scheme. So by the end of the session the Treasury whigs had maneuvered the bank's supporters into a corner. Any option for subscribers to have their guineas or heavy coin taken in at a premium price had now been foreclosed. In order to attract the requisite quantity of subscriptions, they must find some other way of inducing the goldsmiths to sign on. This would require wresting financial concessions from the Treasury: an institution dominated by some of the very men who most wanted to see them fail. The next chapter is a study of how that contest played itself out.

I am not arguing that parliamentary debates on raising the coin or lowering guineas were nothing but quiet struggles over the prospects for a national land bank. Many MPs would have been utterly unaware of the bigger questions at issue and voted on a given measure for reasons of their own. For instance, many of those who plumped for raising the coin did so because they hoped thereby to undermine William's ability to fight a war on the continent.[29] And others may well have been moved to vote in the opposite direction by Locke's argument that raising the coin would constitute a massive subsidy to the monied interest, financed ultimately by landed men. Nevertheless, most MPs were pawns in a larger chess game being played out between the Treasury whigs and supporters of the land bank. The interests, attitudes and prejudices of run-of-the-mill MPs, though hard facts that needed to be taken into account, were all the same being marshalled and manipulated to advance or obstruct larger objectives set out by higher-level politicians.

Notes

1 Horsefield, *British Monetary Experiments*, p. 61.
2 See Li; *Great Recoinage*, pp. 122–29; Horsefield, *British Monetary Experiments*, pp. 73–90; Davison and Keirn, 'John Locke'; and Kelly, Introduction to *Locke on Money*, pp. 33–34.
3 Rubini, 'Politics'; *CTB, Introduction*, pp. xli–lxxiii.
4 Pincus and Wolfram, 'Proactive State?'.
5 The following short account draws upon Kenyon, *Robert Spencer*, pp. 269–77; Horwitz, *Parliament*, pp. 155, 160, 164–66; Rubini, 'Politics'; and Lees, 'Parliament'.
6 Letter of 17 Dec. 1694, Blathwayt Letters to Hill.
7 After its failure, Sunderland defended his support of the National Land Bank on the grounds that 'he thought it would engage the tories in interest to support the government' (Burnet, *History*, p. 4:308). In mid-February 1696, when the whig junto's fortunes were at their very lowest, the king sent for the Duke of Leeds (RCHM, *Hastings Manuscript*, p. 2:255), Nottingham returned to London to pay William court at Kensington (l'Hermitage Reports, 21 Feb. 1696) and there were rumours that they and other tories would soon be returning to office (Horwitz, *Parliament*, p. 166).
8 Burnet, *History*, p. 4:317n.
9 'May it please your lordshipps', memo of 29 Jan. 1695, Mint Papers, fol. 108. Kelly was first to notice the inconsistencies between this memorandum and the later *Report* (Intro. to *Locke on Money*, pp. 106–9). He concluded the *Report* was a statement of the Treasury's official, rather than Lowndes' own, views.
10 The proposal came from Gervaize. The manuscript version hasn't survived. But judging from the description provided in Lowndes' review, it was almost identical to a document that Gervaize published anonymously during the 1695–96

parliamentary session (namely 'A proposal to have all the silver money of England melted down ...', in Gervaize, *Proposal*, pp. 10–29).

11 Gervaize proposed that the Treasury warn everyone hammered coin was going to be demonetized in two years' time and offer to take it off their hands in the meantime for more than it would be worth as mere bullion. To cover the resulting losses, the Treasury should raise the denomination of the silver coin by one-third. To discourage clipping in the interim, compensation should depend on the weight of the clipped coin being submitted. And for their coin, holders should get transferable, interest-bearing bills.

12 This literature is summarized in Horsefield, *British Monetary Experiments*, chapter 5, section IV.

13 RCHM, *Hastings Manuscripts*, pp. 4:310–12. Note that the editor mistakenly dated these minutes to Feb. 1695. They clearly come from Dec. 1695. Judging from the *Commons Journals*, this discussion probably took place on 4 Dec. 1695.

14 *CJ*, 10 Dec. 1695.

15 Bonnet Reports, 10/20 Dec. 1695.

16 L'Hermitage Reports, 20/30 Dec. 1695.

17 Bonnet Reports, 13/23 Dec. 1695.

18 de Beer, *Correspondence*, p. 475. I am following de Beer's guess that the unnamed person to whom Freke referred in this letter was 'the monkey' featured in other letters of Locke's College. And I agree with Kelly that the monkey was Montagu, not Godolphin as some have alleged; see Kelly, 'Monkey Business'.

19 Letter of 7 Jan. 1696, in de Beer, *Correspondence*, p. 507.

20 *CJ*, 28 Oct. 1696.

21 Luttrell, *Brief Historical Relation*, 15 Dec. 1696. Luttrell later reported on the trial in entries for 14 Feb. 1699 and 6 July 1699.

22 Intro. to *Locke on Money*, pp. 33–4.

23 Letter to Locke, 30 Nov. 1695, in de Beer, *Correspondence*, p. 470.

24 Letter to Locke, 2 Jan. 1696, in de Beer, *Correspondence*, p. 500.

25 Letter of Locke to Freke and Clarke, 14 Feb. 1696, in de Beer, *Correspondence*, p. 540.

26 Letter to Locke, 2 Jan. 1696, in de Beer, *Correspondence*, p. 500.

27 *Acts* 19:23–41.

28 It is possible that the goldsmiths were quite willing to accept Montagu's offer but that the two groups, working together, were unable to persuade a majority of MPs to vote for raising the coin. But I consider this unlikely, since there are no traces in the available record of goldsmith-bankers pushing for such an outcome. Judging by reports from Locke's College, land-bank supporters contented themselves rather with arguments for keeping guineas high.

29 Thus two pamphlets against keeping the existing Mint standard bear the marks of being Jacobite productions. The anonymous author of *Money's Mischievous Pilgrimage* alleged that the Dutch had been responsible for most of the clipping and melting and that the recoinage had been designed only to amass all the nation's specie in the Exchequer – much of it to be sent overseas, leaving precious little 'current money' for England itself (pp. 1–3). He predicted that the resulting great scarcity of coin would lead to public rioting by the poor. By implication, raising the coin would have helped keep England's poor well supplied with 'current money'. And *An Abstract of the Consultations and Debates Between the French King and His Council*, dated 12 Dec. 1695, pretends to give inside information of a fantastic French conspiracy to take advantage of England's decision to retain the current Mint standard. Specifically, Louis XIV had arranged to finance an organized ring of agents who would melt and export English specie in an endless arbitrage cycle until the kingdom was entirely drained of all its money.

Bibliography

Manuscript sources

British Library
    Add. MS. 17677 OO-QQ ('l'Hermitage Reports')
    Add. MS 18759 ('Mint Papers')
    Add. MS 56241 ('Blathwayt Letters to Hill')
Geheimes Staatsarchiv, Preußischer Kulturbesitz, Berlin
    I. HA Geheimer Rat, Rep. 11, Nr. 1792–1811 ('Bonnet Reports')

Printed primary sources

An Abstract of the Consultations and Debates Between the French King and His Council, Concerning the New Coyne and Coynage That Is Intended to Be Made in England Wherein Is Contain'd the Political Designs, and Great Hopes the French King and His Council Have to Ruin the English Nation in Divesting and Draining Them of Their New Coyn as Soon as Coyn'd. London: [s.n.], 1695.

Burnet, Gilbert. *History of His Own Time: With Notes by the Earls of Dartmouth and Hardwicke, Speaker Onslow, and Dean Swift: To Which Are Added Other Annotations.* Vol. 4. Ed. Martin Joseph Routh. Oxford: University Press, 1833.

De Beer, E. S. (ed.). *The Correspondence of John Locke.* Vol. 5. Oxford: Clarendon Press, 1979.

[Gervaize, Lewis]. *A Proposal for Amending the Silver Coins of England, and the Possibility of It, Without Any Great Charge to the Nation: Demonstrated in Two Different Ways.* London: printed for the author and to be sold by R. Baldwin, 1696.

[Grascome, Samuel]. *Account of the Proceedings in the House of Commons in Relation to the Recoining the Clipp'd Money, and Falling the Price of Guineas.* [London: s.n., 1696].

Great Britain. Parliament. House of Commons. *Journals of the House of Commons.* London: House of Commons, 1803. Accessed online at http://www.british-history.ac.uk/commons-jrnl/.

Great Britain. Public Record Office. *Calendar of Treasury Books. Introduction to Vols. XI-XVII Covering the Years 1695–1702.* Edited by William Shaw. London: HMSO, 1934.

Great Britain. Royal Commission on Historical Manuscripts. *Report on the Manuscripts of the Late Reginald Rawdon Hastings, Esq., of the Manor House, Ashby de la Zouch.* Volume II. Edited by Francis Bickley. London: HMSO, 1930.

[Locke, John]. *Further Considerations Concerning Raising the Value of Money: Wherein Mr. Lowndes's Arguments for It in His Late Report Containing an Essay for the Amendment of the Silver Coins, Are Particularly Examined.* London: Awnsham & John Churchill, 1695.

Lowndes, William. *A Report Containing an Essay for the Amendment of the Silver Coins.* London: printed by Charles Bill and the executrix of Thomas Newcomb, deceas'd, printers to the kings most excellent majesty, 1695.

Luttrell, Narcissus. *A Brief Historical Relation of State Affairs from September 1678 to April 1714.* 6 vols. Oxford: Oxford University Press, 1857.

Money's Mischievous Pilgrimage: Or, Some Considerations Touching the Ill State of the Coyn of the Kingdom: In a Letter from the Country. [London: s.n., 1696].

Reflections Upon a Scandalous Libel Entituled, An Account of the Proceedings of the House of Commons, in Relation to the Re-Coyning the Clipp'd Money, and Falling the Price of Guinea's. London: printed and sold by the booksellers of London and Westminster, 1697.

Secondary sources

Davison, Lee, and Tim Keirn. 'John Locke, Edward Clarke and the 1696 Guineas Legislation'. *Parliamentary History* 7, no. 2 (1988): 228–40.

Horsefield, John Keith. *British Monetary Experiments, 1650–1710.* Cambridge: Harvard University Press, 1960.

Horwitz, Henry. *Parliament, Policy and Politics in the Reign of William III.* Newark: University of Delaware Press, 1977.

Kelly, Patrick Hyde. Introduction to *Locke on Money*, by John Locke, 1–121. Oxford: Clarendon Press, 1991.

Kelly, Patrick Hyde. '"Monkey" Business: Locke's "College" Correspondence and the Adoption of the Plan for the Great Recoinage'. *Locke Studies* 9 (2009): 139–66.

Kenyon, John P. *Robert Spencer, Earl of Sunderland, 1641–1702.* London: Longmans, Green, 1958.

Lees, R. M. 'Parliament and the Proposal for a Council of Trade, 1695–6'. *English Historical Review* 54 (1939): 38–66.

Li, Ming-Hsun. *The Great Recoinage of 1696 to 1699.* London: Weidenfeld and Nicolson, 1963.

Pincus, Steve, and Alice Wolfram. 'A Proactive State? The Land Bank, Investment and Party Politics in the 1690s'. In *Regulating the British Economy, 1660–1850*, edited by Perry Gauci, 41–62. Farnham, Surrey and Burlington, VT: Ashgate, 2011.

Rubini, Dennis. 'Politics and the Battle for the Banks, 1688–1697'. *English Historical Review* 85 (1970): 693–714.

12 Monetary and financial crisis in England and the plight of the English army in Flanders, spring–summer 1696

In this chapter I describe how the struggle played out between the two camps most interested in the fate of the National Land Bank: the Treasury whigs and the financiers allied with the bank. It was a back and forth contest in which at times one or the other party seemed to have triumphed only to be undone by a surprising turn of events. In the end neither side won but Montagu was able to turn the situation very much to the advantage of the Bank of England – an outcome that simply would not have been possible when the conflict began. But first, in the opening two sections, I sketch the lead-up to, and the actual outbreak of, the severe monetary crisis through which England suffered in the second half of 1696. For that crisis was deliberately incited by the two parties, each for their own ends, and shaped the course of the conflict between them.

Monetary difficulties before 4 May

The recoinage act, passed on 21 January 1696, did not at first have much positive impact on the 'ill state of the coin'. The market price of silver bullion had fallen earlier in the month, perhaps because after 1 January clipped crowns and half-crowns lost much of their currency. But not until the summer did guineas and gold and silver bullion return to the prices that had been normal before the public began losing confidence in clipped coin (see Figures 12.1 and 12.2). And while the Amsterdam and Antwerp exchange rates improved somewhat in January 1696, they declined again in February and remained abnormally low until mid-summer (see Figure 12.3).

This sort of inertia in London's monetary markets suggests that mere passage of the recoinage act had done little to end fears the silver coin might be raised and/or clipped silver demonetized. It may have had to do too with the fact that little other specie was available besides clipped coin. Very little heavy money, either old or new, was making its way into circulation. By contemporary accounts, broad hammered coin remained in hoard at least until late in the year. New milled coin was relatively slow in issuing from the Mint: by the end of March 1696 only £199 thousand.[1] Abbott described the resulting confusion to Hill:

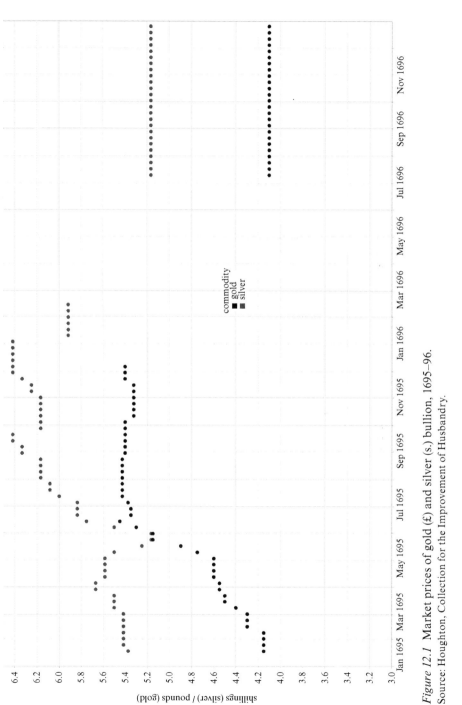

Figure 12.1 Market prices of gold (£) and silver (s.) bullion, 1695–96.
Source: Houghton, Collection for the Improvement of Husbandry.

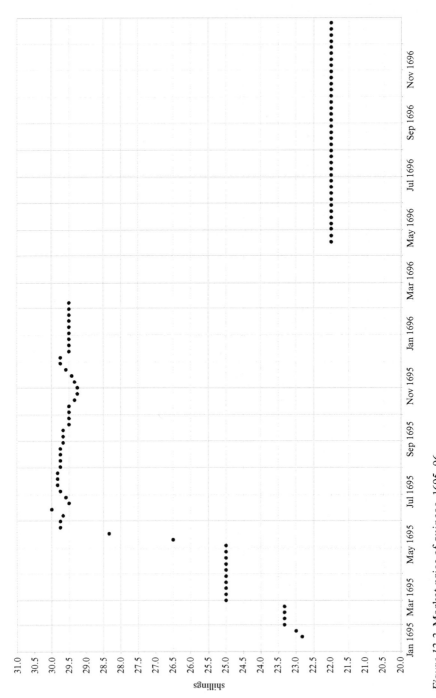

Figure 12.2 Market price of guineas, 1695–96.
Source: Houghton, Collection for the Improvement of Husbandry.

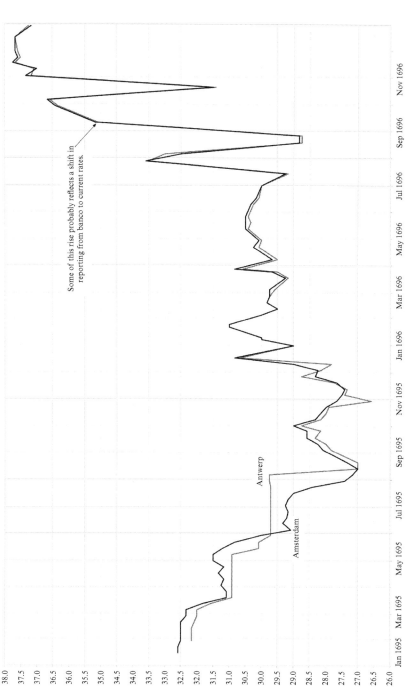

Figure 12.3 London-Amsterdam and London-Antwerp exchange rates, 1695–96.
Source: Houghton, Collection for the Improvement of Husbandry.

You cannot imagine the perplexity we have been and are still in here about our coin ... [A]ll refuse to take the clipped money and we have little else yet passing and guineas continue a dead stock. Some will receive payments on foreign bills [of exchange] only in the Bank of England's notes. Others will not meddle with them but demand [the notes of] the Orphans Fund [another London bank], and there are others will take neither but must have some particular goldsmith's notes. Of all these sorts I have had to do with in the paying of your bills. And it has cost me all this day (as it has done several before) to find out ways to humour 'em all.[2]

The Treasury was already in serious trouble long before the monetary crisis proper broke out in May. This was the result of certain specific features of the recoinage act. It required that all of the clipped money currently in the Exchequer be inventoried, melted down and shipped off to the Mint for recoining. This exercise was carried out in mid-February.[3] Furthermore, whatever money came into the Exchequer thereafter, whether upon loan or in payment of taxes, had likewise to be counted, melted and recoined before any of it could be used. Paterson, writing of this period a few months later, captured the problem very succinctly: 'The king has his coffers full but can make no use of it faster than it is new coined'.[4] Treasury officials, if they hadn't foreseen the resulting difficulties, must have become aware of them very early on. For they had to proceed very differently in fiscal year 1695–96 than they had done in years previous. In the first half of 1695 about two-thirds of all Treasury issues to military paymasters were in specie; by comparison in the first half of 1696 almost all issues were in the form of tallies of fictitious loan.[5] Although we have no systematic records to confirm it, Exchequer tallies must have been falling to significant discounts already in the early months of 1696. Certainly by mid-April the Bank of England was complaining that 'other banks' were discounting tallies at rates of 8 to 12 percent.[6]

The Treasury's problems in turn made life very difficult for military officials. For instance, in February Abbott warned they were going to have trouble sustaining the credit of the bills that Hill in Flanders was drawing upon London to pay for the army's subsistence. Though Ranelagh had been issued funding to answer the bills, it was given in tallies, which at that time no one wanted to accept. 'And the [tax] receivers having no currency and the new money coming out so slowly[,] payments are miserably obstructed'.[7] Similarly, in March the chief officers in the ordnance complained to the treasury lords that they were unable to raise any cash from the tallies they had received and begged for some ready money instead. The Lords responded that by the terms of the recoinage statute it was 'morally impossible to provide ready money at this time because the clipped money (according to the Act) is to be melted down and recoined and when coined must be paid to the several lenders as far as it will go'.[8]

Remittances for the English army in Flanders were also adversely affected well before the crisis proper hit in May. Figure 5.2 shows a sharp decline in the

funding being provided to Hill in Flanders after February 1696. Figure 12.4
shows that this happened not because the Bank stopped remitting bills of
exchange but rather because it cut way back on the frequency with which it
was issuing letters of credit payable at the Antwerp Agency. Few records have
survived of the negotiations between Bank and Treasury on this point. But
it seems very likely that the sharp decline in new credits was in part a result
of the recoinage process itself. Like everyone else, the Bank needed to get its
clipped silver into the Exchequer somehow if it was to avoid suffering large
losses once such coin was reduced to its value by weight. This no doubt is
why, on 18 February, a large part of its specie holdings was converted into
£235 thousand in new public loans and a further £230 thousand in discounted
tallies.[9] The general ledger shows that the Bank's cash holdings fell by about
£300 thousand, or roughly in half, that day (see Figure 3.2). Of course the
Bank would get some of this money back down the road. For by the terms of
the recoinage statute, lenders on Exchequer tallies were first in line for any
new milled coin coming out of the Mint – though they would get only as much
as their clipped coin made when melted down and recoined. But in the meantime, with its specie reserves now greatly diminished, so too was the Bank's
capacity for lending to the Exchequer or for buying foreign bills of exchange
(even if it tried to do so in notes rather than with specie). Normally it could
count upon its remittance operations and tally redemptions to replenish its
store of coin. But in these special times the Treasury had no specie for the
Bank or for anyone else, other than what it was compelled by statute to distribute to Exchequer lenders as their formerly-clipped money came out of the
Mint. This is why, at a meeting with the Treasury in mid-April on the remittances, Bank directors reported that they would be unable to issue Ranelagh
any further letters of credit 'unless they have new money or guineas'.[10] In
other words, they couldn't take payment in tallies or lend the necessary funding; the Treasury would have to pay for any new credits up front in actual
coin. But of course the Treasury too had very little disposable specie at this
time, since by law the Exchequer was compelled to distribute to tally holders
any new money coming out of the Mint. Later that day the treasury lords did
ask John Knight and Bartholomew Burton, cashiers for customs and excise
respectively, if they could convert Ranelagh's tallies into money. (This was
legal since a portion of those revenues was the king's own property and so
was not governed by the terms of the recoinage statute.) Knight and Burton
reported that they could, but warned that they had nothing but clipped silver
for the purpose. Since at this point the date for demonetizing clipped silver in
general circulation was only two weeks away, such an offer would have been
of very little use. A few days later the Treasury asked Knight and Burton instead to secure £30 thousand in guineas[11] – a sum that was later increased to
£40 thousand (since this is the amount that shows up in Hill's general ledger
as cash received from the Bank in May). William then ordered the Treasury
to supply this money to the Bank to assist in its remittance operations.[12] Note
that according to Bonnet the Treasury was unable to obtain guineas at the

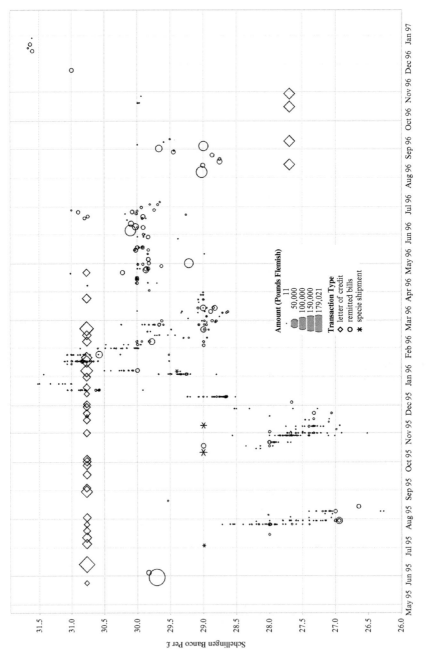

Figure 12.4 Bank transactions with the Antwerp Agency, by exchange rate, 1695–96.
Source: Bank General Ledger 2.

legislated rate of 22s. Instead, to keep within the letter of the law, it instructed goldsmiths to melt the coin down and then bought the resulting bullion from them at an escalated price equivalent to 25s. per guinea.[13]

A genuine monetary crisis breaks out, summer 1696

Sometime in early May, England began to suffer from a sudden collapse of public confidence in paper currencies of all kinds: notes of the Bank and of goldsmiths, foreign and inland bills of exchange and Exchequer tallies. Contemporaries traced this development to a deliberate and sustained attack by London goldsmiths upon the Bank of England. In this judgement they may have been mistaken; specie would have been sufficiently scarce after 4 May to make a spontaneous liquidity crisis perfectly possible. But, as we shall see, the thesis fits with the broad outlines of the monetary politics of these months. And government leaders certainly thought that the goldsmiths had been involved, summoning some of their leaders to Whitehall for a good tongue lashing.

The crisis began when the Bank's cash reserves came under marked pressure. As Figure 3.2 demonstrates, the cash account started upon a steady decline after 24 April. In the first couple of weeks, some of this was of the Bank's own doing. The directors bought about £50 thousand in tallies and £10 thousand in bills of exchange in late April and loaned £50 thousand to the Exchequer on 8 May; presumably they used clipped coin for these purposes, hoping to offload any remaining holdings at face value while they still could. But Figure 3.2 clearly shows that after 1 May the biggest part of the decline in the cash account was caused by a large number of Bank notes returning for encashment. On 6 May, so many people demanded to have new milled money for their notes that the Bank was unable to pay them all.[14] The governor was forced to put in a personal appearance to calm the situation. He tried to persuade people to accept partial payment for now, promising that they would be paid the rest as soon as the Bank was supplied with more milled coin from the Exchequer. Indeed, around this time the Bank introduced a formal system of rotating 10 percent payments on its outstanding notes, designed to distribute its supply of milled coin (continuously replenished from the Exchequer) as equitably as possible to all note holders. This system was to remain in place for months, forcing note holders to queue up and invest large amounts of time to get even a small amount of cash.[15]

The run on the Bank was started by London goldsmiths,[16] inducing a kind of war between the two camps. For the past three months some goldsmiths had accumulated large quantities of Bank notes, intending to present the latter all at once as soon as clipped coin was no longer legal tender. On the appointed day one group alone brought in notes totalling £30 thousand; more requests came from other goldsmiths. The Bank promptly retaliated. The next day, a committee of directors was ordered to meet daily to 'settle the accounts with the goldsmiths', i.e. to demand cash for any outstanding balance of goldsmith notes.[17] But goldsmiths, pleading the Bank's example, claimed that they too did not have enough gold or good silver money to answer their notes. They started paying out only in clipped sixpence coins – which by the terms of the recoinage statute were still legal tender.[18] This had the additional advantage of being time-consuming and troublesome – discouraging many from asking for payment in the first place. Contemporaries suspected that goldsmiths had ample supplies of good coin and were merely hoarding it for their own selfish reasons. L'Hermitage noted for instance that they invariably furnished specie if someone offered them Bank notes at a discount.[19] The situation was aggravated by some foreign-exchange dealers (Sephardic Jews from Portugal, whom contemporaries usually labelled simply as 'the Jews'). They too began refusing payment in notes, of the Bank and goldsmiths alike, and insisted instead upon having milled coin.[20] They were also offering lower rates for bills of exchange when payment was tendered in Bank bills rather than in specie.[21]

Both l'Hermitage and the lords justices thought the goldsmiths were actuated by 'malice' toward the Bank for having made such major inroads into the business of government lending – formerly an area in which they had dominated. Specifically, over the past two years their own credit had declined in proportion as the Bank's had grown.[22] Resentment may well have come into it. But the goldsmiths more likely had the interests of the prospective National Land Bank in view. By bringing the Bank's notes and bills under pressure and draining it of as much specie as possible, they may have hoped to weaken the Bank, at least for a while, as a source of alternative funding for the Treasury (whether directly on war loans or in support of the credit of Exchequer bills). This would make the Treasury more dependent, in the coming weeks and months, upon whatever funding the National Land Bank could hope to provide, and so strengthen the hand of the land-bank commissioners in the negotiations soon to commence on the terms of the impending subscription drive.

Whatever the motivations at work, the lords justices were not amused. They summoned some of the offenders and urged them to stop their current practices, which they interpreted as a deliberate attempt to weaken the credit of their competitors.[23] Shrewsbury, at the time the senior Secretary of State and William's leading minister, wrote the king about these meetings a few weeks later. 'We have taken what pains we could with the Bank, the merchants and the goldsmiths, exhorting some and threatening others, to endeavour to make them easy to one another in this common difficulty'.[24]

This exercise in moral suasion seems to have had very little positive effect. For the goldsmiths continued to hoard their coin and the Bank's specie reserve went on shrinking. In fact the situation quickly grew worse. Though by the recoinage statute both clipped sixpences and unclipped hammered coin remained legal tender, the general public soon began to refuse that kind of money too.[25] Now only guineas and milled silver would do. To aggravate matters, none of the new milled coin issuing from the Mint into the Exchequer, much of which the Bank was paying out in turn to its note-holders, was finding its way into general circulation. As l'Hermitage repeatedly observed throughout the summer, the state of the coin remained exactly as it had been in early May.[26] Finally, the decision by the Bank and goldsmiths to restrict payment on their notes led paper currencies of all kinds, their own included, to start going only at a discount. Since people could no longer be certain of getting coin for their Bank and goldsmith notes, everyone became reluctant to accept the latter currencies in payment of foreign or inland bills of exchange. This led in turn to a general scramble for other means of payment. Some people tried to get their creditors to accept bills of exchange (foreign or inland) drawn on merchants of good reputation. But specie was now sufficiently scarce that even wealthy merchants soon found it hard to honour their bills. So everyone began demanding payment in specie or insisting upon a discount whenever debtors had naught but paper money to offer. Bonnet reports that Bank notes were being discounted at 3 to 4 percent already in the third week of May.[27] Paterson later claimed that the discount on Bank and goldsmith notes fluctuated a great deal that summer, hovering sometimes around 5 to 6 percent but at other times in the ranges of 10 to 12 and 16 to 18 percent.[28] Exchequer tallies, which were being discounted even before 4 May, were now subjected to even higher discount rates. In late May, Bonnet claimed that even tallies on the best funds and with six months or less to maturity were being discounted at 12 to 15 percent, and representatives of the ordnance office reported having to offer a discount of 18 percent on their tallies of fictitious loan.[29]

The correspondence of Roger Hoar, a merchant at Bridgewater, illustrates the pressures at work.[30] The Excise Office in London was holding one of Hoar's bills, for the large sum of £140, and refused to accept payment in anything but coin. Hoar's agent in London, one Obadiah Grevill, asserted that the bill wouldn't have been a problem were anyone else holding it. Had he accompanied it with the offer of just £4 or £5 in specie, many would have been happy to accept the bill as good payment. But the Excise Office was unyielding. Grevill tried to borrow some specie for Hoar but found this 'morally impossible'; there was so little coin around that it might cost Hoar 10 percent to borrow so large a sum for even a month. Grevill had pressed one of Hoar's London debtors, a certain Fisher, to pay half his outstanding bill in specie – explaining that the money was needed to pay Hoar's bill at the Excise lest it be returned protested for non-payment. Fisher responded that most London merchants had stopped worrying about having their bills protested. In normal times this would have been a real blow to their reputations. But he himself had had £1 thousand of his bills returned from the Excise in the last while and didn't care. He would rather see another £10 thousand of his bills protested than submit to their demands for payment in specie. He hoped others would likewise refuse to capitulate. Grevill even tried to offer payment in inland bills of exchange drawn upon Sir Stephen Evance and Sir John Foche, two of the Excise Commissioners. Though those men were at the meeting that day and it caused them great embarrassment to have to refuse their own bills in payment, the commissioners continued to insist on payment entirely in specie. Grevill concluded that Hoar must either send up the necessary cash, let Grevill discount his bill for a 10 percent loss or suffer the bill to be returned protested.

The eventual result, as the payments system came under increasing strain, was a widespread stop of trade. Discounts on paper money gave everyone a strong incentive to hold onto as much as possible of the specie that came through their hands, lest they too be caught short and have to offer a discount on their own paper assets. But the more coin was hoarded, the more reluctant were people to accept paper currencies, generating a vicious circle. It was simply impossible both for everyone to hold onto all their coin and for everyone's bills to be paid in specie. And without ready money to pay suppliers, some simply became unable to keep their businesses going. Again the correspondence of Hoar's merchant company illustrates the process. One of their salt wholesalers (Thomas Minshull) wrote that his customers at Liverpool were refusing to pay in ready money and offering only inland bills of exchange on London. He had no use for such bills because he seldom needed to make payments in London – his excise-tax obligations being the only exception. Conversely, he very much needed coin, because his suppliers were 'poor men' who dealt only in small sums, far smaller than those for which the average bill of exchange was written. So he begged Hoar & Co. several times to pay him half in bills and half in coin. Failing that, he would be forced, with the greatest reluctance, to give up their business.

The monetary crisis also had very grave knock-on effects for the military campaign then under way in Flanders. As Figure 12.4 shows, that spring the Bank had supplied only two relatively small credits: one in March and the other in April. They had agreed to send the latter, for £20 thousand, only after Burton had promised to furnish the Bank with £10 thousand in guineas.[31] In late April the Treasury began negotiating with the Bank to supply a further £100 thousand.[32] This was to be handled in an unusual way. Instead of issuing a letter of credit authorizing Hill to collect funds from de Coninck in Antwerp, the Bank's directors would instruct their agents on the continent to draw bills upon them for payment in London in two months and provide Hill with the cash proceeds. The Bank thought it might be able to supply £80 thousand to £100 thousand in this way (Figure 5.1 shows that it raised a little better than £100 thousand). In return the directors demanded an entry in the Treasury minutes that when the bills came due for payment in two months, the Treasury would provide the necessary cash – paying whatever exchange rates had been negotiated on the bills. As further security, the Treasury also agreed to deposit £120 thousand in wine-tax tallies with the Bank. But even this substantial new tranche of funding did not improve the situation very much. When Abbott wrote Hill to report the new credits, he noted: 'we have not yet (with this £100,000) fully cleared [army subsistence payments for] March nor sent you anything on the account of April'.[33] William, who had left for Flanders as soon as possible after the parliamentary session ended, wrote Shrewsbury in London around this same time to re-port that the English army was in a bad way and to order the Treasury to give immediate attention to the matter. Shrewsbury replied that the lords justices, including Godolphin, had discussed the problem that morning but were not optimistic.[34] Goldsmiths and Bank officials had given 'the dismall-est accounts' of the state of credit in London. In short, it would be all but impossible under the present circumstances to raise any further supplies for the army. The only thing the lords justices thought might help was to call parliament into session as soon as possible to pass an act for restoring currency to clipped money. But Shrewsbury advised William against such a policy. It was the very fear that clipped coin would be remonetized that 'locks up all the gold and good money'; in other words, no one wanted to lend their good money if there was a chance they would be repaid in clipped coin valued by tale. And letting clipped money back into circulation 'would be to undo all that has been done'. William replied in turn that he could see another option: Lowndes' original proposal of raising the silver coin and setting guineas at 24s. or 25s. He acknowledged that he had worked against this outcome in the spring. But 'I now see, too late, that I was in the wrong' and that this was now the only remaining option for securing Exchequer loans. He urged Shrewsbury not to 'be too scrupulous'; 'for all will be lost if credit be not soon found to pay the fleet and the army, especially the troops who are in these parts'. He asked Shrewsbury to do everything possible to assemble parliament in June to pass an act for raising the coin.[35]

Negotiations with the National Land Bank

I turn now to the negotiations that got under way in May between the Treas-ury and the commissioners for the prospective National Land Bank. The salt-tax act had opened the door for the Treasury to begin borrowing right away by means of Exchequer bills – indeed seemed even to assume that this is how it would go. But in fact this option was put off until after the final deadline of 24 June set out in the recoinage act. For otherwise all loan con-tributions would have been made in clipped silver – forcing further large losses upon the crown.[36] Instead the Treasury elected at first to see whether a loan would be forthcoming from a successful National Land Bank.

Commissioners for the bank began meeting with the Treasury toward the end of May to work out a few vital details in preparation for opening their subscription books.[37] These negotiations were headed up by Sir Joseph Herne, Sir Thomas Cook and Sir Thomas Meres. The first two were mon-eyed men with strong connections to the former tory administration. Herne we have already met as one of two goldsmith bankers handling remittances for the army earlier in the decade, but who had since been squeezed out of that line of business by the Bank of England. Cook, a goldsmith banker for many years, had been imprisoned during the parliamentary investiga-tion of 1694–95 for refusing to say what he knew about bribes offered to various members of parliament in 1693 in the quest to secure a new charter for the East India Company (of which he had been governor or deputy governor from 1690–95). Meres was a tory landowner who, during the reigns of Charles II and James II, had held a Commons seat and an important office but was now without either.

The commissioners may have thought they were in a very strong bargaining position. Now that the credit of the Bank of England was thoroughly broken, the Treasury would have no other prospect but a loan from the National Land Bank for raising the funds that William so desperately needed for the army in Flanders. And this in turn put them in line to demand large premia upon the various kinds of specie in which stock subscriptions to the new bank, and so the loan to the government, were to be paid. For in this time of monetary crisis they could argue, with perfect plausibility, that not otherwise would anyone agree to subscribe to the bank. Unless potential investors were confident that the minimum 50 percent target for subscriptions was likely to be attained, none would subscribe – knowing that without incorporation they would earn a far lower rate of return than they could get by discounting tallies instead. So the premia had to be large enough that everyone would know investors were likely to choose bank subscriptions over tally discounting. Which was for the commissioners the larger prize – high premia on their, and their colleagues', specie holdings or a charter for a large new joint-stock bank – is hard to know.

At first the commissioners requested only three concessions. First, they wanted the crown to take their clipped coin at face value, as long as the money was tendered before 24 June. In their estimation this was the key ingredient. There was still lots of clipped silver out there; people would flock to subscribe to the bank if given a chance to rid themselves of it at face value. (What they weren't saying is that prospective bank subscribers would have deliberately held back their clipped coin, not wanting to pay it into the Exchequer upon other loans and so strengthen the government's hand in the bargaining contest now underway.) Second, they wanted the right to take Bank bills on subscription payments, which meant in effect the right to pay such bills to the government in fulfilment of the first quarter instalment payment of their loan. Finally, they asked a premium of 10 percent for any guineas or broad money paid in before 24 June.[38] A few days later they softened the first request by offering to limit contributions in clipped coin to a quarter of the total subscription. But they also added two more asks: to have a mill in the Mint dedicated to coining any plate members might subscribe, and to have the bills of their own bank (once incorporated) be taken on the later instalments of the loan.[39]

The Treasury took these requests to the lords justices, who referred them in turn to the privy council. Everyone agreed that the first proposal was simply illegal. But about the rest there was disagreement. Given the urgency of the army's situation, the lords justices were prepared to consider any demand that wasn't illegal and urged the Treasury to strike a bargain.[40]

Godolphin thought the request for a prompt-payment premium reasonable. He acknowledged that it would be inconvenient to have to take Bank bills on the loan, since this currency was already at a 5 percent discount. But in his estimation the Treasury was better off accepting the commissioners' terms, however harsh, or 'we must take a noble resolution of having no money at all to remit, or to answer bills [drawn from Flanders], and consequently let the army starve'. On Godolphin's telling, however, others in the Treasury did not seem as 'uneasy' about the army's sorry state and were 'full of objections and difficulties' about the proposed terms.[41]

Late in the month the two sides met again.[42] Godolphin began by informing the commissioners that the lords justices would not approve the idea of taking payment in clipped money. But the Treasury was ready to give serious consideration to the rest of their requests. The commissioners insisted on being allowed to contribute a quarter of the loan in clipped coin. Otherwise, they claimed, potential subscribers, knowing that there was so little good-quality specie around, would have the bank at a marked disadvantage and insist upon a stiff premium for any contributions in guineas or milled coin. (More likely they were looking for a way to get out of a corner into which they had painted themselves by having previously refused to pay this clipped money into the Exchequer upon other loans.) The commissioners added that they had discovered a way around the legal obstacle to taking clipped money on their subscriptions. Until 24 June it was still permissible to lend clipped coin to the Exchequer. If the Treasury agreed to the idea in advance, their subscribers would lend their clipped money now (upon other funds), take Exchequer bills in return and offer the latter for the bank's final quarterly instalment payment. In return, the bank would commit to pay its second and third instalments in good specie. The crown would lose nothing on the deal because parliament would surely agree next session to make good any losses suffered from taking part of the loan in clipped coin. Though the treasury lords tried to move on, the commissioners insisted on having a verdict on whether this new strategy was legal. The Treasury promised to speak with the lords justices and get back to them.

Letters written that night by Godolphin and Montagu reveal that negotiations with the land bank commissioners concealed a bigger struggle within the Treasury over whether to use the bank or Exchequer bills to raise the new war loan.[43] Writing to high-level members of the court then in Flanders (William and Blathwayt respectively), both men argued for their preferred outcome on very strategic grounds: by portraying it as the army's best hope. And clearly both were also laying the groundwork for being able to blame the other side should the Treasury fail to find the necessary assistance. In Montagu's estimation, the latest meeting justified his earlier warnings that the land bank's supporters were intent upon doing the government harm. Now 'we are brought by these gentlemen to the greatest difficulties and straits that ever any government was in'. The attempt to set up a new bank had broken the credit of the old one. He claimed to have predicted exactly this: an outbreak of 'faction and party' between the two competing groups of financiers. 'While the monied men of one side are trying to make the run on the other, they have ruined themselves and destroyed all credit on both sides'. Supporters of the National Land Bank were also deliberately keeping back their guineas, both from anger at the losses they had sustained when the price was lowered and in hopes guineas would still be raised. The solution, Montagu urged, was to terminate the whole land-bank project right now and, by implication, move on instead to Exchequer bills. This would force guineas back into circulation; either that or land-bank supporters must 'continue in a very expensive obstinacy'. He closed by arguing that the army would suffer if the Treasury granted the land-bank commissioners' requests. He estimated their total cost at around £500 thousand (50 percent of the first quarter instalment of £641 thousand plus a 10 percent premium on the remaining three quarters). This loss would fall entirely upon the army, since the first £2.1 million of the loan had been strictly appropriated by the Commons for other purposes (the navy and paying interest to the Bank of England).

Godolphin, by contrast, maintained that he could see no other way of finding credit for the army besides the land bank. Those in the Treasury who opposed it were trying to make the commissioners out to be unreasonable in their demands. But the commissioners were being forced to such extremes by the current monetary crisis. The real reason no one else in the Treasury wanted to strike a deal with the land bank is because they 'are possessed with prejudices to the thing & to the persons of the men'. They were also opposing the bank on the mistaken assumption that once it was out of the way, 'they shall be able to set up a credit in the Exchequer from the same funds'. Godolphin believed the Exchequer-bills project would prove a perfect fantasy. And even if it didn't, any funds it provided (since they could not come in until at least 24 June) would arrive late to save the army. By implication, the Treasury had no choice but to grant the terms being offered by the land-bank group.

The lords justices met in late May or early June to discuss the commissioners' new version of their proposal for taking in clipped coin on land-bank subscriptions. No minutes have survived; but an undersecretary of state provided a second-hand report.[44] The Attorney General and Solicitor General began by giving their opinion. The new proposal was indeed legal. But the terms of the salt-tax act were such that the Exchequer must have the express instruction of the king, or in this case his representatives the lords justices, before they could take in any loans, whether in clipped money or otherwise. The lords justices then turned to the question whether to issue such an instruction. The consensus was against it, for two main reasons. First, if loans in clipped money were authorized, there was a risk that the Exchequer would be flooded with clipped coin up to the legislated maximum of £1.5 million, on which sum the king would lose half. Second, the money so contributed would be useless to the crown until it could be recoined. And this would take a long time. For there were already several millions in the Exchequer and by the terms of the recoinage act that money would have to be coined ahead of any money received from the land bank. So in the end the lords justices decided that they were unwilling to order the Treasury to accede to the bank's request.

On 2 June Godolphin delivered the bad news to the land-bank commissioners. The latter continued to press very hard for their measure, citing the view of their own lawyer that in this matter the Treasury could decide for itself and did not need approval from the lords justices. The Treasury minutes for this day are unusually verbose,[45] so that we are treated to Godolphin's wry rejoinder; 'it easy to get such an opinion of any counsel for a five guinea fee'. He added that even if legal, the idea had many disadvantages. Only with great difficulty did the treasury lords get the commissioners to set it aside and start discussing the specifics of their remaining requests. The Treasury began by proposing a concrete plan for an early-payment premium; the minutes cite no specific figure but explain that the premium was to be a per-diem rate – so that the earlier the payment, the larger the payoff. The two parties tussled for a time over the exact size and nature of the premium. The Treasury objected to the commissioners' next request: for taking in Bank of England bills as part of the loan. No one could get cash for Bank bills right now, so 'how shall they become effectual to their lordships and supply the soldiers with subsistence'? The commissioners responded, rather cleverly under the circumstances, that it would improve the Bank's credit should the Treasury agree to accept the Bank's bills for the new loan. Besides, the Bank's bills 'pass as money' and were going at a discount of only 5 percent. Then the commissioners had yet another go at their first proposition. They suggested that, only for bank subscribers, clipped money be taken in by weight as bullion, though with a substantial 'allowance'. They argued this was already being done for plate at the Mint so their case would be no different. They proposed a specific figure of 30 percent for said allowance. They again insisted that without some such measure the whole subscription must fail. Finally, the commissioners pressed for the land bank's own bills to be accepted on later instalments of the loan, once they were a corporation. The commissioners were confident that, though the bank's bills (they may have meant notes) would be payable on demand in specie, 'some of the money will stick and remain with them'. So they would be able to provide the Treasury with cash for their bills 'immediately when required'. The minutes record no final decision on any of the commissioners' requests. It seems rather, from a letter Godolphin wrote Blathwayt that night, that the two sides were feeling one another out and that the Treasury expected the next day to get a formal written proposal.[46] Godolphin warned that he expected his colleagues on the Treasury board to refuse to come to terms. '[F]or the difficulties of getting money will make them [viz. the commissioners] insist upon large demands & we shall be well enough contented to find them unreasonable & take our chance for what is to follow'.

Godolphin's prediction was entirely borne out in the ensuing two final days of negotiation.[47] The commissioners presented their proposals in the form of a written memorial. The Treasury complained that it was very general and did not even explain what was meant by their request for a 10 percent premium. Some of the bank's representatives said the latter figure applied to the whole of whatever they had paid in before the final date, while others thought it applied only to whatever the bank would have paid in before the deadline. The Treasury asked them to compare notes and come back later that day with a clear decision. They urged the commissioners also to make the premium gradual the way the Bank of England had done in 1694 – in other words, a per diem rate that would reward any prepayments in proportion to how early they arrived. Upon their return, the commissioners had altered their proposal to a sliding premium ranging from 5 to 15 percent, with the premium gradually declining as time passed. Montagu seems to have assumed that under these terms the whole loan would be contributed almost right away, so that a 15 percent premium would apply across the whole £2.6 million loan.[48] The treasury lords, Montagu claimed, all thought this 'very extravagant' and got the lords justices to agree, unanimously, that a premium of 5 percent – double what had been afforded to the Bank of England in 1694 – was 'a sufficient encouragement'. The Treasury made this its final offer and ordered the commissioners to commence taking subscriptions – contributing the first £5 thousand in William's name. Given this outcome the commissioners themselves were 'almost in despair of completing their subscriptions'. Luttrell claimed that 'most believe it will not be a bank'. Montagu reported, a day after the subscription books were opened on 4 June, that not a single shilling had been contributed. In his opinion, 'in all probability this project is at an end'. An army official explained that at first many considerable merchants, the East India Company and all the 'lesser banks' had appeared in support of the bank. But once the lords justices had declined the commissioners' demands, they declared themselves unwilling to subscribe.[49]

Again Montagu and Godolphin wrote their respective superiors in Flanders about the outcome, trying to position themselves as well as possible.[50] For Montagu this was, for now, a fairly easy task. He had claimed all along that the land-bank project was a diversion meant to do the king harm. Now he had only to maintain that its failure was none of his doing ('everything had been done to encourage them that could reasonably be expected and yet we were still disappointed') and promise that he would leave no stone unturned in trying to make the Exchequer-bills scheme succeed. He also strengthened his claim to be William's best conduit to war finance. Though the land-bank commissioners had failed the king, he observed, 'the Bank of England is still devoted to him'. Specifically, he was pleased to announce that by this day's post the Bank had sent Hill a credit for 1 million guilders (at the exchange rate agreed upon with the Treasury, about £105 thousand). Godolphin was in a much more difficult position. Throughout the 1695–96 parliamentary session he had espoused the cause of the land bank; its failure was now his as well. So he needed to persuade William that Montagu's interpretation was incorrect and self-serving. The land-bank commissioners really did want the subscription to succeed, he maintained. But they had been stymied by 'the little disposition they find to encourage & assist this bank in I may say almost all those whose countenance is necessary to it'. He even hinted that his opponents had engineered the current financial crisis in a deliberate attempt to sabotage the bank's chances of success. '[I]t's amazing that people should be so blind as not to see that the hasty falling [i.e. lowering] of the guineas must necessarily distress the credit'.[51] A fortnight later he added that the Bank of England had come through with an army loan at this time only 'to furnish an argument for not concluding [i.e. reaching an agreement] with the other [bank]'.[52] He would support the Exchequer-bills project, though only because there was no other alternative now. And, looking again to justify his earlier decision to back the land bank, he repeated his prediction that the Exchequer-bills scheme would fail. He considered it 'very improper at this conjuncture – a time when all paper credit goes at large discounts and everyone demands coin'.

Godolphin was right to have been worried. Upon learning that the subscription drive had failed, William criticized him for 'refusing to lay aside the land bank' project sooner than he had done.[53] And Blathwayt claimed that William now saw Montagu as 'undeniably' on his side, was 'fully satisfied of the truth' of his diagnosis and considered him 'more than justified from all the disappointments or misfortunes that have happened or may yet happen by the different measures that have been taken'.[54] Blathwayt fully accepted Montagu's version of events; 'the new bank have by their extravagant demands put themselves almost out of a capacity of serving the government'. Montagu must now do his best to find supplies by other means.[55]

The experiment with Exchequer bills

The lords justices gave the commissioners a few days to see how the subscription developed. But on 10 June, with only £1.6 thousand having arrived, they concluded that the land-bank project was now a 'real prejudice'. The very prospect of it had locked up specie that might otherwise have found its way into circulation. And it was distracting the administration from finding other ways of raising supplies. So they resolved to move on. The only option left now was 'to issue bills of credit upon the Exchequer'. For this they would have to wait until 24 June, to prevent the loans from being made in clipped coin. But in the meantime they would begin preparing against that day. Godolphin told William he was sure everyone would do their best to make the experiment succeed. But he couldn't resist adding that some would cooperate only so their 'obstruction' of the land bank 'may be the better justified'.[56]

For Exchequer bills to become widely accepted, the Treasury needed to furnish an adequate specie reserve. Already at their first meeting on the new project, the lords justices had given some thought to this problem. They considered authorizing the Treasury to offer prospective contributors a 5 percent premium for good coin – atop whatever rate of return they might earn on their loans proper. This would hardly be unfair. For, as one of them noted, the land bank's supporters had been given, and refused, the same offer.[57] Godolphin thought that a sum of £200 thousand in coin would suffice to circulate the bills. The problem was how to come by this much cash when specie was in very short supply generally and the Treasury had already committed to paying the Bank of England a further £200 thousand, in coin, before the end of July.[58]

But Montagu had already worked up a plan for generating the necessary specie reserve and supporting circulation of the bills more generally. On 23 June he sent a draft, via Blathwayt, for the king's inspection. No copy has survived. But judging from the description provided in Montagu's covering letter, a few details in Blathwayt's reply and the course of action subsequently pursued by the Treasury, it must have run along the following lines.[59] The Exchequer would borrow a £200 thousand specie reserve with which to make the bills payable on demand. To motivate potential lenders and overcome the continued reluctance of many to part with good coin, loan contributions would be accepted in clipped silver (fully demonetized since 24 June).[60] As a further inducement, the coin would be taken in by weight at a premium price, some 10 percent above its current market value as bullion. Lenders would be granted tallies paying interest at 7 percent. With a specie reserve in place or at least well on the way, the Treasury could begin issuing out Exchequer bills to its paymasters, who would offer them in payment to creditors. Hopefully, paying interest at 4.5 percent, most of them would be held as short-term investments, so that there would be relatively little call upon the Exchequer's specie reserve. Montagu also lined up assistance in four cities somewhat distant from London. Men were appointed in each centre and given the task of raising their own small specie reserves to permit encashment of Exchequer bills locally.[61] Further, the Treasury would send some of the proceeds from the £200 thousand loan to the country mints. There it could be offered in exchange for any clipped coin submitted locally, which could then be recoined in turn, hopefully starting a kind of chain reaction. Montagu warned that it would still be exceptionally difficult to make the project work. He believed however that William could put its success beyond doubt by getting the Dutch States General to prohibit their citizens from protesting foreign bills of exchange if payment was offered in Exchequer bills. Given that so many merchants, and the Bank of England, were currently experiencing great difficulties on this front, such a feature would make everyone positively eager to accept the new currency.

Blathwayt wrote back that both he and the king considered Montagu's design 'certainly very good and ... the best that can be thought of'.[62] But

Blathwayt feared there was a great deal of 'malice' at work and that 'all those that deal in money', other than the Bank of England, would 'endeavour to defeat & disappoint it'. In his estimation, not enough was being offered to buy the cooperation of such antagonists: just '4½ percent on bills & 7 percent on tallies'. He urged Montagu to give greater 'encouragements', even if they might in normal times be considered unreasonable. Professing friendship, he warned Montagu of the consequences should Exchequer bills fail. Though he and the king were well pleased with Montagu's efforts to restore the government's credit, if the army was left to starve, Montagu was sure to come under personal attack in the ensuing parliamentary session.

The treasury lords moved quickly to put the new plan into effect. On 2 July they sought formal approval from the lords justices to receive loans in clipped money at 5s. 6d. per ounce.[63] Lenders would be issued tallies on the credit of the Exchequer in general, for the repayment of which parliament could provide next session. In the meantime, the tallies would pay interest at 6 percent. The measure was approved and enacted by way of a privy council order issued the next day.[64] Montagu wrote Blathwayt that if a substantial sum of money came in upon this order, 'our work is done and we will weather this storm'.[65]

But that very day the Exchequer-bills project was dealt a potentially serious setback by the supporters of the land bank. The commissioners, led by Cook and Herne, attended the Treasury with a written version of a proposal they had been discussing for a few days with Godolphin.[66] They noted that no further subscriptions had come in of late. But in their estimation this was only because the 5 percent premium granted by the Treasury was not enough to offset 'the exigent occasions for money and the great advantages to be made thereof upon all securities', both public and private. The commissioners still believed it possible to attain the subscription target necessary for incorporation if the Treasury gave them a somewhat bigger concession. Specifically, they requested an 'allowance' of £300 thousand. The commissioners presented this as a deduction from 'the whole fund of 2,564,000*l*.': equivalent to a fairly reasonable-sounding 11.7 percent discount. But in reality it was merely a revised form of their earlier request to be allowed to take in clipped coin at face value: adjusted now for the fact that this currency had been fully demonetized as of 24 June. For the 'allowance' was surely to be deducted from the one-quarter down payment that must be made upon subscribing to the bank. So instead of having to raise £641 thousand, subscribers would need to pay only about half that amount: £341 thousand. If they used clipped coin for this purpose, even received by weight as bullion it would be almost as if the Treasury were accepting it at face value. The commissioners said they had been warned by counsel that they might be prosecuted for proceeding in this way. Implicitly, then, they were asking for an official commitment that the new strategy would not be deemed illegal. They asked further that this commitment be made public. For with the 50 percent subscription deadline of 1 August fast approaching, they needed something substantial to assure potential investors. At a recent general meeting, all the land-bank commissioners had unanimously agreed that with a Treasury guarantee in place they would subscribe 'as far as their abilities will give them leave'. And others outside that circle had declared that a public declaration of support would lead them too to subscribe 'considerable sums'. The treasury lords promised to consult with the lords justices the next day and deliver their answer as soon as possible.

Montagu wrote Blathwayt later that day to give his assessment of the new proposal.[67] Worried perhaps that it sounded reasonable and might succeed, Montagu quietly did his best to poison the king's mind against it. He began by noting the peculiarity of its timing. The Treasury had heard nothing from the commissioners for almost a month. But now that the Exchequer bills project was under way, 'all of a sudden [they] thought fit to entertain my Lord Godolphin with a new proposition'. The sudden resurgence of the land-bank proposal, at a time 'when it was almost forgotten, has put us back a fortnight' on the Exchequer-bills front. For the very prospect that the bank might succeed after all had caused people to hold onto their specie rather than contribute it to the Exchequer. It had also impaired the credit of the Bank of England.

Montagu also enclosed a very damning document from a source inside the land-bank group. The letter in question, dated 25 June, came he said from someone who had been 'a great promoter of the land bank as long as he thought they meant fairly'. Given that it bore the initials 'J. B.', it was almost certainly written by John Briscoe. Though accused by some of having sold out to the Bank of England in April, Briscoe had been appointed a subscription commissioner and so was eligible to attend the commissioners' meetings. Briscoe informed Montagu of the plan to ask for a £300 thousand allowance and then added a few further technical details. The commissioners also intended to take bills from the Bank of England as well as some £840 thousand in certain tallies slated to be paid out of the land bank's loan.[68] And they planned to give public notice that they would pay a premium of 6d. per ounce (about 10 percent) on any good silver coin, take clipped coin as bullion at a price equivalent to 80 percent of its face value and give subscribers on their second and third instalment payments a premium larger than that being afforded to the bank by the Treasury. None of this was controversial; Briscoe must have reported it solely for the sake of being complete. It showed only that the commissioners were prepared to suffer some significant losses up front in order to reach the 50 percent subscription target required for incorporation, and hoped to make that money back once they were a bank and able to issue their own bills and notes. The really damaging information came later in the letter. The commissioners had ridiculed the Treasury's plan of borrowing a £200 thousand specie reserve by offering a 10 percent premium for clipped coin. (They also complained that the Treasury was willing to offer others a premium of 10 percent when they had been offered only 5 percent.) More importantly, the commissioners were counting upon 'baffling the currency of the Exchequer bills' by selling them for a 20 percent discount on the exchange. They expected this would induce anyone holding Exchequer bills to cash them and use the specie proceeds instead to subscribe to the land bank. In this way the commissioners were hoping 'to bring the Treasury to a compliance with them'.

On 7 July, meeting for some five hours and well into the evening, the lords justices, in privy council, discussed the commissioners' request for a £300 thousand allowance. There are no minutes for this day. We know only from letters written to Flanders that night by Shrewsbury and Godolphin that the council decided against it.[69] They offered three main reasons for their decision. First, the premium being requested was unreasonably large. Second, the Treasury would have great difficulty finding elsewhere the £300 thousand that would thereby be removed from their budget. Finally, and Shrewsbury claimed this was the argument that weighed most with people, there was no guarantee that even with so large an allowance the Bank would be able to raise the whole £2.6 million loan. Under these circumstances the £300 thousand concession, to which the commissioners wanted the Treasury's commitment in advance, might well become something more like a 25 or 50 percent discount. Even Godolphin concluded that the bank project was now 'completely closed off' and that no option remained but to try to make Exchequer bills work.

The treasury lords, accordingly, resumed work on the latter project the very next day. They sent letters to all the leading tax officials, instructing them to order their receivers to accept Exchequer bills in payment of taxes.[70] They issued their first-ever payment in the form of Exchequer bills; Ranelagh was granted £5.6 thousand with which to pay some bills of exchange previously drawn by Hill in Flanders.[71] Finally, they arranged for the new order-in-council for loans in clipped money to be announced in the 6–9 July issue of the *London Gazette*. They added that the arrangement would hold only until 25 July and that the Exchequer would keep a record of the weight and tale of all clipped coin received.[72] This last was a hint that parliament might later provide additional, perhaps even full, compensation. Luttrell reported that 'an office is now fitting up in the Exchequer for issuing out 1,500,000*l*. bills of credit, to make it an Exchequer instead of a land bank'.[73] The first steps in this direction were taken on 14 July, when the Treasury ordered that £40 thousand in new bills be printed and distributed to the four Exchequer tellers, £10 thousand to each. The tellers were instructed to offer the bills to anyone willing to accept them in place of specie.

Very little money had come into the Exchequer under the terms of the new order-in-council: by 14 July just £14 thousand.[74] This, presumably, is why on that day Montagu outlined to the lords justices a revised, much more aggressive, plan for amassing a specie reserve and encouraging the circulation of Exchequer bills more generally. He was asked to present his proposal in writing the next day. Fortunately that document has survived.[75] The plan was to generate some sort of public commitment from large numbers of merchants and traders to accept Exchequer bills as a means of payment. To this end, Montagu proposed that the government prepare a legal instrument by which signatories would bind themselves to take the bills at par from anyone offering them in payment in the signatories' private business dealings. Subscribers would need to declare the maximum value of bills they were prepared to accept and then lend a tenth of this amount to the Exchequer in specie. In return they would be granted interest-bearing tallies for the value of specie contributed and promised interest on the remaining 90 percent of their subscription. The overall subscription target would be set at the full value of the £2.6 million war loan. Subscribers' specie loans would be set aside in the Exchequer as a reserve from which bills could be paid upon demand. The subscription drive should begin with members of the lords justices and privy council and be recommended by them to other prominent persons in London. 'Jews and goldsmiths' – implicitly, the principal backers for the land-bank project – should be required to declare whether they would support or oppose the undertaking.

With this plan Montagu was clearly following Blathwayt's advice and offering substantial encouragements with a view to buying off potential opposition to the Exchequer-bills scheme. For he was quietly affording subscribers an opportunity to earn an exceptionally high rate of return on their specie holdings: 51 percent per annum.[76] Earlier I estimated the return for subscribers to the Land Bank United at the rate of 11.7 percent per annum (see above). Of course the bank's supporters had recently worked to raise that figure considerably with various requests for further concessions. But their proposals would not have generated anywhere near as good a rate of return as Montagu here was quietly offering. His call to force 'the Jews and goldsmiths' to declare their support or opposition was a tactical move of the same kind.

It seems Godolphin tried to clear the way for the new proposal. For on the same day that Montagu made his presentation, the lords justices also received a lengthy memorial from Godolphin's protégé Davenant on the means by which public credit might be restored.[77] Davenant thought it would help to allow bills of the Bank of England, and maybe of some leading goldsmiths, to be received in payment of taxes. But the crucial step would be to get specie circulating again. The 'moneyed men must be invited by large encouragements to let their hoards see the light and be dispersed abroad'. Though this might be thought a capitulation to usurers, those 'who stand possessed of the ready money have in all times and in all countries given the law and hold the rest of the people in their power'. And it was better to pay high interest than let money stagnate as it was doing now. The two available options were paying high premiums for specie or raising the coin. The disease, Davenant repeated, 'cannot be cured at too high a price'.[78]

At least some of the lords justices weren't buying the argument. The minutes record two main objections. The investors would never actually have to take up the other 90 percent of their subscriptions and so would be receiving interest for nothing. There was a risk too that subscribers would refuse to accept bills, pleading they had already taken their full quota. Such claims would be difficult to disprove and cause all the bills out in circulation to come flooding in upon the Exchequer for redemption in specie. On both counts, the design should be reworked so that a much larger proportion of the subscriptions was contributed in cash. Montagu objected that if the terms were made less generous, it was doubtful whether anyone would 'engage their estates' to assist a bank inside the Exchequer – i.e. from which they could not profit as investors in the Bank of England or the land bank might.

Though no decision was taken that day, Montagu remained optimistic. He sent Blathwayt a copy of his new scheme and professed: 'I do not doubt but our Exchequer bills will find credit'.[79] But a week later the lords justices shot down the new plan.[80] They were prepared to authorize interest only on the tenth of subscriptions actually paid in and not on the remaining 90 percent. It needed to look, they insisted, like an association of persons interested only in supporting the government, not in making their private fortunes.

But before even this modest experiment could be attempted, the attention of the lords justices and treasury lords was distracted by a major new development: William's decision to send the Earl of Portland back to London to negotiate an emergency loan for the English army in Flanders. On 14 July Godolphin informed the lords justices of a letter from Blathwayt explaining that unless the Treasury could send funds right away, the army would have to be disbanded. Godolphin then explained that it was impossible for them to furnish a large sum when 'paper credit was so broken'. The only disposable coin they had was £14 thousand in clipped silver received upon the recent order-in-council. And this was reserved to support the circulation of Exchequer bills. The only solution was for the king to find a loan on the continent. Shrewsbury wrote Blathwayt later that day to deliver the bad news. In a letter of his own, Godolphin added that a decision by legal officials in Amsterdam to uphold the protests being registered for non-payment of bills of exchange at London had 'given the last stroke to our credit'. The Treasury couldn't even find the money with which to repay the Bank of England, as in June they had solemnly promised to do. William replied a week later, in despair, that it was even more impossible to find money on the continent. If the necessary funds could not be raised in England, 'all is lost and I must go to the Indies [i.e. into exile]'.[81] It was at this point that he decided to send Portland back to London. He said this was so Portland could consult with the lords justices and decide whether in this great emergency to recall parliament immediately.[82] But no doubt, believing that only 'malice and faction' was keeping milled money out of circulation, he also hoped Portland could put an end to the infighting and himself rescue the government's credit.[83]

In the meantime, the Treasury endeavoured to find some immediate relief for the army in Flanders. By 28 July they had reached a tentative agreement with two London bullion merchants, Peter Floyer and John Johnson. Floyer and Johnson were to supply a total of £200 thousand in instalments, starting with an immediate £10 thousand credit at the current market exchange rate. In return they wanted the king's license, granted by parliament earlier that year, to export £200 thousand in silver bullion and the Treasury's promise that each instalment credit would be repaid within a fortnight.[84] They also received security in the form of Exchequer bills, which they promised not to cash at least until the Treasury's promised payment date had arrived.

Portland arrived in London on Sunday, 26 July and met the next day with the lords justices in privy council.[85] The group quickly decided to declare that parliament would not meet until at least 1 September. For only so could Portland hope to find a loan for the army right away.[86] If parliament were immediately called into session, the nation's entire specie supply would be utterly locked away for a time. It would take three weeks to gather all the MPs in London. In the meantime people would be expecting the Commons to restore clipped coin to its face value, raise the silver coin and set a higher price on guineas. They opted instead to look for some group willing to come to the government's assistance with a large quantity of specie. Though no one said so out loud, this money would be used to support the circulation of Exchequer bills – thereby restoring public credit in an instant.

This presented supporters of the land bank with an opportunity to rescue their project through the back door. Though the specie would be used to support Exchequer bills, by organizing its provision they would buy the goodwill of William and parliament alike and so put themselves in the strongest possible position to secure a charter of incorporation next session.[87] They were in a very strategic position in this regard. For, as Godolphin explained to William, in this time of general monetary stringency they were the only ones with a large amount of specie ready to hand.[88] Godolphin repeated his previous claim that the land-bank men had all along been very willing to lend to the crown. But they had been 'mortified' and 'discouraged' by some in the administration, 'as if they had been persons who had designed nothing else all along than to distress the government'. He hoped Portland, now he was on the scene, would quickly 'set that matter right'. Shrewsbury too maintained that 'those gentlemen' did not want to see the army reduced to extremities.[89] Foley and Harley had assured him that, with good treatment and the proper financial inducements, the land bank's backers would come through with a substantial emergency loan. The financiers refused to deal with the whig-dominated Treasury and wanted instead to meet directly with Portland, Godolphin and Shrewsbury.[90]

On 28 July, Portland held preliminary discussions with a large group of London merchants.[91] Though all professed good will toward William, they doubted whether much could be done. The land bank having failed, potential lenders had foreseen that the government would have no other means of getting money and would have to accept whatever terms were offered them. This had ruined public credit and pushed tallies to discounts of 30 to 40 percent. Many of their associates would rather deploy their cash that way than join with them in lending to the government. But several of the group promised to see what they could do. They were not heard from again.

Shrewsbury and Godolphin then invited some of the principals of the land bank to meet with Portland on 29 July. Acting as emissaries were Sir Stephen Fox, Sir Stephen Evance, Sir Joseph Herne, Sir John Banks, Charles Duncombe, Henry Guy and Floyer and Johnson. Shrewsbury and Godolphin also begged Portland to get Sir Josiah Child to attend and see what he could do to bring the group to agree among themselves.[92] These were wealthy, monied men, all but the latter two tories with strong connections to public finance under the former tory administration.[93] Fox was a Treasury lord allied with Godolphin; Duncombe was Excise cashier and an associate of Sunderland and Guy. The financiers were sure they could find £200 thousand for the government.[94] Their asking price was steep: tallies (on the Exchequer in general) bearing interest at 6 percent, a premium of 12 percent on their money (contributed it would seem in clipped money taken by weight) and assignment of the license granted the king in the previous parliamentary session to export £200 thousand worth of bullion.[95] It seems Portland accepted these terms. The group headed off to raise subscriptions.

But on the morning of 31 July, five emissaries returned to inform Portland that their associates were unwilling to commit to a loan.[96] Their colleagues were worried that in the king's absence the whigs in the Treasury would somehow manage to undermine them. Before anyone would agree to participate, they wanted the king's prior assurance of a royal charter for the land bank. Portland warned his visitors that, by delaying in this way (it would take a week or longer to get the king's reply) and setting further conditions, the group was doing itself serious harm. The emissaries agreed to start collecting loan subscriptions without any further delay, a resolution in which they were keenly supported by Foley and Harley.

But they returned that afternoon with bad news; they had been able to gather commitments for no more than £40 thousand.[97] For this they now blamed the Treasury whigs. They pointed specifically to an agreement that Montagu had struck earlier that day with several merchants to send a further £20 thousand for the army in Flanders. To others, even Godolphin, the deal seemed perfectly above-board.[98] Pereira (also a bread contractor for the army) and two associates had agreed to provide bills of exchange at 10 guilders per English pound – the same rate as Godolphin had negotiated a few days earlier with Floyer and Johnson. But Pereira and friends were prepared to make do without an accompanying right to export a corresponding amount of bullion. The Treasury quickly informed Floyer and Johnson that their services would no longer be required. The tory financiers meeting with Portland maintained that the Treasury deal was a deliberate strike at them; Montagu had offered Pereira good terms in order to tie up cash that would otherwise have been pledged for their loan. Portland doubted their claims but promised to give them the same terms that had been offered to Pereira and associates. At this point, Portland wrote William, the group fell silent and the meeting came to an end. The lords justices waited a few more days, but no further subscriptions were forthcoming.[99] Portland, Shrewsbury and Godolphin were forced to conclude that the tories could not deliver what they had promised. Even the ardently-tory MP Francis Gwyn, in private correspondence, had to admit that Portland would now 'go away satisfied that Mr. Montagu, etc. have acted very wisely in refusing the land bank', since the tory financiers could not deliver even £200 thousand, let alone a loan of £2.6 million.[100]

Gwyn, like the land-bank negotiators, blamed the failure of the subscription drive upon backroom maneuvering. 'The animosity of land bank & old Bank seems to men almost as high as Jacobite & Williamite'. When the prospect of an emergency land-bank loan first presented itself, Foley 'was in great exaltation of spirit ... & thought he should get the better of his enemy Charles & the Bank of England'. But Montagu defeated him in the end through a strategy of divide and conquer. He had offered something under the table to Pereira and somehow threatened Guy and Duncombe into withdrawing their support. Sunderland too had quietly worked against the scheme. He might have been worried that 'encouraging these subscriptions will set up one party of men too high & too much pull down Montagu etc.'. Or perhaps Somers had 'prevailed with him'.

But a simpler and far less conspiratorial explanation is available. The tory financiers' ultimate objective was to secure a charter for the land bank. But in the short term their specie loan would be used to establish the credit of Exchequer bills. Once the latter currency had met with public acceptance, the Treasury might have little further need for them. So in the coming parliamentary session they might fail to win incorporation and thus another shot at a large war loan. This would explain why they pressed Portland to have William's written promise of a charter *before* agreeing to lend anything and why the subscription drive failed as soon as Portland refused that demand. The group hardly wanted to contribute to setting a rival project on foot – an outcome that might do them irreparable harm.

On 5 August the lords justices summoned Portland and the treasury lords to a special meeting to determine the best way forward.[101] The Treasury whigs were quick to point out that the land-bank men had done nothing more than cost the administration a couple of weeks. For the crown's financial situation was exactly where it had been before Portland arrived. In principle the Treasury was free to carry on with the Exchequer-bills project and seek a specie loan on its own. The group gave serious consideration to this possibility but eventually decided against it. The minutes are very clipped so it is hard to know how the debate ran. But it seems two options were considered and both found lacking. One was to approach the City of London for a loan. There were grave doubts whether the request would prove successful; the very fact that London merchants were having great difficulties paying the bills of exchange drawn upon them suggested they had little spare cash. And it was pointed out that the Treasury would be much worse off than now if the City should refuse a loan or respond only half-heartedly. The other option was a general subscription drive. This raised the same issue that had been under discussion on 22 July before news of Portland's mission had arrived. Some argued that while a few might subscribe 'only in consideration of the public', most would be unwilling to contribute to a loan without a significant premium. It seems that in the end the lords justices decided to set the whole Exchequer-bills project aside, unable to agree on how to structure the premium. The best clues as to their reasoning come from a letter Montagu wrote Blathwayt about a week later.[102] The plan Montagu had sent Blathwayt in mid-July, for a subscription drive supported by a large premium, 'was baffled by the new treaty with the other [viz. the land-bank] gentlemen'. For the lords justices were unwilling to approve terms as generous as those Portland had offered the tory financiers; yet if anything less than this were proposed for a public subscription drive, the latter would be sure to fail.

In the end the lords justices decided to take an entirely different approach: seeking a short-term loan of £200 thousand from the Bank of England. This would be enough to finance the several military services until parliament could be called into session in September to provide a more permanent solution.[103] Implicitly this amounted to a resolution to abandon the pursuit of a specie reserve with which to support the circulation of Exchequer bills. For the Bank of England did not have large available stores of specie that it could contribute for said purpose; if anything it needed more specie to support its own operations. Rather the Bank would lend by way of having bills of exchange drawn upon itself, due in two months, for which the Treasury could repay the Bank gradually out of the normal flow of specie coming into the Exchequer upon public taxes.

The Exchequer-bills project, therefore, quietly faded away. A few small attempts were made to keep it alive. On 14 August two officials with the Excise commission arranged to send letters encouraging their collectors, and cashier Duncombe, to take Exchequer bills in payment of excise duties.[104] And that same day the lords justices extended for another month the order permitting the Exchequer to receive loans in clipped silver at 5s. 8d. per ounce.[105] A month later the order was extended one more time.[106] But it seems these measures had very little effect. For in the end only a small number of Exchequer bills were ever issued this year. A short Treasury account shows total issues of £133,709.[107] The account was for the period between 10 July and 28 September, suggesting the experiment had been completely discontinued by the latter date.

The Bank of England returns

To properly understand the nature of the negotiations between Treasury and Bank for a new £200 thousand loan, we must first backtrack a little to see how the Bank tried to cope with the effects of the monetary crisis. At a general meeting on 13 May 1696, shareholders agreed to have the midsummer dividend postponed indefinitely. The directors also encouraged them to keep all their cash with the Bank and offered that anyone 'under any uneasiness for want of his money' could have 'good tallies' upon request.[108] At another general meeting later that month, shareholders rejected a proposal to call in the next 20 percent of their stock subscriptions by way of a six-month loan at 6 percent interest.[109] Two weeks later, however, they approved the idea.[110] This was in order to finance a new £100 thousand loan to the government: offered, Godolphin believed, to give the Treasury less reason to capitulate to the subscription terms being proposed by the commissioners of the National Land Bank. The Bank of England arranged for the shareholder loan to be paid in two instalments, with deadlines of 30 June and 20 July.[111] In return the Treasury promised to furnish the Bank with the specie it would need to pay £100 thousand in bills of exchange that had been drawn in late April for the army in Flanders. The Treasury was to provide £50 thousand on 18 June and another £50 thousand on 1 July. The Treasury was made to promise too that the latest £100 thousand loan would 'positively' be repaid on the last day of July. The Bank also decided, effective 10 June, to raise interest on its bills by 50 percent to about 4.6 percent per annum – a rate the directors promised to maintain for the next six months.[112] Figure 3.2 suggests that the measure helped, since for the next two months the quantity of bills in circulation stayed pinned to the legal maximum of £1.2 million.

Unfortunately for the Bank, it soon became clear that the Treasury would not be honouring its promise to provide the specie needed to pay the £100 thousand in bills of exchange coming due in late June. The Bank would somehow have to find a way of honouring those bills at a time when it had relatively little specie of its own on hand and everyone was refusing to accept Bank notes and bills.

The Bank responded in two main ways. First, on 23 June the directors announced they were prepared to give out special 'specie notes' to anyone bringing in milled coin or guineas, entitling the bearer to repayment, upon demand, in the same coin originally deposited. The very offer suggests that people were hoarding good specie in part for fear clipped coin would soon be remonetized – raising the prospect that deposits made in the first medium might be repaid in the second. These special notes also represented a promise to repay the entire sum on demand, rather than putting note holders through the wringer to get back even 10 percent of the cash owing, as with regular Bank notes. The offer doesn't seem to have had any impact at first. So a week later the directors made an additional concession: that specie notes would pay interest at 6 percent per annum as long as the sum was for £50 or more.[113] This did the trick, for specie notes began to be issued that very day. Figures 12.5 and 12.6 show that there was considerable turnover but that on balance specie notes helped to build the Bank's cash reserves.

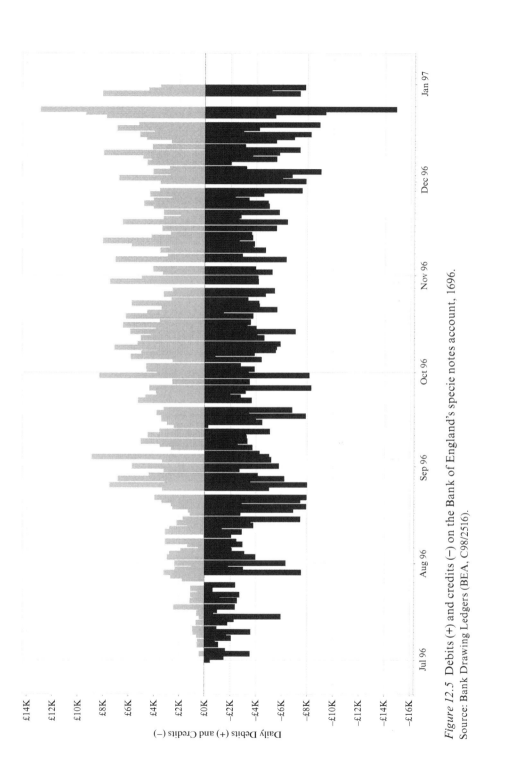

Figure 12.5 Debits (+) and credits (−) on the Bank of England's specie notes account, 1696.
Source: Bank Drawing Ledgers (BEA, C98/2516).

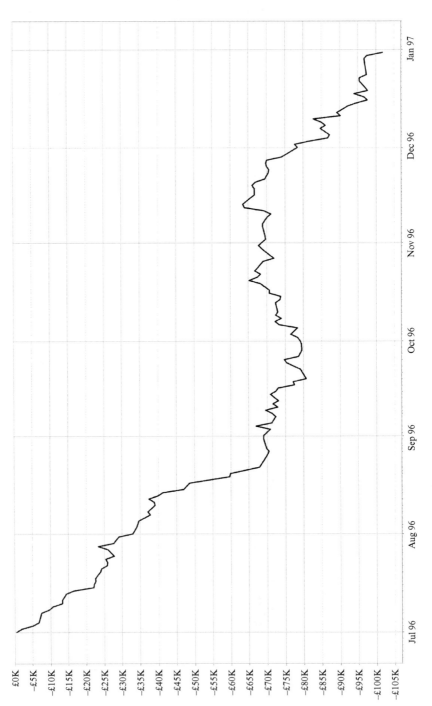

Figure 12.6 **Running net debits on the Bank's specie notes account, 1696.**
Source: Bank Drawing Ledgers (BEA, C98/2516).

Second, the Bank tried to get creditors to accept payment on all foreign bills of exchange half in Bank notes and half in specie. Staff were ordered very early on to take payment this way when collecting on any foreign bills of exchange owned by the Bank.[114] By this means the directors probably hoped to make the practice general in London, to the Bank's own subsequent benefit. If so, the strategy failed. For creditors insisted that foreign bills of exchange be paid entirely in specie. In late June some of the Bank's bills were protested when they were not paid in this way. In early July the directors banded together with several city merchants to complain to the lords justices about a recent judgement in Amsterdam upholding a protest for non-payment of a bill on London even though payment had been offered half in money and half in Bank notes.[115] The Bank also urged the Treasury to try to get the Amsterdam judgement reversed.[116] The lords justices did, on 13 July, issue an order prohibiting London's public notaries for the next fourteen days from registering a protest on bills offered to be paid half in specie.[117] And Lord Villiers, England's ambassador to The Hague, was sent to Amsterdam to see whether he could get the States General to agree to a compromise. But the council order was not renewed when it expired at the end of July.[118] And Villiers got nowhere with the Dutch.[119]

In sum, by late July the Bank was in some ways in a less precarious situation than it had been during the worst weeks of the crisis in early June. Figure 3.2 shows that it had managed to pay off the best part of the short-term borrowing by which it had financed remittance operations over the past year. And cash reserves, though still nowhere near their former heights, were much better than in June. But these gains had been achieved only at considerable expense: by running down the Bank's holdings of Exchequer tallies and taking out large new short-term loans from shareholders and specie-note holders at an interest rate of 6 percent per annum. And protests for non-payment of the Bank's foreign bills of exchange had really injured its credit on the continent and so its ability to borrow short-term by drawing from thence upon itself.

This was the situation when in early August the Treasury approached the Bank for another large loan for the army. The lords justices called the Bank governor in on 6 August to stress the urgency of the request.[120] They had been forewarned by treasury lords Montagu and Smith that the Bank, while well-disposed to the king, was hardly in a good position to furnish a new loan. Governor Houblon then pointed out that the directors had several very good reasons to decline the government's latest request. The Bank had loaned £200 thousand for Flanders earlier in the summer upon a solemn promise of repayment in July – which the Treasury had not honoured. They had lost £80 thousand on their remittance contract in the past year. Leading members of the administration had recently sold their Bank stock – a gentle hint that some had done their best to establish a competitor despite an implicit promise in 1694 that parliament would incorporate no other banks. Houblon promised to consult with shareholders but wanted to know what

terms the lords justices were prepared to offer for a loan. No terms were settled that day; the two sides merely agreed to meet again in the near future.

The whig treasury lords attended the lords justices a few days later to
relay the Bank's conditions.[121] They began by asserting that the Bank was
now their only hope for supply and then laid out the directors' demands:
a) to be compensated for their remittance losses; b) to be repaid the £200
thousand they had loaned earlier that summer; and c) that the lords justices
would set a public example by buying Bank stock. The second demand was
of course impossible; if the Treasury had the means to repay the Bank at
this time, it would not be asking them for a further loan for the army. But
the lords justices did promise to buy Bank stock, give them 'protection and
favour' and advise William to grant any 'reasonable' request for compensation. By promising to buy stock themselves, the lords justices were in effect
giving substance to their commitment to protect and favour the Bank –
which everyone understood to mean that the government would stop trying
to establish a competing bank. With these assurances in hand the directors
were able to persuade shareholders, at a general meeting on 15 August, to
unanimously approve a new loan for £200 thousand.[122] They met with the
lords justices later that day and promised to call another general meeting
the following week to decide how to raise the necessary funds.[123] But they
immediately furnished a £50 thousand letter of credit for Ranelagh to send
Hill in Flanders.[124] Montagu hastened to take credit for the new loan; he
wrote Blathwayt: 'I assure you, unless I had taken particular care and pains
in it, we should not have obtained it'.[125]

It took months for the two sides to agree upon a hard number for the
Bank's remittance losses. The directors' initial demand was for £170 thousand.[126] A little later they lowered their ask to an absolute minimum of £67
thousand (the sum of their losses for calendar year 1696 to date) and left any
further compensation (namely for losses incurred in 1695) to the Treasury's
discretion.[127] Then Ranelagh spotted an error that lowered the Bank's original request to £135 thousand and, after questioning a number of the directors' assumptions, urged the Treasury to reduce the claim still further. Not
until January did the two sides finally settle upon a figure of £77 thousand;
tallies for this amount were made over to the Bank in early February.[128]

Fortunately for the army, the directors did not keep to their original as-
sertion that they would deliver the rest of the £200 thousand loan only after
the Treasury had granted compensation for the Bank's remittance losses.[129]
On 8 September they furnished a further £50 thousand in return only for being granted tallies on the salt tax for both this and the earlier £50 thousand
credit.[130] By early October the directors had already seen Ranelagh's initial
report on their claim, which made it clear that the Treasury would ultimately
agree to provide something more than the £67 thousand upon which they had
originally insisted. So on 14 October they furnished a further £50 thousand
loan instalment.[131] They delivered the final £50 thousand on 30 October after receiving the Treasury's promise (as it turns out, not honoured) that the

account would be settled later that week.[132] To help finance the loan, the directors called in a further 20 percent of the par value of the stock (amounting to £240 thousand), giving shareholders until 10 November to pay their respective contributions.[133] The results are visible in Figure 3.2.[134]

While the Treasury and Bank were negotiating on the terms of the new remittance loan, William was working on a strategy that promised to raise an even larger sum by alternative means. Very likely he pursued the idea because it would have freed him from having to depend upon the Bank. This would have been advantageous to him both financially (he could have refused the Bank's demands for compensation) and politically (by freeing him from having to build the court's financial program during the coming session around the Bank's supporters). The very same factors probably explain why the Treasury whigs and a whig-dominated cabinet strongly opposed the strategy. The idea probably came from Godolphin, since it required inside knowledge of the Treasury's operations and was passed along to Portland just a few days after the lords justices had been forced to turn to the Bank of England for assistance. Portland outlined the plan to William in a letter of 11 August, suggesting it could be used to raise £300 or £400 thousand.[135] Treasury officials had come to suspect some land-tax receivers of defrauding the crown. The individuals in question had bought up large quantities of clipped coin at discounted prices and paid it into the Exchequer, before 24 June, on pretence of having received it from tax payers at full face value. This raised the possibility of treating the receivers' payments into the Exchequer not as tax proceeds but rather as loans made by private citizens. In that case the money would no longer be bound by the terms of the recoinage and land-tax acts and so could be used for whatever purpose the Treasury chose – which in this case, obviously, would be to pay the army in Flanders. The only difficulty, Portland maintained, would be to find out how much of the money paid into the Exchequer on the land tax qualified for this kind of treatment. Upon this problem the treasury lords made a start the next day. They ordered land-tax commissioners in every county to send up their records of local receipts, which could then be compared with the sums that land-tax receivers claimed to have been paid.[136] William pressed the idea very strongly upon Shrewsbury, urging him to secure an order from the lords justices for its implementation.[137] He opined that even if the money, having coming in upon the land tax, was still deemed to be appropriated to the purposes specified in the relevant act, parliament would surely grant the Treasury a legal indemnity next session for having redirected it to the army – the latter's need being so obvious and so great. Blathwayt also wrote the treasury lords separately asking them to pursue the idea (no record of his letter has survived). The lords justices summoned the three whig treasury lords to ask their opinion.[138] They argued very strongly against the idea. It would not only violate strict parliamentary appropriations, but also destroy public confidence in tax receivers and cause people to stop paying their taxes. The nation was already under great financial and political strain; 'this was not a time of day for the king's officers to appear as criminals in parliament'. Furthermore, the allegations would be difficult to prove, for land-tax commissioners had not responded to their requests for information. The treasury lords speculated, finally, that a political trap was being laid for them; for the letter from Blathwayt urging them to pursue a potentially illegal strategy was in a clerk's hand rather than as usual in his own. Shrewsbury wrote William that night to report that in the end all the lords justices had agreed the project was not feasible. The treasury lords, in their own reply to Blathwayt, expressed their opposition at great length. They acknowledged that the tax receivers had acted illegally and that the sums involved were very large – perhaps as much as £1.4 million. But they offered numerous practical and legal objections against the proposed strategy.[139] The very vehemence of their response suggests they were keen to defeat it and wanted the Bank to be central to any rescue that might be organized for the army.

Foley and Harley made one final attempt to undermine the Bank, but in the end were defeated once more by Montagu. To the Treasury whigs' dismay, a week before the new session of parliament began (on 20 October 1696), William spent 2.5 hours meeting with the two country-party leaders.[140] A few days later William asked the Treasury's thoughts on a plan Foley had submitted for retiring the very large quantity of unpaid tallies with which the government now found itself saddled.[141] From the few details available it appears Foley had proposed setting up an independent corporation that would look after retiring not only the tallies but also the government's debts to the Bank. People would be invited to subscribe their tallies and Bank bills into this corporation, and in return would be issued transferable receipts. Over the next decade the corporation, endowed with some appropriate parliamentary fund, would then gradually pay off the principal, with interest, to those currently holding the receipts.[142] Since in the meantime the Bank would be prohibited from issuing any further bills, at the end of that time its charter could be terminated and the organization disbanded. But Foley was out-manoeuvered. First, Godolphin, his biggest supporter inside the Treasury, was manipulated into resigning at the end of October; his offer to resign, made he thought pro forma, was to his surprise quickly accepted by William.[143] In effect, in the internal battle for supremacy, Montagu's group had emerged victorious. This gave Montagu free rein to appropriate Foley's plan, but with one decisive twist: the corporation charged with gradually retiring the debt would be the Bank of England itself (and naturally its own bills would *not* be retired). Foley protested at length against involving the Bank in this process.[144] But in the end parliament agreed to implement Montagu's version. By a statute enacted in April 1697, the Bank was authorized to accept new stock subscriptions, to a maximum of £5.2 million (the total value of the tallies needing to be retired). Interested investors would need to pay 4/5ths of their subscriptions in the relevant Exchequer tallies and 1/5th in Bank notes and/or bills (8 & 9 Will. 3, c. 20). The Commons simultaneously extended several existing taxes to 1707, estimating that this would suffice to pay off all the tallies in question over that period. The Bank would then hold the tallies on behalf of the subscribers. The Exchequer would periodically make blended principal and interest payments to the Bank, which in turn would distribute the proceeds out to its shareholders by means of regular dividend payments. In return for taking on this function, the Bank was granted the guarantee for which it had been looking ever since the idea of a National Land Bank was first broached: that 'no other bank or any other corporation, society, fellowship, company or constitution in the nature of a bank shall be erected or established, permitted, suffered, countenanced or allowed by act of parliament within this kingdom'. And it received three additional very significant benefits: a) a five-year extension on its charter; b) the right to issue more bills; and c) a large, new and very regular influx of specie from the Exchequer (namely the principal and interest payments on the subscribed tallies).[145] The Bank's future, so dim just a year ago, now looked quite rosy.

Notes

1 Kelly, Intro. to *Locke on Money*, p. 118.
2 Abbott Letters, 17 Mar. 1696.
3 See NA, MINT 1/6, fol. 7.
4 Paterson, *Review*, p. 26.
5 The record of Treasury disbursements (*CTB*, 1693–96 and 1696–97) shows that of £2.8 million and £2.2 million in military funding provided in the two periods, 35.0 percent and 96.4 percent respectively were granted in the form of tallies of fictitious loan. In 1695, the first tallies of fictitious loan weren't given out until mid-March, by which point the Treasury had already issued over £1 million to its paymasters.
6 *CTB*, Minutes, 17 Apr. 1696.
7 Abbott Letters, 21 Feb. 1696.
8 *CTB*, Minutes, 27 Mar. 1696.
9 Bank General Ledger 1.
10 *CTB*, Minutes, 17 Apr. 1696.
11 *CTB*, Warrants, etc., 21 Apr. 1696.
12 *CTB*, Warrants, etc., 22 Apr. 1696.
13 Bonnet Reports, 12/22 May 1696.
14 Luttrell, *Brief Historical Relation*, 6 May 1696.
15 A contemporary reported that 'they strain you through the eye of a needle' (letter of Obadiah Greville at London to Roger Hoar & Co., 13 June 1696, in NA, C104/12, part I [hereafter 'Hoar Letter Book']). Note holders had to come at 6 AM on a certain day to register their request for cash. There were so many people queuing up to get their names on the list that 'you are ever pressed to death'. Then they had to come again on the morrow and wait to hear their name called. But this could take days, for the Bank called names alphabetically, only 6 or 7 letters a day and about 200 names per letter. And if someone wasn't there at the very moment their name came up, they had to start the whole process over again. Another contemporary noted that 'the Bank of England is so haunted all day long, that there's never less than 200 or 300, and more than 1000 every morning, & happy is he that can get 10 percent of his money, be his occasions

never so great' (letter of Henley to Blathwayt, 9 June 1696, BL, MS 9727, fols. 142–43 [hereafter 'Henley Letter to Blathwayt']).

16 L'Hermitage Reports, 8/18 May 1696.

17 Bank Minutes, 7 May 1696.

18 Lords Justices Minutes, 13 May 1696; Paterson, *Review*, pp. 27–28.

19 L'Hermitage Reports, 28 July/7 Aug. 1696.

20 L'Hermitage Reports, 19/29 May 1696.

21 Lords Justices Minutes, 14 May 1696.

22 L'Hermitage Reports, 8/18 May.

23 *CSPD*, 14 and 15 May 1696.

24 Letter to William, 29 May/8 June 1696, in Coxe, *Correspondence,* pp. 119–20.

25 See Paterson, *Review*, pp. 27–30. An army official wrote Blathwayt that tax receivers had refused to take some hammered money that was better than any he had seen in years (Henley Letter to Blathwayt). A circuit-court judge, trying to forestall public unrest, ordered a local market official to proclaim that anyone refusing sixpences or good punched money would be arrested (letter of Charles Price to Secretary of State William Trumbull, 14 June 1696, in RCHM, *Downshire Manuscripts*, p. 669).

26 See for instance l'Hermitage Reports, 23 June, 30 June and 10 July 1696.

27 Bonnet Reports, 22 May 1696.

28 Paterson, *Review*, p. 36.

29 Bonnet Reports, 22 May 1696; *CTB*, 25 May 1696.

30 See the first fifteen or so folios of Hoar Letter Book.

31 Bank Minutes, 22 Apr. 1696.

32 *CTB*, Minutes, 28 and 29 April and 5 May 1696; Bank Minutes, 27–29 April and 4–5 May 1696.

33 Abbott Letters, 5 May 1696.

34 Letter to William, 15/25 May 1696, in Coxe, *Correspondence*, p. 116.

35 Letter of 25 May/4 June 1696, in Coxe, *Correspondence*, p. 118.

36 Letter of Godolphin to William, 12 June 1696, in *CSPD*; letter of Montagu to Blathwayt, 23 June 1696, in BL, Add. MS 34355 (hereafter 'Montagu Letters').

37 *CTB*, Minutes, 22 May 1696.

38 Letter of Godolphin to William, 22 May 1696, University of Nottingham, MS Pw A 476; *CTB,* Minutes, 22 May 1696. L'Hermitage maintains that the three requests were part of a package proposal to pay the four quarters of the £2.6 million loan respectively in clipped money, guineas and heavy coin (received at a 10 percent premium), Bank notes and lottery tickets and, finally, tallies (l'Hermitage Reports, 26 May/5 June 1696).

39 *CTB*, Minutes, 25 May 1696; *CSPD*, 26 May 1696; *CJ*, 25 Nov. 1696.

40 Letter of Shrewsbury to William, 29 May/8 June 1696, in Coxe, *Correspondence*, pp. 119–20; *CTB*, Minutes, 29 May 1696.

41 Letter to William, 22 May 1696, University of Nottingham, MS Pw A 476.

42 *CTB*, Minutes, 29 May 1696; letter of Godolphin to William, 29 May 1696, in NA, SP 8/16 (hereafter 'Godolphin Letters to William'); *CJ*, 25 Nov. 1696.

43 Letter of Montagu to Blathwayt, 29 May 1696, in Montagu Letters; letter of Godolphin to William, 29 May 1696, in Godolphin Letters to William.

44 Letter of Yard to Stanhope, 2 June 1696, Kent History and Library Centre, U1590/059/5.

45 This is so unlike the minutes in all other respects that the treasury lords must have wanted, in so crucial an affair, to have a record of exactly what had been said and by whom.

46 Letter of 2 June 1696, Koninklijk Huisarchief, Willem III, XI G Nos. 179–94 (henceforth 'Godolphin Letters to Blathwayt').

47 *CTB,* Minutes, 3 June 1696; *CJ,* 25 Nov. 1696; letter of Godolphin to William, 5 June 1696, in Godolphin Letters to William; letter of Montagu to Blathwayt, 5 June 1696, in Montagu Letters; Luttrell, *Brief Historical Relation,* 4 June 1696; l'Hermitage Reports, 5/15 Jun. 1696.

48 He claimed that the proposed premium would absorb all that the crown had been authorized by parliament to borrow on the funding provided that year for the civil list. Parliament had authorized William to borrow £515 thousand on the civil list that year (*CJ,* 28 Mar. 1696). So Montagu must have been exaggerating somewhat, given that 15 percent of the total loan came only to £385 thousand.

49 Henley Letter to Blathwayt.

50 Letter of Montagu to Blathwayt, 5 June 1696, in Montagu Letters; letter of Godolphin to William, 5 June 1696, in Godolphin Letters to William.

51 Godolphin raised the same idea with Blathwayt two weeks later. He claimed that the bank's problems must ultimately be attributed to 'the wrong step of forcing the guinea by a law to 22s. at a time when the silver money was melting down to be recoined' (letter of 19 June 1696, in Godolphin Letters to Blathwayt). Sunderland had put the same proposition to William's entourage a little earlier. 'Money is very scarce and it is found that guineas should not have been so much lowered' (letter to Portland, 23 May 1696, University of Nottingham, MS Pw A 1251). This suggests they were trying to blame Montagu or the whig junto more generally, even though it had been William's own preference.

52 Letter to William of 17 June 1696, NA, SP 8/15/75-76; note that this letter is incorrectly catalogued in *CSPD* as 17 June 1694.

53 Letter of Godolphin to William, 17 June 1696, in Godolphin Letters to William.

54 Letter to Montagu, 11 June 1696, Montagu Letters.

55 Perhaps William's thinking had been swayed by news that the Bank of England had provided a large credit for the army. For just three days earlier he had been very angry with Shrewsbury for having failed to reach an agreement with the land bank group. Now was not the time, William wrote, to worry about whether their demands were reasonable. They must 'pass over things which we should not do at other times; for there is no alternative but to perish or find credit' (letter to Shrewsbury, 8/18 June 1696, in Coxe, *Correspondence,* p. 121).

56 Letter of Godolphin to William, 17 June 1696, NA, SP 8/15/75-76.

57 *CSPD,* 10 June 1696.

58 Letter of Godolphin to William, 23 June 1696, in Godolphin Letters to Willialm; *CTB,* Minutes, 4 June 1696. This was in repayment of the Bank's two latest loans for the army in Flanders and had been a condition for obtaining the second credit.

59 Letter of Montagu to Blathwayt, 23 June 1696, in Montagu Letters.

60 This feature may also have been designed to undermine the position of the land bank somewhat. For everyone knew its supporters were sitting on large pools of clipped coin.

61 See also *CTB*, Minutes, 30 June 1696.

62 Letter to Montagu, 2/12 July 1696, in Montagu Letters.

63 Lords Justices Minutes, 2 July 1696.

64 The order is reproduced in full in *CSPD,* 2 July 1696.

65 Letter to Blathwayt, 3 July 1696, in Montagu Letters.

66 *CTB,* Minutes, 3 July 1696.

67 Montagu Letters.

68 They would ask the Exchequer to take the latter in payment by cancelling them against the loan amount. Briscoe observed that the Treasury would much rather have specie, since by paying cash on some tallies it could substantially lower the discount on all of them.

69 Letter of Godolphin to Blathwayt, 7 July 1696, in Godolphin Letters to Blathwayt; letter of Shrewsbury to Blathwayt, 7 July 1696, in RCHM, *Buccleuch Manuscripts*, p. 365; see also Luttrell, *Brief Historical Relation*, 9 July 1696.

70 *CTB*, Minutes, 8 July 1696.

71 Two further small issues, for a total of £4.5 thousand, were ordered on 10 July.

72 The loan deadline was subsequently extended to 20 August and 29 September. See issues of *London Gazette* for 27–30 July and 27–31 August.

73 Luttrell, *Brief Historical Relation*, 9 July 1696.

74 Lords Justices Minutes, 14 July 1696.

75 It is stored as Senate House Library, University of London, MS 65, fols. 1–2, and printed in Li, *Great Recoinage*, pp. 322–23. Though the original bears no title or date and the author is unnamed, it matches exactly with the summary of Montagu's plan that was given in the minutes of the lords justices for 15 July 1696. Though it is usually attributed to Montagu himself, it was presented to the lords justices as 'Eyle's project' (Lords Justices Minutes, 14 July 1696). This was a reference to Sir Francis Eyles, who became a director of the Bank of England in 1697 and was the governor in 1707–9 when Bank and Treasury cooperated in a second and much more successful attempt at circulating Exchequer bills. The minutes of the lords justices for 15 July provide a little additional information.

76 For a £1 thousand subscription, signatories would have had to invest £100 in specie up front. This would have cost them just £91.18, since loans were to be contributed in clipped silver taken by weight at a price of 5s. 8d. per ounce. In return subscribers were promised interest of £46.5 in the first year: 6 percent on the one-tenth of their subscription contributed in cash and 4.5 percent on the rest.

77 'Memoriall Concerning Credit', BL, Harley MS 1223, fols. 71–95; printed in Davenant, *Two Manuscripts*, pp. 67–108.

78 Davenant, *Two Manuscripts*, pp. 98, 70, 102.

79 Letter to Blathwayt, 17 July 1696, in Montagu Letters.

80 Lords Justices Minutes, 22 July 1696.

81 Letter to Shrewsbury, 20/30 July 1696, in Coxe, *Correspondence*, p. 129.

82 Letter to Shrewsbury, 21/31 July, in Coxe, *Correspondence*, p. 130.

83 Letter of Hill to Shrewsbury, 27 July / 6 Aug. 1696, in RCHM, *Buccleuch Manuscripts*, p. 373.

84 *CTB*, Minutes, 28 July 1696; letter of Godolphin to William, 28 July 1696, in Godolphin Letters to William.

85 Luttrell, *Brief Historical Relation*, 28 July 1696.

86 Letter of Shrewsbury to William, 28 July/7 Aug. 1696, in Coxe, *Correspondence*, pp. 130–31; letter of Portland to William, 28 July/7 Aug. 1696, in Japikse, *Correspondentie*, pp. 180–82.

87 Shrewsbury letter to William, 31 July/10 Aug. 1696, in Coxe, *Correspondence*, p. 133.

88 Letter to William, 28 July 1696, SP 8/15/111-12; note that in *CSPD* this letter is mistakenly catalogued as 1694.

89 Letter of Shrewsbury to William, 28 July/7 Aug. 1696, in Coxe, *Correspondence*, pp. 130–31.

90 Letter of Gwyn to Halifax, 3 Aug. 1696, in BL, Add. 75370.

91 Letter of Portland to William, 28 July/7 Aug. 1696, in Japikse, *Correspondentie*, pp. 180–82.

92 Letter of Portland to William, 28 July 1686, in *CSPD*; Luttrell, *Brief Historical Relation*, 30 July and 1 Aug. 1696.

93 Fox had been appointed a Treasury Lord when Leeds was the chief minister. Evance and Herne had held the army remittance contract before the Bank of England came along. Guy was of course the former Treasury Secretary, ousted from his post by the efforts of the whig junto and especially of Montagu.

Duncombe had been the Excise cashier since 1680 and was a protégé of Leeds. Banks had loaned extensively to the crown during the tory years. Child was widely believed to have offered £5 thousand in guineas to Leeds in 1693 to help secure a new charter for the East India Company.

94 Letter of Godolphin to William, 31 July 1696, in Godolphin Letters to William.
95 Lords Justices Minutes, 5 Aug. 1696. The lords justices thought the bullion-export license was worth £20 thousand and so that in total the consortium was asking for a 30 percent rate of return on their loan. Montagu claimed that they had asked the Treasury to take clipped coin by weight at 6s. 6d.–14.7 percent better than the price of 5s. 8d. already being offered to the general public. The group asked for a bank charter since this could no longer be attained through salt-tax act – the 1 August deadline being almost upon them. With corporate status already in hand, they hoped to secure a large war loan next session.
96 Letter of Portland to William, 31 July / 10 Aug. 1696, in Japikse, *Correspondentie*, pp. 182–84.
97 Letter of Portland to William, 31 July / 10 Aug. 1696, in Japikse, *Correspondentie*, pp. 182–84.
98 Godolphin, Letter to William, 31 July 1696, in Godolphin Letters to William; *CTB,* Minutes, 31 July 1696.
99 Letter of Shrewsbury to William, 4/14 Aug. 1696, in Coxe, *Correspondence,* p. 134.
100 Letter of Gwyn to Halifax, 3 Aug.1696, BL, Add. MS 75370.
101 Lords Justices Minutes; letter of Shrewsbury to William, 7/17 Aug. 1696, in Coxe, *Correspondence*, p. 135.
102 Letter of 14 Aug. 1696, in Montagu Letters.
103 Letter of Shrewsbury to William, 7/17 Aug. 1696, in Coxe, *Correspondence*, p. 135.
104 *CTB*, Warrants, etc., 14 Aug. 1696.
105 *CTB*, Warrants, etc., 14 Aug. 1696.
106 *CTB*, Warrants, etc., 8 Sep. 1696.
107 Senate House Library, MS 54.
108 Bank Minutes, 13 May 1696; Luttrell, *Brief Historical Relation*, 14 May 1696.
109 Bank Minutes, 26 May 1696; Luttrell, *Brief Historical Relation*, 28 May 1696.
110 Bank Minutes, 4 June 1696; Luttrell, *Brief Historical Relation*, 11 June 1696.
111 The results of this cash call are clearly visible in Figure 3.2.
112 Bank Minutes, 4 June 1696; Luttrell, *Brief Historical Relation*, 6 June 1696.
113 Bank Minutes, 1 July 1696.
114 Bank Minutes, 10 June 1696.
115 Bank Minutes, 9 July 1696; Lords Justices Minutes, 10 July 1696. The Bank had been asking for such an order since early June (*CSPD*, 4 June 1696). But the lords justices had been reluctant to issue it, fearing it might destroy rather than improve the Bank's credit.
116 *CTB,* Minutes, 10 July 1696.
117 Luttrell, *Brief Historical Relation*, 14 July 1696; l'Hermitage Reports, 14 July 1696.
118 L'Hermitage Reports, 28 July 1696.
119 See the proposal that he drew up for the Dutch, dated 22 July (in RCHM, *Buccleuch Manuscripts*, p. 372) and his letter to Shrewsbury, 31 July 1696 (in RCHM, *Buccleuch Manuscripts*, p. 376).
120 Lords Justices Minutes, 6 Aug. 1696.
121 Lords Justices Minutes, 11 Aug. 1696.
122 Bank Minutes, 15 Aug. 1696; Luttrell, *Brief Historical Relation*, 15 Aug. 1696.
123 Lords Justices Minutes, 15 Aug. 1696.

124 Bank Minutes, 15 Aug. 1696; *CTB,* Minutes, 19 Aug. 1696. The credit was negotiated at a rate of 9 guilders per £ sterling. This was equivalent to 27.7 schellingen banco per £, at a time when the market exchange rate on Antwerp was
being quoted at 28.75.

125 Letter to Blathwayt, 14 Aug. 1696, in Montagu Letters.

126 Ranelagh furnished a detailed analysis, in which report a copy of the Bank's original claim is also contained. The whole report is available in BEA, M5/13. It is
very revealing as to the processes by which the Bank managed its remittance
business.

127 Bank Minutes, 26 Aug. 1696; *CTB*, Minutes, 4 Sep. 1696.

128 Bank Minutes, 3 Feb. 1697.

129 Bank Minutes, 4 Sep. 1696; *CTB*, Minutes, 4 Sep. 1696.

130 Bank Minutes, 8 Sep. 1696; Hill Account Book.

131 Bank Minutes, 14 Oct. 1696; Hill Account Book.

132 Bank Minutes, 30 Oct. 1696; Hill Account Book.

133 Note that the new resources weren't actually used to support the Bank's remittance operations. Hill's new letters of credit were financed instead by way
of a large new loan from the States General (equivalent to £120 thousand) and
credits that the Bank had previously built up with George Clifford, an Amsterdam banker (Bank General Ledger 2). This freed the directors to use the new
subscriber cash call to retire a large quantity of the Bank notes in circulation
(in which currency most of the call was received) and rebuild the Bank's specie
reserve. The directors further bolstered the Bank's short-term cash position by
committing to pay interest of 6 percent per annum on Bank bills for the next
six months (Bank Minutes, 1 Oct. 1696) and selling £50 thousand in bills of
exchange (drawn upon an Amsterdam banker) to London merchants interested
in obtaining credits on the continent. So as soon as proceeds from the cash call
began coming in, cashiers were ordered to begin paying off, in full, all Bank
running-cash notes upon which £5 or less remained owing and to increase the
frequency with which they were offering partial payment on notes above that
cut-off (Bank Minutes, 21 and 23 Oct. 1696).

134 Note that while the payment deadline was set for 10 Nov., shareholders were
offered a discount of 1 percent if they paid on or before 26 October (Bank Minutes, 5 Oct. 1696).

135 Letter to William, 11/21 Aug. 1696, in Japikse, *Correspondentie*, pp. 192–94.

136 *CTB*, Minutes, 12 Aug. 1696.

137 Letter to Shrewsbury, 24 Aug./3 Sep. 1696, in Coxe, *Correspondence*, p. 138.

138 Lords Justices Minutes, 1 Sep. 1696.

139 *CTB*, Warrants, etc., 8 Sep. 1696.

140 Horwitz, *Parliament*, p. 183.

141 *CTB*, Minutes, 21 Oct. 1696. Details on the plan are sketchy. No copy survives;
we have nothing but William's questions about it and a couple of hints from
Vernon (Undersecretary of State) about a version Foley laid before the Commons on 10 Nov. 1696 (letter to Shrewsbury, 10 Nov. 1696, in Vernon, *Letters
Illustrative*, p. 55). But the gist of the plan suggested by William's queries
matches up very well with the report Vernon gives of Foley's verbal remarks.
And Vernon himself later noted that a similar scheme presented by Montagu a
few weeks later had built from Foley's own ideas (letter to Shrewsbury, 26 Nov.
1696, in Vernon, *Letters Illustrative*, p. 83).

142 Much the same plan (minus the Bank element) was put forward, around this
very time, in *Sure and Effectual Method*. So Foley may have been behind its
publication.

143 Letter of Somers to Shrewsbury, 31 Oct. 1696, in Coxe, *Correspondence*, p. 420.

144 Letter of Vernon to Shrewsbury, 26 Nov. 1696, in Vernon, *Letters Illustrative*, p. 83.

145 By the terms of the statute, the Bank became entitled to raise the ceiling on its note issue by an amount equal to the value of any bills and notes paid in by the new subscribers.

Bibliography

Manuscript sources

Bank of England Archive
  ADM7/1-2 ('Bank General Ledger 1' and 'Bank General Ledger 2')
  G4/1-2 ('Bank Minutes')
  M5/13
British Library
  Add. MS 9727 ('Henley Letter to Blathwayt')
  Add. MS. 17677 OO-QQ ('l'Hermitage Reports')
  Add. MS 34355 ('Montagu Letters')
  Add. MS 75370
  Harley MS 1223
Geheimes Staatsarchiv, Preußischer Kulturbesitz, Berlin
  I. HA Geheimer Rat, Rep. 11, Nr. 1792–1811 ('Bonnet Reports')
Kent History and Library Centre, Maidstone
  U1590/O59/5
Koninklijk Huisarchief, Amsterdam
  Willem III, XI G Nos. 179–94 ('Godolphin Letters to Blathwayt')
National Archives
  C104/12, part I ('Hoar Letter Book')
  MINT 1/6
  SP 8/15
  SP 8/16 ('Godolphin Letters to William')
  SP 44/274 ('Lords Justices Minutes')
Senate House Library, University of London
  MS 54
  MS 65
Shropshire Archives (Attingham Collection)
  X112/1/2/1 ('Abbott Letters')
  X112/1A/1 ('Hill Account Book')
University of Nottingham
  MS Pw A 473–76
  MS Pw A 1251

Printed primary sources

Coxe, William (ed.). *Private and Original Correspondence of Charles Talbot, Duke of Shrewsbury, with King William, the Leaders of the Whig Party, and Other Distinguished Statesmen.* London: Longman, Hurst, Rees, Orme & Brown, 1821.
Davenant, Charles. *Two Manuscripts by Charles Davenant.* Edited by Abbott Payson Usher. Baltimore: Johns Hopkins University Press, 1942.
Great Britain. *Statutes of the Realm.* Edited Alexander Luders and John Raithby. London: G. Eyre and A. Strahan, 1810–22. Accessed online at http://www.british-history.ac.uk/statutes-realm/.

Great Britain. Parliament. House of Commons. *Journals of the House of Commons.* London: House of Commons, 1803. Accessed online at http://www.british-history. ac.uk/commons-jrnl/.

Great Britain. Public Record Office. *Calendar of State Papers, Domestic Series, of the Reign of William and Mary.* London: HMSO, 1898–. Accessed online at http:// www.british-history.ac.uk/search/series/cal-state-papers--domestic--will-mary.

Great Britain. Public Record Office. *Calendar of Treasury Books.* Volume X: *January 1693 to March 1696.* Edited by William Shaw. London: HMSO, 1931. Accessed online at http://www.british-history.ac.uk/cal-treasury-books/vol10.

Great Britain. Public Record Office. *Calendar of Treasury Books.* Volume XI: *April 1696 to March 1696–7.* Edited by William Shaw. London: HMSO, 1931. Accessed online at http://www.british-history.ac.uk/cal-treasury-books/vol11.

Great Britain. Royal Commission on Historical Manuscripts. *Report on the Manuscripts of the Duke of Buccleuch and Queensberry, K.G., K.T., Preserved at Montagu House, Whitehall.* Vol. 2: *The Shrewsbury Papers.* Ed. R. E. G. Kirk. London: HMSO, 1903.

Great Britain. Royal Commission on Historical Manuscripts. *Report on the Manuscripts of the Marquess of Downshire Preserved at Easthampstead Park, Berks.* Vol. 1: *Papers of Sir William Trumbull.* London: HMSO, 1924.

Japikse, Nicolaas (ed.). *Correspondentie van Willem III en van Hans Willem Bentinck, Eersten Graaf van Portland.* 's-Gravenhage: Martinus Nijhoff, 1927.

Luttrell, Narcissus. *A Brief Historical Relation of State Affairs from September 1678 to April 1714.* 6 vols. Oxford: Oxford University Press, 1857.

[Paterson, William]. *A Review of the Universal Remedy for All Diseases Incident to Coin, With Application to Our Present Circumstances: In a Letter to Mr. Locke.* London: Awnsham & John Churchill, 1696.

A Sure and Effectual Method for the Recovery of Credit and Making Good the Deficiency of Parliamentary Funds: Humbly Proposed by a Merchant of London. [London: s.n., 1696].

Vernon, James. *Letters Illustrative of the Reign of William III, from 1696 to 1708, Addressed to the Duke of Shrewsbury, by James Vernon, Esq., Secretary of State: Now First Published From the Originals.* Ed. G. P. R. James. 3 vols. London: Henry Colburn, 1841.

Contemporary periodicals

London Gazette.

Secondary sources

Horwitz, Henry. *Parliament, Policy and Politics in the Reign of William III.* Newark: University of Delaware Press, 1977.

Kelly, Patrick Hyde. Introduction to *Locke on Money*, by John Locke, 1–121. Oxford: Clarendon Press, 1991.

Li, Ming-Hsun. *The Great Recoinage of 1696 to 1699.* London: Weidenfeld and Nicolson, 1963.

Concluding remarks

Specie was clearly the scarlet thread that ran throughout the monetary politics of our period. As the only medium accepted without question as a final means of payment, it was the nation's preeminent form of money. Being both indispensable for certain kinds of payments (e.g. taxes and wages) and constantly in fairly short supply, it conferred power upon those who had it and made those who lacked it open to being imposed upon by others. Consequently, contemporaries were constantly working to improve, or at least maintain, their access to specie. And because the largest quantities of specie moved through the nation's public-revenue and -expenditure systems, this struggle for power played itself out in competitions for appointment to key tax and spending offices and for the right to handle large public loans.

The creation of the Bank of England, and the introduction of substantial quantities of Bank bills and notes, changed none of this. The new currencies made it easier for members of the general public to make do without specie when clearing their payment obligations. But because for many kinds of transactions, especially those involving taxes and wage bills, specie remained the sole acceptable means of payment, it still paid handsomely to insert oneself somehow into the flow of public specie. Several of the land-bank projects were potential game-changers in this respect. The Chamberlen and Briscoe banks in particular amounted to proposals to add a new final means of payment to England's monetary system, threatening to completely alter the existing allocation of monetary power in favour of landowners. But neither project was able to win parliamentary approval. So the struggle for power unfolded instead in the form of a competition between two specie-based banks: the Bank of England (dominated by whig merchants) and the Land Bank United or National Land Bank (associated in large part with tory goldsmiths). There was also some lesser play, along the sidelines so to speak, in regard to what I have called recoinage banks – proposals to use the recoinage itself to secure access to large quantities of silver or gold specie.

This power struggle came about in the first place because the new Bank of England had generated a great deal of resentment. Theodore Janssen, when campaigning in 1697 to become a Bank director, maintained that the first slate of directors should have been content to take deposits without interest and lend them on to the government at interest of no more than 3 percent. Instead they had aimed for 'vast exorbitant gains' with a design that 'create[d] envy and enemies'. It was 'their ambition of grasping at all' that led them to pay interest on their bills (which the goldsmiths had not done). And with their decision to start trading in foreign bills of exchange, the Bank 'disobliged abundance of people and drew upon itself the hatred of the merchants'.[1] This widespread resentment was to prove exceedingly dangerous to the Bank.

For it led to a contest of rival financial powers that ended up intersecting with a conflict internal to the administration, and with the whig-tory struggle for control of the administration more generally. The Bank was quickly hamstrung by this struggle, left to its own devices to muddle through as best it could. But this did not leave the field open to its competitor, the prospective National Land Bank. For the Treasury whigs had their own reasons for wanting that undertaking to fail. It was politically unviable for them to push for the new war loan to come instead from the Bank of England. So they devised the project of establishing a bank in the Exchequer. This would allow for the new war loan to be raised by means independent of both the Bank of England and the National Land Bank, while offering better returns to the actual lenders (those holding Exchequer bills) than would have been afforded them by either private bank. Specie holders would still be able to profit very handsomely by contributing their money to the reserve that would be needed to circulate Exchequer bills. And to further help defeat the National Land Bank, the Treasury whigs arranged for clipped money to be completely retired from circulation for several months and tried to bribe goldsmiths with the offer of high-salary offices, a guaranteed price for their guineas and a sizeable windfall gain on their holdings of heavy silver coin. If the administration eventually sought to lower guineas to their pre-crisis value, this happened not because it had bought into Lockean dogma, but because the goldsmiths decided to hold out for the prospect of a second parliamentary bank – by which they could still hope to realize gains close to those that Montagu had been offering by other means.

After the monetary crisis hit in May 1696, many in the administration, William among them, concluded that it had been a mistake not to raise the coin. This was a political rather than a technical diagnosis. All along the currency situation had been a contest of wills. In pushing early on for keeping the existing Mint standard and lowering the market price of guineas to 22s., William had sought to break widespread public expectations of a rise in the coin. Like Locke, he must have been sure that with no remaining prospect for greater rewards, those hoarding guineas and heavy silver coin would break down and return their money to circulation. As Montagu himself wrote in late May:

> One great reason of keeping up the gold was the expectation of an advantage from the establishment of this [land] bank. The gentlemen concerned

have taken guineas in at high rates. And the vexation and anger they have at the loss they sustained by crying them down, makes them continue still to lose by hoarding them, to justify their opinion who would have kept them up, and who they hope will yet be able to relieve them. But if the design of setting up another bank were entirely laid aside, the gold must appear or the gentlemen continue in a very expensive obstinacy.[2]

But as long as the general public continued to believe that the coin was indeed going to be raised, there would be strong pressure on the state to do exactly this – making the prophecy almost self-fulfilling. And, albeit late in the game, land-bank supporters did their very best to nourish and sustain such expectations. So in the end the question of whether or not to raise the coin turned upon whether prospective subscribers to the National Land Bank would continue to see it as their right to earn large profits on their holdings of guineas and heavy and clipped silver coin and so to go on hoarding that money until they got what was coming to them. Locke was almost fanatical in his belief that the nation owed the goldsmiths nothing and that the state would have been in the right to try to impose all the losses from clipping upon them. In effect he wanted the crown to call their bluff and believed they could be forced to fold. The goldsmiths obviously thought otherwise. There was no objective right or wrong here – only a power struggle. In changing his mind ex post, William was acknowledging only that he had erred in supposing the crown capable of winning this contest of wills.

Though in this sense specie did confer power, that power proved to be limited in its reach. The Bank of England, for instance, far from being able to dictate terms to the government, was coerced into taking on the army remittances contract, harassed to lend more and more and tossed aside when the crown thought it could do better by another lender. The National Land Bank, despite having the government over a financial barrel, could not get the lords justices to agree to their terms. This was in part because Montagu had outmaneuvered them by getting the Exchequer-bills scheme into place as a credible, low-cost fallback. But at the end of the day the new bank failed because the lords justices, other than Godolphin, could not bring themselves to approve large handouts to the financiers. They could not grasp, perhaps, the potent forces at work during a time of monetary crisis, nor the impossibility of raising funds without capitulating to those who had access to specie at a time when the state did not. So it was perhaps a case of power misunderstood, mistakenly left unacknowledged, rather than an outright power failure.

Notes

1 Janssen, *Discourse*, pp. 3–7.
2 Letter to Blathwayt, 29 May 1696, in Montagu Letters.

Bibliography

Manuscript sources

British Library
  Add. MS 34355 ('Montagu Letters')

Printed primary sources

[Janssen, Theodore]. *A Discourse Concerning Banks.* London: James Knapton, 1697.

Index